Competition Law in Cyprus

Competition Law in Cyprus

Achilles C. Emilianides
Anastasios A. Antoniou

This book was originally published as a monograph in the International Encyclopaedia of Laws/Competition Law.

Founding Editor: Roger Blanpain
General Editor: Frank Hendrickx
Volume Editors: Francesco Denozza & Alberto Toffoletto

Wolters Kluwer

Published by:
Kluwer Law International B.V.
PO Box 316
2400 AH Alphen aan den Rijn
The Netherlands
E-mail: international-sales@wolterskluwer.com
Website: lrus.wolterskluwer.com

Sold and distributed by:
Wolters Kluwer Legal & Regulatory U.S.
7201 McKinney Circle
Frederick, MD 21704
United States of America
E-mail: customer.service@wolterskluwer.com

ISBN 978-94-035-3824-2

e-Book: ISBN 978-94-035-3825-9
web-PDF: ISBN 978-94-035-3830-3

The Authors

Achilles C. Emilianides is a Professor, Dean of the School of Law at the University of Nicosia, and a practicing advocate, senior partner of the law firms Achilles & Emile, Constantinos Emilianides LLC, and A&E C. Emilianides, C. Katsaros and Associates LLC. He holds a PhD in Law and an LLM from the Aristotle University of Thessaloniki and an LLM from Leicester University. He has been elected as a founding member and first Secretary-General of the Cyprus Academy of Sciences, Letters and Arts, and as a member of the European Academy of Sciences and Arts. He is also the national representative to All European Academies (ALLEA), the Chair of the Royal Commonwealth Society Cyprus Branch, and a board member to a number of scientific organisations and journals. He has been involved in high profile civil litigation, as well as legal consultancy and funded research. Recent publications in the IEL series include: *Tort Law in Cyprus* (Kluwer, 2020), *Civil Procedure in Cyprus* (Kluwer, 2020), *Religion and Law in Cyprus* (3rd ed., Kluwer, 2019), *Constitutional Law in Cyprus* (2nd ed., Kluwer, 2019), *Family and Succession Law in Cyprus* (2nd ed., Kluwer 2019), *Labour Law in Cyprus* (2nd ed., Kluwer, 2019), and *Media Law in Cyprus* (2nd ed., Kluwer, 2019).

Anastasios A. Antoniou is a practicing advocate and partner at Antoniou McCollum & Co. LLC. He has been ranked as the leading lawyer on EU law and competition law in Cyprus by *The Legal 500 (Hall of Fame)*. He is a member of the European Competition Lawyers Forum, in which senior practitioners and officials from the European Commission engage in an open dialogue on competition law issues and reform. He advises and acts for multinational companies and governments on regulatory and competition law matters. He has been involved in high profile civil litigation and international arbitration.

The Authors

Table of Contents

The Authors 3

List of Abbreviations 11

Preface 15

General Introduction 17

§1. General Background of the Country 17
I. Geography 17
II. History 17
III. Political System 20

§2. Economic System 21

§3. Legal System 24
I. Sources 24
A. Constitution 24
B. EU Law 25
C. International Treaties 26
D. Ordinary Legislation 28
II. Position of the Judiciary 29

§4. Historical Background of Antitrust Law 30

Part I. Structure of Antitrust Law and Its Enforcement 35

Chapter 1. Sources of Antitrust Law 35

§1. National Sources 35

§2. International Sources 37

§3. Secondary Sources 39

§4. Sources' Relation and Hierarchy 41

§5. Role and Authority of Precedents 42

Chapter 2. Scope of Application 43

§1. Territorial Reach 43

§2. Special Sectors 45
A. Electronic Communications 45
B. Energy 51

§3. State-Owned Enterprises and Public Utilities 52

§4. Sensible Effect and De Minimis 54

Chapter 3. Overview of Substantive Provisions 56

§1. Restrictive Agreements 56

§2. Dominant Undertakings 57

§3. Concentrations 57

§4. Tests of Illegality 57
I. Per Se Prohibitions 57
II. Balancing Tests 58
III. Merger Tests 59

Chapter 4. Overview of Main Notions 60

§1. Undertaking 60

§2. Relevant Market 61

§3. Market Power/Dominant Position 62

§4. Agreements and Concerted Practices 63

§5. Restriction of Competition 65

§6. Monopolisation and Abuse of Dominance 65

§7. Concentrations 67

§8. Joint Ventures 68

Chapter 5. Consequences of Violations and Enforcement Institutions 69

§1. ADMINISTRATIVE ENFORCEMENT 69
I. Antitrust Authorities 69
A. Formation and Composition 69
B. Term and Working Conditions 72
C. Investigating Powers 74
D. Adjudicating Powers (Ascertaining and Sanctioning) 74
E. Other Institutional Tasks (Consultancy to Parliament/Government) 75
F. The Service 75
II. Government Direct Enforcement Activities 76
III. Other Administrative Agencies Applying Antitrust Rules 77
IV. Administrative Fines 78
A. Infringements 78
B. Procedure and Guidelines 79
C. Leniency Programme 83
V. Administrative Injunctions and Other Restrictive Orders 86
VI. Interim Measures 86

§2. CIVIL ENFORCEMENT 87
I. Competent Civil Courts 87
II. Sanctions 87
A. Nullity 87
B. Damages 88
C. Interim Measures 93

§3. CRIMINAL ENFORCEMENT 94
I. Criminal Sanctions for Antitrust Violations 94
II. Role of Prosecutors 94
III. Competent Criminal Courts 95

Part II. Application of the Prohibitions 97

Chapter 1. Restrictive Agreements 97

§1. HORIZONTAL AGREEMENTS 97
I. Cartels 97
A. Introduction 97
B. Price-Fixing 97
C. Market/Client Allocation 101
D. Production/Innovation Limitation 103
E. Group Boycott 105
II. Information Exchange Practices 105
III. Cooperation Agreements 107

A. Research and Development Agreements 107
B. Specialisation Agreements 108
C. Standardisation Agreements 109
D. Joint Production Agreements 110
E. Joint Purchasing Agreements 111
F. Joint Selling Agreements 112

§2. VERTICAL AGREEMENTS 113
I. General 113
II. Distribution 115
A. Exclusive Distribution 115
B. Exclusive Dealing 116
C. Selective Distribution 116
D. Franchising 118
III. Technology Licensing 119
A. Patent Licensing 119
B. Trademark Licensing 121
C. Know-How and Trade Secret Licensing 121

Chapter 2. Dominant Undertakings' Prohibited Practices 124

§1. INTRODUCTION 124

§2. EXPLOITATIVE PRACTICES 126
I. Excessive/Unfair Pricing 126
II. Discrimination 129

§3. EXCLUSIONARY PRACTICES 132
I. Predation 132
II. Tying 132
III. Rebates 132
IV. Refusal to Deal 133
V. Margin Squeeze 136

Chapter 3. Concentrations 138

§1. HORIZONTAL MERGERS 138

§2. VERTICAL MERGERS 140

§3. PURE CONGLOMERATE MERGERS 142

§4. JOINT VENTURES 143

Part III. Administrative Procedure 147

Chapter 1. Administrative Investigations Before the Antitrust Authority 147

§1. Initiative 147
I. General Sectors Inquiries 147
II. Ex-Officio Investigations 148
III. Complaints 148

§2. Powers 150
I. Requests for Information 150
II. Investigating and Search Powers 152
III. Cooperation with Other State Institutions 154

§3. Right of Defence 157
I. Content and Notification of Opening Decisions 157
II. Proceedings: Hearings, Access to File, and Briefs 158
III. Decision 159

Chapter 2. Voluntary Notifications and Clearance Decisions Merger Control 160

§1. Preliminary Filing Obligations 160
I. Criteria and Thresholds 160
II. Turnover Calculation 160
III. Market Share Calculation 162

§2. Structure of Proceedings 163
I. Preliminary Assessment and Full Investigation 163
A. Notification 163
B. Preliminary Assessment 167
C. Full Investigation 167
II. Time Framework 169
III. Right of Defence 170

§3. Clearance and Conditional Clearance 172
I. Conditions and Undertakings 172
A. Content 172
B. Timing 175

§4. Relations with Other Merger Control Authorities 176
I. Other Authorities Within the Local Jurisdiction 176
II. International Coordination 176

Chapter 3. Challenging of the Administrative Decision 181

§1. Competent Courts 181

§2. Time Limits 183

§3. Scope of Judicial Review 183

§4. Confidential Information 191

Selected Bibliography 195

Index 197

List of Abbreviations

Antitrust Damages Law	Claims for Compensation for Violations of Competition Law113(I)/17
BEREC	Body of European Regulators for Electronic Communications
CECPR	Commissioner of Electronic Communications and Postal Regulation
CERA	Cyprus Energy Regulatory Authority
CJEU	Court of Justice of the European Union
CIC	Cyprus Import Corporation Ltd
CLR	Cyprus Law Reports
COLA	Cost of Living Allowance
Concentrations Law	Control of Concentration of Undertakings Law 83(I)/14
CPC	Commission for the Protection of Competition
CPC Law	Protection of Competition Law 13(I)/2008
CYTA	Cyprus Telecommunications Authority
EBITDA	Earnings Before Interest, Tax, Depreciation and Amortisation
ECHR	European Convention on Human Rights
ECtHR	European Court of Human Rights
ECJ	European Court of Justice
ECN	European Competition Network
EEC	European Economic Communities
Electricity Market Law	Law Regulating the Electricity Market 122(I)/03
EU	European Union
GDP	Gross Domestic Product
HHI	Herfindahl-Hirschman Index

List of Abbreviations

Horizontal Agreements Guidelines	Guidelines on the applicability of Article 101 of the Treaty on the Functioning of the European Union to horizontal co-operation agreements
Horizontal Merger Guidelines	Guidelines on the assessment of horizontal mergers under the Council Regulation on the control of concentrations between undertakings
Leniency Programme	The Immunity from and Reduction of Administrative Fines in cases of Restrictive Collusions Infringing Section 3 of the Law and/or Article 101 of the TFEU
LLDP	Linear Low-Density Polyethylene
Mergers Regulation	Council Regulation (EC) No. 139/2004 of 20 Jan. 2004 on the control of concentrations between undertakings
Modernisation Regulation	Council Regulation (EC) No. 1/2003 of 16 December 2002 on the implementation of the rules on competition laid down in Articles 81 and 82 of the Treaty
MoU	Memorandum of Understanding
OCECPR Law	Regulation of Electronic Communications and Postal Services Law 112(I)/04
Principles of Administrative Law	General Principles of Administrative Law 158(I)/99
R&D	Research and Development
R&D Block Exemption Regulation	Commission Regulation (EU) No. 1217/2010 of 14 December 2010 on the application of Article 101 §3 of the Treaty on the Functioning of the European Union to certain categories of research and development agreements
SBA	Sovereign Base Areas
SME	Small or medium-sized enterprises
Specialisation Block Exemption Regulation	Commission Regulation (EU) No. 1218/2010 of 14 December 2010 on the application of Article 101 §3 of the Treaty on the Functioning of the European Union to certain categories of specialisation agreements
TEC	Treaty establishing the European Community
Technology Transfer Guidelines	European Commission Guidelines on the application of Article 101 TFEU to technology transfer agreements
TEU	Treaty on European Union
TFEU	Treaty for the Functioning of the European Union

TRNC	Turkish Republic of Northern Cyprus
TTBER	Commission Regulation (EU) No. 316/2014 of 21 March 2014 on the application of Article 101 §3 of the Treaty on the Functioning of the European Union to categories of technology transfer agreements
UN	United Nations
VBER	Commission Regulation (EU) No. 330/2010 of 20 April 2010 on the application of Article 101 §3 of the Treaty on the Functioning of the European Union to categories of vertical agreements and concerted practices
Vertical Merger Guidelines	Guidelines on the assessment of non-horizontal mergers under the Council Regulation on the control of concentrations between undertakings

List of Abbreviations

Preface

This study consists of an analysis of Cypriot competition law. It is the first time that a comprehensive monograph about Cypriot competition law has been published in the English language. A significant part of Cypriot competition law derives from EU instruments, which are directly applicable, or have been implemented, or apply *mutatis mutandis*, in the Cypriot legal order. Since this is a national monograph which forms part of a multi-volume encyclopaedia, the authors have avoided any extensive analysis of such EU legal instruments and case law, to the extent that their application in the Cypriot legal order does not present any peculiarities, or to the extent that they have not been interpreted by Cypriot case law. This is the reason why this monograph does not contain extensive analysis of some important aspects of competition law where Cypriot law is not idiosyncratic, but merely reflects the provisions of the EU instruments. The reader is referred to many general works of EU competition law for a more extensive analysis of such areas.

General Introduction and Parts I and III were written by Achilles C. Emilianides. Part II was written by Anastasios A. Antoniou.

Achilles C. Emilianides wishes to express his gratitude to the many individuals who have collaborated with him over the years and have helped him expand his views on competition law, most notably colleagues in his law firms and the University of Nicosia, his family and friends, and particularly his late father Constantinos Emilianides.

Anastasios A. Antoniou wishes to express his gratitude to his parents and colleagues for facilitating his practice of competition law, and particularly his partner at Antoniou McCollum & Co. LLC, Christina McCollum.

General Introduction

§1. General Background of the Country

I. Geography

1. Cyprus, officially the Republic of Cyprus, is the third largest Mediterranean island, after the Italian islands of Sicily and Sardinia. It is situated in the Eastern Mediterranean, at a distance of 300 km to the north of Egypt, 90 km to the west of Syria, 60 km to the south of Turkey and 360 km to the north-west of Greece. It covers an area of 9,251 sq. km (3,572 sq. miles) and has 648 km of coastline. It is divided into six districts, namely Nicosia, Limassol, Famagusta, Larnaca, Paphos and Kyrenia. The capital of the island is the town of Nicosia. Cyprus also has two mountain ranges: the Pentadaktylos range which runs along the entire northern coast and the Troodos massif in the central and south-western parts of the island. The geographical position and the small size of Cyprus signify both the advantages and the disadvantages of the country. The island is situated in the far north-eastern end of the Mediterranean Sea and is at the crossroads of three continents – Europe, Asia and Africa. This strategic position has represented, over the years, a temptation to foreign aggressors who sought to obtain control of the Middle East, while its small size intensified its vulnerable position. The history of Cyprus begins with the early Neolithic period, dating back to the 8th or even 10th millennium BC and has been characterised by successive conquests and lengthy periods under foreign rule.

II. History

2. The constitutional history of the Republic of Cyprus is characterised by continuous attempts to overthrow, modify or replace the constitutional structure.[1] The Republic of Cyprus was established as an independent and sovereign republic on 16 August 1960, when its Constitution came into force and the British sovereignty over Cyprus, as a crown colony, ceased. The establishment of the Republic was the outcome of the Zurich and London Agreements of February 1959, on which the fundamental provisions of the Constitution were based. As a result, the constitutional

1. *See, in general,* A. Emilianides, *Beyond the Constitution of Cyprus* (Sakkoulas 2006, in Greek); K. Chrysostomides, *The Republic of Cyprus: A Study in International Law* (Martinus Nijhoff 2000).

structure of Cyprus was essentially decided without the participation of the people of Cyprus. Consequently, the people of Cyprus considered that the Constitution had been imposed on them.

3. The structure provided by the Zurich Agreements was considered as a compromise between the Greek demand for union with Greece and the Turkish demand for partition of the island. Furthermore, the United Kingdom retained – and continues to retain – sovereignty over two Base Areas, one in Akrotiri and the other in Dhekelia, which cover 250 sq. km of the land area of the island of Cyprus. The Constitution is unique in its perplexity and the multiplicity of safeguards that it provides for the principal numerical minority of the island, namely the Turkish community. The principle of bi-communality permeates the constitutional structure, according, in many respects, equal status to the Greek community, representing 82% of the population, and to the Turkish community, representing the remaining 18%.

4. Not surprisingly, the Zurich Agreement failed to establish cooperation between the Greek and the Turkish communities of the island and proved to be unworkable in practice. In 1963, there was an outbreak of violence on the island, which led to a constitutional breakdown.[2] In 1964, a United Nations ('UN') Peacekeeping operation was deployed on the island and has remained there since. The UN Security Council with Resolution 186/1964, and the General Assembly of the UN on 18 December 1965, called upon all States to respect the sovereignty, unity, independence and territorial integrity of the Republic of Cyprus and to refrain from intervening in it. The Government of the Republic of Cyprus continues to be recognised by the international community as the only legitimate representative of the Republic.

5. Inter-communal talks began with the aim of achieving a satisfactory solution to the Cyprus Problem. However, in July 1974 the Republic of Turkey, one of the guarantor powers of the independence, sovereignty and territorial integrity of Cyprus, invaded the country with its armed forces and occupied its northern part.[3] Turkey alleged that its invasion had the purpose of restoring the constitutional order following a coup against President Makarios by the Greek military government (junta), which was then in power in Greece,[4] pursuant to the provisions of the Treaty of Guarantee signed between Cyprus, Greece, Turkey and the United Kingdom, as part of the Zurich and London Agreements, However, this allegation was not accepted by the international community.[5] UN Resolution 360/74 expressed the official contempt on behalf of the Security Council of the unilateral military force undertaken against the Republic of Cyprus, while UN Resolution 3212/74 of the

2. *See* S. Kyriakides, *Cyprus: Constitutionalism and Crisis Government* (University of Pennsylvania Press 1968); T. Ehrlich, *Cyprus 1958–1967: International Crises and the Role of Law* (Oxford University Press 1974).
3. C. Tornaritis, *The Turkish Invasion of Cyprus and Legal Problems Arising therefrom* (Nicosia 1975).
4. *See* L. Loucaides, *The Legal Effect of the Coup of 15 July 1974* (2d ed., 1976, in Greek).
5. *See* I. Brownlie, *The Prohibition of the Use of Armed Force for the Solution of International Differences with Particular Reference to the Affairs of the Republic of Cyprus, in International Law Conference on Cyprus* 198–213 (Cyprus Bar Council 1979); R. McDonald, *International Law and*

General Assembly demanded that all foreign armed forces leave at once from the Republic of Cyprus and that any foreign intervention in the Republic of Cyprus' affairs should cease immediately. The latter Resolution was endorsed by UN Resolution 365/74 of the Security Council.

6. As a result of the Turkish invasion, the Greeks and other Christians of the region were displaced to the southern part of the island. The Turks of the southern part of the island were forced to move to the north. The area occupied by Turkey amounts to 36.4% of the territory of the Republic of Cyprus. The Turkish invasion resulted in grave human suffering and material economic loss. Its effects are still evident today, with more than one-quarter of the population of the island being displaced, and more than 1,000 people being classified as 'missing persons'. About 43,000 Turkish military troops, armed with the latest military weapons, continue to be situated illegally on the island. The Turkish occupation in Cyprus continues to the present day; therefore, the Republic of Cyprus is prevented from exercising its powers over the occupied territory. Several attempts to achieve a solution for the Cyprus Problem have so far failed. Cyprus became a full member of the European Union ('EU') on 1 May 2004.[6] However, the application of the *acquis communautaire* in the occupied areas has been suspended, until a solution to the Cyprus Problem is found. Moreover, the *acquis* does not apply to the British Sovereign Base Areas (SBAs).

7. As far as the population is concerned, pursuant to the official census of 1960, the population of Cyprus was 573,666, out of whom 441,656 (77%) were of Greek origin and adhered to the Orthodox Christian religion, while 104,492 (18.3%) were of Turkish origin and adhered to the Islamic religion. The ratio between Greek and Turkish Cypriots had not been materially affected prior to the Turkish invasion of 1974. Since the Turkish invasion, providing precise figures with respect to the population of Cyprus has presented certain difficulties, due to the abnormal situation prevailing on the island. According to the 2011 official census the population of Cyprus (excluding Turkish Cypriots residing in the occupied areas) was 840,407, out of whom 667,398 (79.41%) were Cypriots, 106,270 (12.64%) were European citizens and 64,113 (7.62%) were third-country nationals (the majority being Asian or Russian nationals). The remaining 0.33% was unidentified. The actual number of Turkish Cypriots residing in Cyprus is difficult to estimate with precision, as the numbers of settlers from Turkey currently residing in Cyprus cannot be determined with accuracy. It is estimated, however, that more than 100,000 settlers from mainland Turkey are currently residing in the occupied areas. These settlers are not included in any estimation of the current population of Cyprus, as it was considered that any

---

the Conflict in Cyprus, 19 *Canadian Yearbook of International Law* 3 (1981). For the Turkish position, *see* Z. Necatigil, *The Cyprus Question and the Turkish Position in International Law* (2d ed., Oxford University Press 1993).

6. S. Lauhlé-Shaelou, *The EU and Cyprus. Principles and Strategies of Full Integration* (Martinus Nijhoff 2010).

potential legalisation of the Turkish settlers would illegally modify the demographic structure of the island and threaten the stability and security of the Republic.[7]

III. Political System

8. The Republic of Cyprus is a presidential democracy. The main state organs provided for in the Constitution are the President, the Council of Ministers, the Parliament, called the House of Representatives, and the Supreme Court. The President is the Head of State, representing the Republic in all its official functions. The President belongs to the Greek Cypriot community and is elected for a five-year term directly, by universal suffrage, and secret ballot. The President appoints and dismisses the members of the Council of Ministers, and in general, has wide executive powers. The Council of Ministers is composed of eleven ministers who are chosen from outside the House of Representatives. The Council of Ministers exercises the executive power alongside the President. The House of Representatives exercise the legislative power of the Republic. The representatives are elected for a term of five years in free, general and direct elections. The number of representatives is currently fifty-six. The judiciary is independent of the executive and the legislative organs, and it is a powerful factor in both legal and social life. The highest Cypriot court is the Supreme Court of Cyprus, which functions as both the supreme constitutional court and the supreme appellate court of the Republic. Many of the Court's decisions have been on the highest legal and political impact.[8]

9. In accordance with the principle of bi-communality, Cyprus is a unitary state, comprised of two communities, the Greek community and the Turkish community. It was therefore, provided that a Greek-Cypriot President should be elected by members of the Greek Community, while a Turkish-Cypriot Vice-President should be elected by members of the Turkish Community. The President and the Vice-President would retain broad powers of veto on decisions of the Council of Ministers concerning foreign affairs, defence and security, as well as with respect to the laws enacted by the House of Representatives on the same issues. It was further provided that the Council of Ministers would comprise of seven Greek Cypriots appointed by the President of the Republic and three Turkish Cypriots appointed by the Vice-President. The House of Representatives would consist of fifty Representatives. Once again, 70% of the members of the House of Representatives were to be elected separately by the members of the Greek community, while 30% were to be elected separately by the members of the Turkish community. The Constitution

7. L. Loucaides, *Expulsion of Settlers from Occupied Territories: The Case of Turkish Settlers, in Essays on the Developing Law of Human Rights* 108–138 (L. Loucaides ed., Martinus Nijhoff 1995); A. De Zayas, *The Annan Plan and the Implantation of Turkish Settlers in Northern Cyprus, The Cyprus Yearbook of International Relations* 163–178 (2006); Council of Europe, 2 May 2003, Doc. 9799, *Colonisation by Turkish Settlers of the Occupied Part of Cyprus* (Rapporteur Mr Laakso).
8. *See, in general,* A. Emilianides, *Constitutional Law in Cyprus* (2d ed., Kluwer 2019).

also provided for two communal chambers: a Greek communal chamber and a Turkish communal chamber, which should have legislative power in educational, cultural, religious and other matters of purely communal nature.

10. In its essence, the structure provided by the Constitution aimed at ensuring that each community would enjoy partial administrative autonomy, while the numerically smaller Turkish community would effectively participate in the exercise and functions of the Government in such a way so as to avoid a de facto supremacy of the larger community. As a result of the Cyprus Problem and the abnormal constitutional situation prevailing in the island, constitutional provisions which refer to the Turkish-Cypriot Community have not been in force for over fifty-five years, even though they are considered to be fundamental and thus not subject to modification. Thus, there is no Turkish Vice-President, Ministers or Representatives. A doctrine of necessity has been accepted by the Supreme Court of Cyprus, so that the House of Representatives may enact laws, even contrary to those provisions of the Constitution which are temporarily not in force because of the Cyprus Problem. This has resulted in a fundamental differentiation between the written form of the 1960 Constitution and the living Constitution as has been applied in Cypriot case law and practice since 1964. No analysis of the constitutional order of Cyprus might be accurate, without understanding the importance of the doctrine of necessity in the perseverance, interpretation and function of the Constitution.[9]

§2. Economic System

11. The Constitution does not specify a particular economic system. However, certain fundamental decisions by the framers of the Constitution provide for a set of conditions that have to be met when structuring the economic system. Among them are the freedom of property, the freedom to work or trade, the right to enter into a contract and the right to form associations; it is further provided that a person is bound to contribute towards the public burdens according to his means. The right to strike is also constitutionally safeguarded. The Cypriot economy is in general based on the free market system, with the private sector being the backbone of economic activity. The Government's role is limited to safeguarding a transparent framework for the operation of market mechanisms, the exercise of indicative planning and the provision of public utilities. Although the blow inflicted on the economy by the Turkish invasion of 1974 was devastating, considering the occupied part at that time accounted for almost 70% of Gross Domestic Product ('GDP'), recovery was remarkable. In the post-1974 period, Cyprus has converted from an exporter of agricultural products and minerals into a services-oriented economy, with tourism and provision of services being the main pillars of the economic growth. International

9. On the doctrine, *see* A. Emilianides, C. Papastylianos and C. Stratilatis, *The Republic of Cyprus and the Doctrine of Necessity* (Sakkoulas 2016, in Greek); P. Polyviou, *The Case of Ibrahim, The Doctrine of Necessity and the Republic of Cyprus* (Chryssafinis and Polyviou 2015).

trade is of considerable importance to the economy of Cyprus; Cyprus has been sought after as a base for several companies for its highly developed infrastructure, as well as for the tax incentives it offers.

12. Since its accession to the EU, Cyprus has undergone significant economic and structural reforms, which have transformed its economic landscape; tariffs and quantitative restrictions have been eliminated for all manufactured goods and agricultural products originating in EU countries. Trade and interest rates have also been liberated, while price controls and investment restrictions have, as a principle, been lifted. Private financing has been introduced for the construction and operation of infrastructural projects, while the State monopoly in the telecommunications sector has been abolished. EU Law provisions concerning competition and public procurement now form part of Cypriot internal law, with superior force. As of 1 January 2008, Cyprus has adopted the Euro as the national currency. Following a financial collapse in early 2013, Cyprus agreed to a Eurogroup scheme for the recapitalisation of the Cypriot banking sector by forcing the depositors in the two major Cypriot banks to bail-in. A Memorandum of Understanding ('MoU') was signed with Troika, the tripartite committee composed of the European Commission, the European Central Bank and the International Monetary Fund in order to finance the Cypriot economy;[10] the agreement introduced a series of austerity measures in the island. Structural adjustments included public spending cuts and tax increases, reform of the system of distribution of public benefits, as well as a privatisation scheme for profitable semi-governmental organisations. Improvement in the financial situation led to the completion of the financial support programme and eventual exit from the MoU in 2016.

13. The key to understanding the 'Cypriot corporatist model'[11] is by examining its reliance on cooperation between a set of organised interests and the State. It is, in effect, a tripartite structure of cooperation between the trade unions, the employers' associations and the Government of the Republic (through the Ministry of Labour, Welfare and Social Insurance) – the three social partners that constitute the 'model'. A tradition of smooth cooperation between the social partners exists in the industrial arrangement of the country. The 'corporatist culture' of the island has been the main variable in securing a climate of cooperation between the social partners over time. The success of the system of industrial relations in Cyprus rests upon the willingness of the social partners to cooperate and on voluntariness rather than legislative imposition. Following the Turkish invasion of 1974 and the catastrophe which occurred to the fabric of Cypriot society, the social partners showed a capacity to cooperate with one another in order to alleviate the problems created. They

10. *See, in general,* C. Ioannou and A. Emilianides, *The Haircut of Cypriot Deposits and the Protection of Fundamental Rights*, 2 *Cyprus Human Rights Law Review* 141–166 (2013); C. Ioannou and A. Emilianides, *Cyprus and EU Following the Haircut of Deposits, in Cyprus in a New Era: Geostrategy, Economy, Foreign Policy* 124–153 (C. Ioannou, D. Sotiropoulos and A. Emilianides eds., Foreign Affairs: Hellenic Edition and Hippasus 2014, in Greek).
11. C. Ioannou, *The Development of the Cypriot Corporatist Model, the Emergence of a Corporatist Culture and its Impact on the Process of Europeanisation,* 10 *Cyprus and European Law Review* 700–736 (2009); A. Emilianides and C. Ioannou, *Labour Law in Cyprus* (2d ed., Kluwer 2019).

agreed to suspend the Cost of Living Allowance ('COLA') system, which had been a major achievement of years of struggles by the working force. In other words, during the period from 1974 to 1978 (when COLA was re-introduced) wages stopped rising. This reduced the overall cost to the economy, helping it to recover sooner. This suspension of the COLA system is considered to be a great sacrifice on the part of trade unions during a crisis point. In other words, the experience has been incorporated into a vision of the essentially cooperative nature of the Cypriot model. The same agreement between social partners was reached following the 2013 financial collapse and helped the economy.

14. The accession of Cyprus to the EU in 2004 was seen as the culmination of a long history of attempts to find a viable solution to the political division of the island. The rationale behind the country's application for EU membership was primarily political. A clear connection was made between the Cyprus Problem and the approach of the country to the EU, to the extent that the two became almost synonymous. As a result, the harmonisation process, in relation to the transposition of the various directives of the *acquis communautaire* regarding social policy, was mostly conflict-free as it was thought likely to promote the long-anticipated solution to the Cyprus Problem. This was the dominant perception among the Cypriot political elite as well as the wider public, who linked accession to the EU to the solution of the country's political problem. Thus, while the process was largely politicised on a high politics field, it was largely apolitical on the lower politics field.[12] The wider objectives of the Cypriot adjustment process were to achieve reunification of the island by focusing on the 'higher' politics field and, at the same time, to convince the other members – through a smooth adjustment path – that the country is a 'good European'.[13]

15. This rather 'enthusiastic' process of Europeanisation reached its apogee on 1 May 2004, when the country acceded to the EU. Since accession, there has been increasing Euroscepticism as well as disappointment among Cypriot public opinion regarding the expected benefits arising from EU membership and its effects on Cypriot social policy. Euroscepticism reached its climax during the recent financial crisis and especially following the decisions of the Eurogroup in March 2013. Increase in unemployment and a cheaper labour force due to migration of workers led to changes in the landscape and effective application of the Cypriot model. Many employers viewed the economic crisis as an opportunity to restrict the rights of employees previously agreed by collective agreements and to violate their obligations towards their employees; fear of unemployment has led many employees to accept various forms of violations of their rights. The maintenance of economic

12. *See, in detail*, C. Ioannou, *The Europeanisation of Cypriot Social Policy: An 'Apolitical' Europeanisation Process, Journal of Modern Hellenism* 97–128 (2008–2009).
13. C. Ioannou and G. Kentas, *Social and Societal Aspects of EU Membership, in An Island in Europe: The EU and the Transformation of Cyprus* 89–111 (J. Ker-Lindsay, H. Faustmann and F. Mullen eds., I.B. Tauris 2011).

growth and industrial peace in a period of economic crisis remains a major challenge for the future of the Cypriot economic model, the COVID-19 pandemic having led to further deterioration.

§3. Legal System

I. Sources

A. *Constitution*

16. The Constitution of Cyprus is a written and lengthy document, consisting of 199 articles and three annexes.[14] Article 179 §1 provides that the Constitution shall be the supreme law of the Republic, while Article 179 §2 provides that no law or decision of the House of Representatives, or of any of the Communal Chambers, and no act or decision of any organ, authority or person in the Republic exercising executive power or any administrative function shall in any way be repugnant to, or inconsistent with, any of the provisions of the Constitution. The Constitution of Cyprus is accordingly the supreme law of the Republic and any ordinary laws, or international law instruments must not be inconsistent with the Constitution. A detailed list of the constitutionally safeguarded fundamental rights is included in Part II of the Constitution of Cyprus under the heading 'Fundamental Rights and Liberties'.[15]

17. Legislation which is contrary to the provisions of the Constitution safeguarding individual human rights may be declared unconstitutional by the trial court. It has been held that the fundamental rights and liberties safeguarded by the Constitution have to be narrowly construed and in case of doubt, should always be interpreted in favour of the individual protected, rather than in favour of the State. It is further noted that the Constitution safeguards minimum rights; the legislator may always opt to afford wider protection of a right or establish a new right; however, in the latter cases such right shall not enjoy a constitutional level of protection, but shall only be protected by ordinary legislation. Authorities of the Republic, legislative, executive and judicial are bound, in accordance with Article 35 of the Constitution, to secure within the limits of their respective competence, the effective application of the provisions of Part II of the Constitution.[16]

18. Article 33 of the Constitution explicitly provides that the fundamental rights and liberties guaranteed by the Constitution shall not be subject to any other limitations or restrictions other than those provided in Part II of the Constitution. Such

---

14. *See*, in detail, A. Emilianides, *Constitutional Law in Cyprus* (2d ed., Kluwer 2019).
15. *See*, in general, C. Tornaritis, *The State Law of the Republic of Cyprus* (Cyprus Research Centre 1982, in Greek); A. Loizou, *Constitution of the Republic of Cyprus* (2001, in Greek); C. Paraskeva, *Cypriot Constitutional Law: Fundamental Rights and Freedoms* (Nomiki Vivliothiki 2015, in Greek).
16. *Police v. Georghiades* [1983] 2 CLR 33.

limitations may further only be introduced by legislation enacted by the House of Representatives or legislation deemed to be part of Cypriot law under Article 188 of the Constitution, or, since the accession of the Republic of Cyprus to the EU, legislation which forms part of EU law. It is further stipulated in Article 33 §2 of the Constitution, that limitations or restrictions to the fundamental rights safeguarded by the Constitution should be interpreted strictly and should not be applied for any purpose other than those for which they have been prescribed. Interference with constitutional rights should never be given wider effect that what clearly and beyond doubt is warranted by their context.

B. EU Law

19. The Court of Justice of the European Union ('CJEU') has long considered that the Treaty on European Union ('TEU') is different from other treaties in that it has established a new legal order for the benefit of which the Member States have permanently limited their sovereign rights.[17] The CJEU has therefore considered that the supremacy and primacy of EU law extend even against the provisions of the national constitutions of the Member States of the Union.[18] Following the accession of the Republic of Cyprus to the EU, the Constitution was amended with the Fifth Constitutional Amendment of 2006, 127(I)/2006, which aimed at facilitating the exercise of the rights and obligations of the Republic of Cyprus as an EU Member State.

20. The newly added paragraph 4 of Article 169 of the Constitution provides that the Republic may exercise any option and discretion provided for in the Treaty Establishing the European Community ('TEC') or the TEU and to any treaties substituting or modifying them. Amended Article 179, paragraph 2 of the Constitution provides that no law or decision of the House of Representatives, or of any of the Communal Chambers, and no act or decision of any organ, authority or person in the Republic exercising executive power or any administrative function shall in any way be repugnant to, or inconsistent with, any obligation imposed upon the Republic as a result of its participation as a Member State of the EU.

21. Furthermore, the newly inserted Article 1A of the Constitution provides that no constitutional provision is considered to invalidate any laws, acts or measures which are deemed necessary due to the obligations of the Republic of Cyprus as a Member State of the EU, or may impede the legal effect and application of regulations, directives or other EU legal instruments of a binding nature in the Republic.[19] As a result, EU law has an intra-constitutional effect, in the sense that it is considered as an integral part of the Constitution, and no constitutional provision

17. Case 26/62, *Van Gend en Loos*, ECLI:EU:C:1963:1; Case 6/64, *Costa v. ENEL*, ECLI-:EU:C:1964:66.
18. Case 11/70, *InternationaleHandelsgesellschaft*, ECLI:EU:C:1970:114.
19. *See also* C. Lycourgos, *The Application of EU Law in Cyprus: Selected Aspects, The Cyprus Yearbook of International Law* 43 (2012); S. Laulhe-Shaelou, *Back to Reality: The Implications of EU*

may invalidate any provision of a binding nature of EU law. It should be noted that it is the Constitution itself which provides for the facilitation of EU law within the Cypriot legal order and its specific primacy. EU law is therefore accorded a constitutional status by the Constitution itself, in the sense that no other provision of the Constitution may be invoked so as to declare the provisions of EU law unconstitutional. Such effect is purely intra-constitutional as far as the Cypriot legal order is concerned.

C. *International Treaties*

22. Article 169 §1 of the Constitution provides that every international agreement with a foreign state or with any international organisation, relating to commercial matters, economic cooperation (including payments and credit) and *modus vivendi*, shall be concluded under a decision of the Council of Ministers. Any other treaty, convention or international agreement shall be negotiated and signed under a decision of the Council of Ministers, in accordance with Article 169 §2 of the Constitution, and it shall only be operative and binding on the Republic of Cyprus when approved by a law made by the House of Representatives whereupon it shall be concluded. The above are subject to the veto right of the President of the Republic, provided for in Article 50 of the Constitution if the decision of the Council of Ministers relates to foreign affairs, defence or security. An international treaty, convention or agreement that has been concluded in accordance with the procedure described above shall have as from its publication in the Official Gazette of the Republic superior force to any municipal law, on condition that such a treaty, convention or agreement is also applied by the other party thereto, in accordance with Article 169 §3 of the Constitution.

23. In view of the above, the Constitution provides for a dualistic approach with respect to the relationship between national and international laws. An international treaty, convention or agreement will therefore not become part of the Cypriot legal order, unless and until it has been ratified by the Council of Ministers, approved by law by the House of Representatives and published in the Official Gazette of the Republic. It is only through publication in the Official Gazette that the international law instrument may be invoked before the Cypriot courts and be applied in the Cypriot legal order. Such an international law instrument has superior force over any ordinary domestic legislation, not in the sense of an obligation to repeal any inconsistent domestic law, but in the sense of having superiority and precedence in its application. International law, once incorporated into the national legal order and published in the Official Gazette, is superior to any other municipal law, irrespective of whether such law is prior or subsequent to the international law instrument.

Membership in the Constitutional Legal Order of Cyprus, in Brave New World. Application of EU Law in the New Member States 471–502 (A. Lazowski ed., TMC Asser Press 201):.

An international law instrument may not be implicitly repealed through the enactment of conflicting subsequent municipal legislation.[20] Hierarchically, international law instruments are therefore placed above any municipal legislation, with the exception of the Constitution. The Constitution, as the supreme law of the Republic, does not fall within the definition of municipal law of Article 169 §3 of the Constitution.

24. It should be further noted that, while an international law instrument has to be ratified and published in the Official Gazette in order to become part of the Cypriot legal order, its interpretation is governed by the principles and interpretation of international law and particularly those contained in the Vienna Convention on the Law of Treaties. The rules and principles of interpretation of ordinary statutes do not apply with respect to the interpretation of international law instruments. Article 169 §3 of the Constitution introduces the condition of reciprocity, namely the condition that the international law instruments, either treaties, conventions or agreements, have to be applied also by the other party thereto, in order to enjoy superior force over municipal legislation. It has been held, however, that the nature, objective and function of certain international treaties and conventions are such so as to exclude the condition of reciprocity. These are multilateral conventions, the object of which is not to create any subjective or reciprocal rights for the contracting parties themselves, but rather to promote certain principles of law, moral and legal values, and which a contracting party signs and ratifies only for the realisation of this objective. Examples of such international conventions are those which protect human rights, or those whose aim is the improvement and formulation of common rules and the achievement of social justice. The latter are self-executing.[21]

25. The most important self-executing international convention that is applicable in the Cypriot legal order is the European Convention on Human Rights ('ECHR'). Part II of the Constitution of Cyprus, which guarantees the fundamental rights and liberties, is modelled on the ECHR. However, the provisions of the ECHR have been extended and enlarged in some respects with a number of social and economic rights added in order to meet the basic requirements of a modern society.[22] The ECHR itself was ratified and was incorporated in the internal legal order by the European Convention for the Protection of Human Rights (Ratification) Law 39/1962.[23] Pursuant to Article 169, paragraph 3 of the Constitution, the ECHR and its Protocols have superior force to any municipal law; however, the constitutional provisions shall prevail in case of any inconsistency between them. To the extent, however, that it has been incorporated in constitutional provisions and to the degree

20. *Malachtou v. Armefti and Another* [1987] 1 CLR 207. *See also* C. Tornaritis, *The Introduction of International Law into the Legal System of Cyprus,* 3 *Cyprus Law Tribune* 460–474 (1990); C. Tornaritis, *The Treaty Making Power, especially under the Law of the Republic of Cyprus* (1973).
21. *Malachtou v. Armefti* [1987] 1 CLR 207.
22. Acknowledged in several judgments of the Supreme Court of Cyprus, such as *Attorney-General v. Ibrahim* [1964] CLR 195, 225; *Attorney-General v. Afamis* 1 RSCC 121.
23. *See* A. Loizou, *Cyprus*, in *Fundamental Rights in Europe: The European Convention on Human Rights and Its Member States, 1950–2000* 219 (R. Blackburn and J. Polakiewicz eds., Oxford University Press 2001).

that its provisions have not been altered during incorporation, the ECHR enjoys limited constitutional status. Cypriot courts frequently invoke the case law of the European Court of Human Rights ('ECtHR'), with respect to not only the interpretation of the ECHR but also the interpretation of the corresponding constitutional articles. Therefore, the courts will try, wherever possible, to interpret the relevant constitutional provisions in a manner which is consistent with the interpretation adopted by the ECtHR.[24]

D. *Ordinary Legislation*

26. Article 61 of the Constitution provides that the legislative power of the Republic shall be exercised by the House of Representatives in all matters except those expressly reserved to the Communal Chambers under the Constitution. Following the self-dissolution of the Greek Communal Chamber, the whole of the legislative power of the Republic has been transferred to the House of Representatives. The House of Representatives may exercise its legislative power in relation to not only general matters but also matters of specific nature, such as loans, guarantees or similar legal obligations of the Government. The exercise of the legislative power of the House is, however, subject to the application of the principle of separation of powers in the sense that the legislative power of the House of Representatives may not interfere with the powers of the executive or the judiciary.

27. The main source for legislation, including constitutional amendments, is the Official Gazette of the Republic of Cyprus. Article 82 of the Constitution explicitly provides that a law or decision of the House of Representatives shall come into operation on its publication in the Official Gazette of the Republic, unless another date is provided by such law or decision. In accordance with Article 188 of the Constitution, all laws in force on the date of the coming into operation of the Constitution shall, until amended, whether by way of variation, addition or repeal as the case may be, continue in force on, or after, that date, and shall be construed and applied with such modification as may be necessary to bring them into conformity with the Constitution; no provision in such law shall continue to be in force, if it is contrary to, or inconsistent with, any provision of the Constitution, save as otherwise provided for in the Constitution itself. The Laws of Cyprus in force on 1 April 1959, before independence, were compiled by the former Attorney-General of the Republic Criton Tornaritis and are separated into six volumes and 354 Chapters (Caps) each Cap. corresponding to a single law. Laws which continue to be in force after independence are referred to by their respective Cap. in the 1959 edition (e.g., Interpretation Law is Cap. 1, Advocates Law is Cap. 2, and so on).

---

24. *See further* A. Loizou, *Cyprus and the European Convention on Human Rights* (Sakkoulas 2003, in Greek).

II. Position of the Judiciary

28. The Constitution provides for the establishment of a Supreme Constitutional Court and a High Court. In accordance with Article 133 of the Constitution, the Supreme Constitutional Court was to be composed of a Greek Cypriot, a Turkish Cypriot and a neutral judge (not a subject or citizen of the Republic of Cyprus, Greece, Turkey or the United Kingdom and its Colonies) who would act as the President of the Court, whereas the High Court was to be composed of two Greek Cypriots, a Turkish Cypriot and a neutral judge who would act as the President of the Court. However, following the constitutional breakdown in 1963, the neutral Presidents of the Supreme Constitutional Court and the High Court decided to leave Cyprus and, as a result, the highest courts of the land could not function. Furthermore, the administration of justice, as well as the very existence of the Republic of Cyprus, was in immediate danger.[25] In view of the aforementioned problems, the House of Representatives enacted, by virtue of the doctrine of necessity, the Administration of Justice (Miscellaneous Provisions) Law 33/1964, according to the provisions of which, a newly established Supreme Court would exercise the jurisdiction and powers of the Supreme Constitutional Court and the High Court, 'until such time as the people of Cyprus may determine such matters'.[26] Since 1964, the Supreme Court has been exercising all the competencies conferred by the Constitution to the Supreme Constitutional Court and the High Court. The seat of the Supreme Court is in Nicosia. The Supreme Court is currently composed of thirteen Greek Cypriot judges, one of whom is appointed as the President of the Court.

29. The Supreme Court is the highest appellate court in the Republic and has jurisdiction to hear and determine all civil and criminal appeals from any court (with the exception of the Family Courts) and all administrative appeals. In civil and criminal appeals, the Supreme Court is composed of three judges, unless it is decided that the case should be reviewed by the Full Bench of the Court. In addition, the Supreme Court exercises its original jurisdiction in cases of maritime law; one single judge may exercise such original jurisdiction. The Supreme Court further has exclusive jurisdiction to adjudicate finally on any election petition with regard to the elections of the President, or of members of the House of Representatives or of any Communal Chamber, to determine any conflict between the original Greek and Turkish texts of the Constitution and to interpret the Constitution in case of ambiguity, to hear and determine recourses filed by virtue of Articles 137–139 and 143 of the Constitution, references for opinion filed by virtue of Articles 141–142 of the Constitution and motions in accordance with Article 147 of the Constitution. It also has the power to grant the prerogative orders of habeas corpus, mandamus, prohibition, quo warranto and certiorari; such writs have their origin in English common law. The jurisdiction of the Supreme Court to issue the

25. *See, inter alia, The Attorney-General of the Republic v. Ibrahim* [1964] CLR 195.
26. Preamble of Law 33/64. *Attorney-General v. Ibrahim* [1964] CLR 195. *See also Charalambides and another v. Republic and another*, Administrative App. 99/2016, Supreme Court Judgment of 4 Apr. 2018 (in Greek).

prerogative writs is a significant one, since it enables the Court to review the action of lower courts or organs, outside the exercise of the appellate jurisdiction.

30. Articles 134 and 154 of the Constitution stipulate that the sittings of the Supreme Court for the hearing of all proceedings shall be public, but the Court may hear any proceedings in the presence of only the parties and the officers of the Court, if it considers that such a course will be in the interest of the orderly conduct of the proceedings, or if the security of the Republic or public morals so require. As an exception, it is provided in Article 134 §2 that where a recourse filed before the Supreme Court, while exercising its powers as the Supreme Constitutional Court of the Republic, appears to be prima facie frivolous, the Court may, after hearing arguments by or on behalf of the parties concerned, dismiss such recourse without a public hearing if satisfied that such recourse is in fact frivolous. This is also reiterated in the rules of procedure enacted by the Supreme Court. In practice, the Supreme Court does not often use its powers to dismiss recourses as frivolous without a public hearing.

31. Article 162 of the Constitution provides that the Supreme Court shall have jurisdiction to punish for any contempt of itself, and any other court of the Republic shall have power to commit any person disobeying a judgment or order of such court to prison until such person complies with such judgment or order and in any event for a period not exceeding twelve months. The power of the Court to punish any person disobeying its judgments or orders has always been regarded as an inherent and significant power of the courts. The notion of contempt is further expanded in Article 44 of the Courts of Justice Law 14/60 where, *inter alia*, acts of disrespect, obstruction or disturbance of any judicial proceedings, including publications which are capable of prejudicing the fair trial of such proceedings, witness tampering or dismissing an employee for giving evidence in judicial proceedings, are penalised, and wrongdoers are liable to imprisonment up to six months.[27]

§4. Historical Background of Antitrust Law

32. The first Cypriot legislative instrument, which aimed to regulate competition law, was the Protection of Competition Law 62/1983.[28] The objective of Law 62/83 was to introduce comprehensive antitrust legislation in the Republic of Cyprus, so as to protect competition. It was considered that the need to introduce antitrust legislation had become imperative, due to the growing efforts of undertakings to distort competition through the creation of monopolies and oligopolies, and the concerted practices of their policies in several sectors of the economy. The stated objective of Law 62/83 was to achieve resource efficiency, improve production and

27. *See*, in general, A. Emilianides, *Contempt in the Face of the Court and the Right to a Fair Trial*,13 *European Journal of Crime, Criminal Law & Criminal Justice* 401–412 (2005); A. Emilianides, *Reflections on the Law of Contempt in Light of Recent Cypriot Jurisprudence*, 2 *Cyrus Human Rights Law Review* 221–226 (2012).

28. For a historical background of, and a general introduction to, Cypriot antitrust law, *see also* P. Agisilaou et al., *Competition Policy in Cyprus 1989-2009* (Nomiki Vivliothiki 2011, in Greek): 50ff.

distribution of goods and services to the benefit of consumers, and preclude the distortion of competition. Law 62/83 was to enter into force by a relevant order issued by the Council of Ministers. This never happened. Eventually, Law 62/83 was abolished, without ever entering into force.

33. The Republic of Cyprus undertook the obligation to introduce antitrust legislation by the Protocol for the application of the second stage of the Agreement of Association between the Republic of Cyprus and the European Economic Communities ('EEC'). The Agreement of Association had been in force since 1972, but the Protocol was signed in 1987 and explicitly provided for the introduction of legislation for the protection of competition, in a manner analogous to the Treaty of Rome establishing the EEC. Conforming to such obligations, the Republic of Cyprus enacted the Protection of Competition 207/89. Law 207/89 entered into force on 8 June 1990 and had the objective to protect free competition and to introduce in the Republic of Cyprus analogous provisions to the competition provisions of the TEC.

34. Law 207/89 contained substantive provisions prohibiting agreements and concerted practice which may prevent, restrict or distort competition, and also the abuse of dominant position by undertakings, similar to Articles 85 and 86 TEC as they then were (subsequently, Articles 81 and 82 TEC, and eventually Articles 101 and 102 TFEU). It further established for the first time in Cyprus, the institution of the Commission for the Protection of Competition (CPC), as an independent administrative organ having wide powers for the protection of competition, equivalent to those of the European Commission. The CPC comprised of seven members was appointed by the Council of Ministers for a four-year term. The first Chair of the CPC was former Minister of Justice and advocate Christodoulos Chrysanthou, who served until 1998. CPC issued its first decision on 1 December 1990, a case which referred to an application for individual exception by thirty insurance companies with regard to insurance for seismic danger. However, the total number of cases examined by the CPC during the 1990s was few, and its actual impact remained relatively insignificant. The powers of the CPC were further enhanced in 2000, in advance of the potential accession of the Republic of Cyprus to the EU, and with the objective to strengthen the CPC and increase its effectiveness. Amending Law 155(I)/2000 restricted the number of the members of the CPC from seven to five, and increased the term of the members to five years. Furthermore, the position of the Chair of the CPC became full-time, and the CPC was granted the power to carry out sudden searches in the establishments of the undertakings. Another amending legislation, Law 87(I)/2000, granted the CPC power over public undertakings.

35. The above-mentioned legislative amendments, as well as the momentum of the accession of Cyprus to the EU, helped establish the CPC as an important new regulator in the market. Advocate Christodoulos Tselepos was appointed as the second Chair of the CPC in 1998 and served until 2005. However, Tselepos' term was terminated prematurely by the Council of Ministers, when he was prosecuted for alleged forgery of the minutes of the CPC. Tselepos had signed a minute approving the applications of the Cyprus Football Association and a TV subscription company for individual exception for the transmission of football matches, by reference to an alleged meeting of the CPC that had not taken place on that date. The Council of Ministers held that the Chair of the CPC has abused his position so that continuation of his term would be detrimental to the public interest. Tselepos was convicted by the First Instance Court, but the Supreme Court eventually decided by a 2-1 majority to acquit Tselepos from all criminal charges; it observed, however, that despite his acquittal, Tselepos had not acted in the fair and proper manner that a high officer is expected to.[29] Tselepos filed a recourse against the termination of his term, but to no avail; the Plenary of the Supreme Court affirmed the validity of the decision of the Council of Ministers.[30]

36. Another advocate, and former member of the House of Representatives, Giorgos Christofides, was appointed as the third Chair of the CPC. His term, however, was also cut short. The media showed that Christofides had established cameras and surveillance system in the CPC, which could monitor parties and advocates appearing before the CPC, as well as the CPC personnel, thus infringing their personal data and right to privacy. The employees of the CPC organised a strike for several days, and Christofides was forced to resign after having served as Chair of the CPC for only two years. The fourth CPC Chair was the former Supreme Court judge Panayiotis Kallis. Following his appointment, the Plenary of the Supreme Court held that the previous composition of the CPC had been unlawful, because one of its members, Kostis Efstathiou, was concurrently serving at a municipal board.[31] This meant that the CPC had to effectively revoke and revaluate from the beginning, nearly all decisions it had issued. Kallis resigned on his own after serving for only a few months, citing lack of resources to fight the cartels and protect consumers, particularly the lack of sufficient personnel and the fact that the members of the CPC were serving part-time only. Kallis' disappointment can also be explained by the following: the CPC was appointed by the Council of Ministers in June 2006, as the competent authority for the application of Articles 81 and 82 TEC (subsequently Articles 101 and 102 TFEU), pursuant to Article 35 of Regulation 1/2003 ('Modernisation Regulation').[32] However, despite such appointment, it could not exercise such competences due to a lack of a domestic legislative framework.

37. Law 207/89 was eventually abolished and replaced by Law 13(I)/2008 ('CPC Law'). The objective of the CPC Law was to apply effectively the Modernisation Regulation in the Republic of Cyprus, and to protect competition in areas where the EU competition law does not apply. The CPC Law provides that the Chair and the four members of the CPC shall be full-time, thereby significantly enhancing

29. *Tselepos v. Police* [2008] 2 CLR 457 (in Greek).
30. *Tselepos v. Republic* [2010] 3 CLR 410 (in Greek).
31. *Cyprus Telecommunications Authority v. Republic* [2007] 3 CLR 560 (in Greek).
32. Council Regulation (EC) No. 1/2003 of 16 December 2002 on the implementation of the rules on competition laid down in Articles 81 and 82 of the Treaty, as amended by Regulations 411/2004 of 26 Feb. 2004, 1419/06 of 25 Sep. 2006, 169/09 of 26 Feb. 2009, 246/09 of 26 Feb. 2009, and 487/09 of 25 May 2009.

their role. The former Director of the House of Representatives, Costakis Christoforou, was appointed by the Council of Ministers as the new Chair of the CPC. However, his appointment was declared as unlawful by the Full Bench of the Supreme Court, which held that the decision to appoint him had not made any mention that the Chair fulfilled the qualifications required by CPC Law, and in particular, specialised knowledge and experience in law, and the ability to contribute to the realisation of the objectives of CPC Law. Any decision taken with the participation of the Chair was declared void.[33]

38. Under its new Chair Loukia Christodoulou, the CPC had to once again revoke and revaluate from the beginning, nearly all decisions it had issued, many of them dating from the mid-2000s. Further confusion occurred when the Administrative Court annulled the appointment to the CPC of one of its members, Christos Tsingis, because he was concurrently serving as a member of the central committee of a political party. However, the Supreme Court eventually set aside the judgment of the Administrative Court by a 7-4 majority and held that the appointment of Tsingis, who had in the meantime resigned from his office, was lawful.[34]

39. Three decades after the CPC was first established, and despite the best intentions and efforts of its members, and its Service, the CPC had long been widely perceived as a relatively unsuccessful regulator, largely due to problems with its composition. The successive annulment of its membership led the CPC to effectively terminate a number of investigations due to a lack of interest from complainants to further pursue their complaints, years after they initially submitted them before the CPC. The CPC further decided to terminate a number of ex-officio investigations due to failure to deal with its excess workload, following the need to re-examine decisions it had taken that were set aside by the courts. Undertakings and consumers alike, however, are gradually growing conscious of the importance and role that the CPC is able to perform in the market. As has become evident from the volume and quality of decisions over the past few years and the targeted nature of its investigation, the CPC appears determined to fulfil its statutory mandate and has been demonstrating increased rigour in investigating potential infringements of the CPC Law.

33. *Exxon Mobil Ltd and others v. Commission for the Protection of Competition* [2011] 3 CLR 449 (in Greek).
34. *Commission for the Protection of Competition v. Cyprus Telecommunications Authority*, Apps 2/16 and 7/16, 3 Mar. 2017 (in Greek).

Part I. Structure of Antitrust Law and Its Enforcement

Chapter 1. Sources of Antitrust Law

§1. National Sources

40. The main source of Cypriot competition law is the CPC Law, as amended by Law 41(I)/2014. The CPC Law establishes the CPC and the Service of the CPC, and provides for the powers of the CPC, the prohibited conduct by undertakings, and the relevant exceptions, as well as other incidental provisions. The CPC Law has been partly enacted in implementation of the Modernisation Regulation. The objective of competition policy is to encourage economic activity and maximise efficiency by enabling goods and resources to flow freely among Member States according to the operation of normal market forces. The concentration of resources resulting from such activity functioning on a transnational, rather than a national, scale is intended to increase the competitiveness of European industry in a world market. In addition to this primary goal, and sometimes conflicting with it, EU competition policy seeks to protect and encourage small and medium-sized enterprises so that they too may be part of the competitive process.[35]

41. The CPC Law is a restriction of the right to enter freely into any contract, which is safeguarded by Article 26 of the Constitution. Article 26 provides that every person has the right to enter freely into any contract subject to such conditions, limitations or restrictions as are laid down by the general principles of the law of contract. In *Chimonides v. Manglis*, the majority of the Supreme Court held that Article 26 safeguards only the right to enter into a contract and not the obligations arising out of an agreement resulting from an exercise of the right to contract.[36] Rights arising out of a contract were therefore not considered to be guaranteed by Article 26 of the Constitution as fundamental rights. The Supreme Court, however, in a recent unanimous judgment, partly reversed the *Chimonides* majority ruling and held that the right safeguarded under Article 26 of the Constitution, includes the right to determine the content of the contract in accordance with the free will of the parties. Accordingly, any subsequent interference by the legislator is not consistent

35. Case 1023/12, *Pancyprian Organisation of Cattle Public Company Ltd v. Commission for the Protection of Competition*, 30 Nov. 2012 (in Greek).
36. [1967] 1 CLR 125.

with the freedom of contract, except under the circumstances provided for in the Constitution and to the extent that they do not prejudice the substance or core of the right.[37]

42. Irrespective of whether Article 26 safeguards only the right to freely enter into contract only, or the content of the contract as determined by the free will of the parties as well, the provisions of antitrust law should be considered as being in accordance with the Constitution. Article 26 stipulates that a law shall provide for the prevention of exploitation by persons who are commanding economic power, and this constitutional provision has been interpreted as a sufficient legal basis for the enactment of the CPC Law and the imposition of restrictions and limitations to the right of the parties to a contract. It has further been held that in any event Article 26 of the Constitution should be interpreted in line with the need to realize the objectives of the EU in the field of competition law.[38] To the extent that the CPC applies EU law directly, this is anyway accorded a constitutional status pursuant to Articles 1A, 169 §4 and 179 §2 of the Constitution.

43. The other important national legal source is the Control of Concentration of Undertakings Law 83(I)/14 ('Concentrations Law'), which repealed and substituted the previously applicable Control of Concentration of Undertakings Law 22(I)/99. The Concentrations Law was enacted pursuant to the provisions of Regulation 139/2004 ('Merger Regulation').[39] The Concentrations Law has introduced a system of notification and *a priori* examination of concentrations by the CPC.

44. Furthermore, the Claims for Compensation for Violations of Competition Law, Law 113(I)/17 ('Antitrust Damages Law'), has implemented Directive 2014/104/EU[40] in the domestic Cypriot order. The Antitrust Damages Law is an important instrument, as it provides that persons, who have suffered harm caused by an infringement of competition law, may claim full compensation for that harm.

45. While Cyprus has yet to transpose Directive 2019/1[41] into its legal order, it carried out a public consultation in 2020 on a draft bill intending to implement the said Directive.[42] Directive 2019/1 introduces provisions to guarantee the necessary

37. *President of the Republic v. House of Representatives*, App. 1/2014, 31 Oct. 2014 (in Greek), *President of the Republic v. House of Representatives*, App. 4/2014, 31 Oct. 2014 (in Greek).
38. Case 1023/12, *Pancyprian Organisation of Cattle Public Company Ltd v. Commission for the Protection of Competition*, 30 Nov. 2012 (in Greek).
39. Of 20 Jan. 2004 on the control of concentrations between undertakings.
40. Council Regulation (EC) No. 139/2004 of the European Parliament and of the Council of 26 November 2014 on certain rules governing actions for damages under national law for infringements of the competition law provisions of the Member States and of the EU.
41. Directive (EU) No. 2019/1 of the European Parliament and of the Council of 11 December 2018 to empower the competition authorities of the Member States to be more effective enforcers and to ensure the proper functioning of the internal market.
42. Public consultation carried out by the CPC between 11 May and 12 June 2020 on the draft bill titled 'Protection of Competition Law of 2021'.

independence, resources and enforcement and fining powers for national competition authorities in the EU and strengthens mutual assistance between national competition authorities.

§2. International Sources

46. Articles 101 and 102 TFEU (formerly Articles 81 and 82 TEC) apply directly to the Republic of Cyprus and have superior effect to any municipal legislation. Moreover, section 50 of the CPC Law expressly provides that where an issue is not dealt with by the Law itself, EU Law shall be applied, *mutatis mutandis*. Article 101 §1 TFEU provides that all agreements between undertakings, decisions by associations of undertakings and concerted practices which may affect trade between Member States, and which have as their object or effect the prevention, restriction or distortion of competition within the internal market, shall be prohibited as incompatible with the internal market. This refers, in particular, to those agreements, decisions and concerted practices, which: (a) directly or indirectly fix purchase or selling prices or any other trading conditions; (b) limit or control production, markets, technical development, or investment; (c) share markets or sources of supply; (d) apply dissimilar conditions to equivalent transactions with other trading parties, thereby placing them at a competitive disadvantage; (e) make the conclusion of contracts subject to the acceptance by the other parties of supplementary obligations which, by their nature or according to commercial usage, have no connection with the subject of such contracts.

47. Any prohibited agreements or decisions shall be automatically void. However, the provisions of Article 101 §1 TFEU may be declared inapplicable in the case of any agreement or category of agreements between undertakings, any decision or category of decisions by associations of undertakings, or any concerted practice or category of concerted practices: (a) which contributes to the improvement of the production or distribution of goods or to the promotion of technical or economic progress; (b) while allowing consumers a fair share of the resulting benefit; and (c) which does not impose on the undertakings concerned restrictions which are not indispensable to the attainment of these objectives, or afford such undertakings the possibility of eliminating competition in respect of a substantial part of the products in question.

48. Article 102 TFEU provides that any abuse by one or more undertakings of a dominant position within the internal market or in a substantial part of it shall be prohibited as incompatible with the internal market in so far as it may affect trade between Member States. Such abuse may, in particular, consist in: (a) directly or indirectly imposing unfair purchase or selling prices or other unfair trading conditions; (b) limiting production, markets or technical development to the prejudice of consumers; (c) applying dissimilar conditions to equivalent transactions with other trading parties, thereby placing them at a competitive disadvantage; and (d) making the conclusion of contracts subject to acceptance by the other parties of supplementary obligations which, by their nature or according to commercial usage, have no connection with the subject of such contracts.

49. Article 105 TFEU further provides that the European Commission shall ensure the application of the principles laid down in Articles 101 and 102 TFEU. On application by a Member State or on its own initiative, and in cooperation with the competent authorities in the Member States, which shall give it their assistance, the European Commission shall investigate cases of suspected infringement of these principles. If it finds that there has been an infringement, it shall propose appropriate measures to bring it to an end. If the infringement is not brought to an end, the European Commission shall record such infringement in a reasoned decision, and authorise Member States to take the measures, the conditions and details of which it shall determine, needed to remedy the situation.

50. Article 106 TFEU further provides that in the case of public undertakings and undertakings to which Member States grant special or exclusive rights, Member States shall neither enact, nor maintain in force, any measure contrary to the rules contained in the Treaties. Undertakings entrusted with the operation of services of general economic interest or having the character of a revenue-producing monopoly shall be subject to the rules contained in the Treaties, in particular to the rules on competition, in so far as the application of such rules does not obstruct the performance, in law or in fact, of the particular tasks assigned to them. The development of trade must not be affected to such an extent as would be contrary to the interests of the EU.

51. Article 103 TFEU provides that the Council shall lay down the appropriate regulations or directives to give effect to the principles set out in Articles 101 and 102 TFEU, on a proposal from the European Commission and after consulting the European Parliament. Such regulations or directives shall be designed in particular: (a) to ensure compliance with the prohibitions laid down in Articles 101 and 102 TFEU by making provision for fines and periodic penalty payments; (b) to lay down detailed rules for the application of Article 101 §3 TFEU, taking into account the need to ensure effective supervision on the one hand, and to simplify administration to the greatest possible extent on the other; (c) to define, if need be, in the various branches of the economy, the scope of the provisions of Articles 101 and 102 TFEU; (d) to define the respective functions of the European Commission and of the CJEU in applying the provisions; and (e) to determine the relationship between national laws and EU competition law. Pursuant to Article 103 TFEU, the Council has enacted the Modernisation Regulation, in order to implement the rules on competition laid down in Articles 101 and 102 TFEU. This is complemented by two sectoral Regulations, i.e., Regulation (EC) 411/2004[43] for the air transport sector and Regulation (EC) 1419/06[44] for the maritime transport sector.

52. The Modernisation Regulation allows for competition rules previously applied by the European Commission to be enforced on a decentralised basis by EU countries' competition authorities. It thus enhanced the role of national antitrust authorities and courts in implementing EU competition law. This allows the European Commission to focus its resources on enforcing the most serious competition infringements with a cross-border dimension.[45] The CPC is the national authority responsible for applying the provisions of the Modernisation Regulation in the Republic of Cyprus. The Modernisation Regulation has been further implemented by Commission Regulation (EC) 773/2004.[46] Another important legal instrument, as already mentioned, is the Mergers Regulation. The Commission has issued a number of additional regulations and guidelines, which will be referred to in the appropriate sections. This monograph will not engage in a detailed interpretation of the provisions of the TFEU, or the provisions of either the Modernisation Regulation or the Mergers Regulation, or other provisions of EU law, since its focus will be the national provisions and practice. Accordingly, there will be reference to EU law only to the extent necessary to assess domestic law and practice.[47]

§3. Secondary Sources

53. The Immunity from and Reduction of Administrative Fines in cases of Restrictive Collusions Infringing section 3 of the Law and Article 101 of the TFEU Regulations of 2011 ('Leniency Programme')[48] are secondary legislations. Their objective is to define the leniency or exemption from administrative fines of an undertaking and/or associations of undertakings wishing to cooperate with the CPC

43. Council Regulation (EC) No. 411/2004 of 26 February 2004 repealing Regulation (EEC) 3975/87 and amending Regulations (EEC) 3976/87 and (EC) 1/2003, in connection with air transport between the Community and third countries.
44. Council Regulation (EC) No. 1419/06 of 25 September 2006 repealing Regulation (EEC) 4056/86 laying down detailed rules for the application of Articles 85 and 86 of the Treaty to maritime transport, and amending Regulation (EC) 1/2003 as regards the extension of its scope to include cabotage and international tramp services.
45. *See*, in general, Communication from the European Commission – Ten Years of Antitrust Enforcement under Regulation 1/2003: Achievements and Future Perspectives, COM (2014) 453, 9 Jul. 2014, Commission Staff Working Document SWD (2014) 230 – Ten Years of Antitrust Enforcement under Regulation 1/2003, SWD (2014) 230/2, 9 Jul. 2014, Commission Staff Working Document SWD (2014) 231 – Enhancing competition enforcement by the Member States' competition authorities: institutional and procedural issues SWD (2014) 231/2, 9 Jul. 2014.
46. Of 7 Apr. 2004 relating to the conduct of proceedings by the European Commission pursuant to Articles 81 and 82 of the EC Treaty.
47. *See*, e.g., A. Jones et al., *Jones & Sufrin's EU Competition Law* (7th ed., OUP 2019); R. Whish & D. Bailey, *Competition Law* (9th ed., OUP 2018).
48. 463/11, [2011] III(I) OJ 3189.

to uncover illegal cartels. The Leniency Programme codifies the procedure, the conditions and the criteria for granting an exemption or reduction of the administrative fine imposed by the CPC in such cases. The introduction of a Leniency Programme mirrors the European Commission Notice on Immunity from fines and reduction of fines in cartel cases, which sets out the framework for rewarding cooperation in the Commission investigation by undertakings which are or have been party to secret cartels affecting the Community.[49] A revised leniency framework intended to replace the Leniency Programme was placed in public consultation in 2020.[50]

54. The Council of Ministers has further issued a number of block exemptions to the competition rules. These include Vertical Agreements and Concerted Practices,[51] Agreements for Research and Development,[52] Licensing Agreements for Transfer of Technology,[53] certain categories of transport,[54] and insurance.[55] These exemptions mirror block exemptions issued pursuant to Article 101 §3 TFEU, and essentially provide for the, *mutatis mutandis*, application of the respective EU block exemptions, respectively Regulation 330/10,[56] Regulation 461/10,[57] Regulation 1217/10,[58] Regulation 316/14,[59] Regulation 906/09,[60] Regulation 169/09,[61] Regulation 1218/10,[62] and Regulation 267/10.[63]

49. Commission Notice on Immunity from fines and reduction of fines in cartel cases, OJ C 298, 8 Dec. 2006, OJ C 144, 23 Apr. 2016.
50. Public consultation carried out by the CPC between 11/5/2020 and 12/6/2020 on draft subsidiary legislation prepared to replace the Leniency Programme.
51. 141/14, [2014] III(I) OJ 483; 140/14, [2014] III(I) OJ 482.
52. 70/19, [2019] III(I) OJ 364.
53. 67/19, [2019] III(I) OJ 361.
54. 64/19, [2019] III(I) OJ 358, 65/19, [2019] III(I) OJ 359, 66/19, [2019] III(I) OJ 360, 68/19, [2019] III(I) OJ 362, 69/19, [2019] III(I) OJ 363.
55. 139/14, [2014] III(I) OJ 481.
56. Commission Regulation (EU) No. 330/2010 of 20 April 2010 on the application of Article 101 (3) of the Treaty on the Functioning of the European Union to categories of vertical agreements and concerted practices.
57. Commission Regulation (EU) No. 461/2010 of 27 May 2010 on the application of Article 101 (3) of the Treaty on the Functioning of the European Union to categories of vertical agreements and concerted practices in the motor vehicle sector.
58. Commission Regulation (EU) No. 1217/2010 of 14 December 2010 on the application of Article 101 (3) of the Treaty on the Functioning of the European Union to certain categories of research and development agreements.
59. Commission Regulation (EU) No. 316/2014 of 21 March 2014 on the application of Article 101(3) of the Treaty on the Functioning of the European Union to categories of technology transfer agreements.
60. Commission Regulation (EC) No. 906/2009 of 28 September 2009 on the application of Article 81(3) of the Treaty to certain categories of agreements, decisions and concerted practices between liner shipping companies (consortia).
61. Council Regulation (EC) No. 169/2009 of 26 February 2009 applying rules of competition to transport by rail, road and inland waterway.
62. Commission Regulation (EU) No. 1218/2010 of 14 December 2010 on the application of Article 101(3) of the Treaty on the Functioning of the European Union to certain categories of specialisation agreements.

55. The CPC forms part of the European Competition Network (ECN), which was established as a system of parallel competences in which the national competition authorities of Member States apply the competition rules. The ECN provides a framework for cooperation between the EU Commission and the national competition authorities in cases in which Articles 101 and 102 TFEU apply. The competition authorities, including the CPC, have adopted a number of ECN recommendations, concerning the powers of investigation that they should have, as well as their powers to take decisions on the application of the competition rules. The Recommendations are intended to be used as supporting documents, or for the purpose of determining competition policy. These are: (a) ECN Recommendation on Investigative Powers, Enforcement Measures and Sanctions in the context of Inspections and Requests for Information; (b) ECN Recommendation on the Power to Collect Digital Evidence, including by Forensic Means; (c) ECN Recommendation on Assistance in Inspections conducted under Articles 22(1) of Regulation (EC) No. 1/2003; (d) ECN Recommendation on the Power to set Priorities; (e) ECN Recommendation on Interim Measures; (f) ECN Recommendation on Commitment Procedures; and (g) ECN Recommendation on the Power to Impose Structural Remedies.

§4. Sources' Relation and Hierarchy

56. As already indicated, EU law is accorded a constitutional status. This includes the legal effect not only of TFEU provisions but also of Regulations and directives as harmonised in the domestic legal order, as well as other EU legal instruments of a binding nature. No law or decision of any organ, authority or person in the Republic, exercising executive or legislative power, or administrative function, may be in any way repugnant to, or inconsistent with obligations imposed upon the Republic as a result of its participation as a Member State of the EU. Considering that even the domestic competition law rules have been adopted as part of the obligations imposed upon the Republic because of its participation as a Member State of the EU, it would seem that the main legislative sources of Cypriot competition law have a superior hierarchical status. Statutory legislation may not, however, be inconsistent with the provisions of the Directive it aims to harmonise in the domestic legal order.

63. Commission Regulation (EU) No. 267/2010 of 24 March 2010 on the application of Article 101(3) of the Treaty on the Functioning of the European Union to certain categories of agreements, decisions and concerted practices in the insurance sector. This Regulation is no longer in force since 31 Mar. 2017.

§5. Role and Authority of Precedents

57. The principles of common law and equity apply in the Republic of Cyprus.[64] Previous judgments of the Supreme Court are binding for lower courts; thus, case law is of great significance with regard to the interpretation of legal provisions.[65] The Supreme Court itself may depart from its earlier decisions whenever it concludes that a previous decision is founded on an indisputably wrong principle of law, or a principle leading to manifest injustice, or a principle which cannot be reconciled to changed legal or social circumstances. It is accordingly noted that previous case law is only binding so far as a subsequent law with different content has not been enacted. The legal rule which must be applied is the *ratio decidendi*, or the legal principle on which the previous decision was founded. The *ratio* of the case is distinguishable from obiter dicta, which are statements on principles of law made in the course of a decision, but on which the decision does not depend. Having a substantially codified legal system, Cyprus applies common law principles where there is no Cypriot legislation in force and in so far as existing Cypriot legislation is not contradicted.

64. L. Loucaides, *The Dependence of Cypriot Law from Common Law*, in *Topics of Cypriot Law* 36–77 (1982, in Greek); G. Pikis, *The English Common Law: The Rules of Equity and their Application in Cyprus* (1981, in Greek).

65. C. Artemides, *The Principle of Commitment of Courts to Case-Law in English Common Law*, in *Aspects of Cypriot Law* Vol. I, 219–231 (Asselia 1981, in Greek); S. Nikitas, *The Principle of Judicial Precedent in English Common Law*, in *Corpus de Jure Cyprii* Vol. I, 119–133 (Legal Studies Council, 1987, in Greek).

Chapter 2. Scope of Application

§1. Territorial Reach

58. The CPC exercises its powers in the territory of the Republic of Cyprus, pursuant to the provisions of the CPC Law, the Concentrations Law and other related instruments. It does not exercise its competences, however, to the areas of the Republic which continue to be occupied by Turkey. Following the Turkish invasion in 1974, then Turkish Cypriot leader announced the unilateral establishment of the so-called 'Turkish Cypriot Federal State'.[66] The UN Security Council expressed, with Resolution 367/75, its dissatisfaction for the unilateral statement. On 15 November 1983, the Turkish-occupied area declared itself, as the 'Turkish Republic of Northern Cyprus' ('TRNC'). That entity is recognised only by Turkey. The UN Security Council has condemned the declaration of the so-called 'TRNC' with Resolution 541/83 in which it declared that such declaration was legally invalid.[67] The Security Council called upon all Member States to abstain from recognising any other state in Cyprus, apart from the internationally recognised Republic of Cyprus. Similar was the reaction of other international organisations, including the EU and the Council of Europe. The fact that the Government of the Republic of Cyprus is the only internationally recognised government, and that the occupied areas continue to form part of the Republic of Cyprus, has also been recognised by various decisions of international Courts, such as the European Court of Justice (ECJ) (as it then was)[68] and the ECtHR,[69] as well as British[70] and US courts.[71] The ECtHR has confirmed in both the *Loizidou* judgment and the inter-state judgment of *Cyprus v. Turkey*, that 'Turkish armed forces of more than 30,000 personnel are stationed throughout the whole of the occupied area of Northern Cyprus, which is constantly patrolled and has checkpoints on all main lines of communications.' In view of the above, it was held that 'TRNC' should be properly considered to be a subordinate administration to Turkey.

66. *See* C. Tornaritis, *The Alleged Constitution of the So-Called Turkish Cypriot Federal State* (1978, in Greek); C. Tornaritis, *The Legal Effect of the Establishment of a Turkish Cypriot Federal State* (1975).
67. *See also* L. Clerides, *The Legal Invalidity of the Unilateral Declaration of an Independent State from the Turkish Cypriot Leadership*, 7 Cyprus L. Rev. 1198–1203 (1984) (in Greek).
68. Case C-432/92, *R v. Minister of Agriculture, Fisheries and Food*, ex p. *S. P. Anastasiou (Pissouri) Ltd and Others*, ECLI:EU:C:1994:277; Case C-219/98, *R v. Minister of Agriculture, Fisheries and Food*, ex p. *S. P. Anastasiou (Pissouri) Ltd and Others*, ECLI:EU:C:2000:360, Case 140/02, *R v. Minister of Agriculture, Fisheries and Food ex p. S.P. Anastasiou (Pissouri) Ltd & Others*, ECLI-:EU:C:2003:520.
69. *Loizidou v. Turkey*, Judgment of 23 Mar. 1995 and 18 Dec. 1996; *Cyprus v. Turkey*, Judgment of 10 May 2001. *See further* L. Loucaides, *The Judgment of the European Court of Human Rights in the Case of Cyprus v. Turkey*, 15 Leiden J. Intl. L. 225–236 (2002) ; G. Cohen-Jonathan, *L'Affaire Loizidou devant la Cour Européenne des Droits de l'Homme: Quelques Observations*, 46 *Revue Général de Droit International Public* 123–144 (1998).
70. *Caglar v. Billingham (Inspector of Taxes)* [1996] STC (SCD) 150; *Veysi Dag v. Secretary of State for the Home Department* (2002) 122 ILR 529; *R v. Secretary of State for Transport* (2010) EWCA Civ 1093.
71. *Autocephalous Greek – Orthodox Church of Cyprus and Another v. Goldberg and Another* 917 F.2d 278 (1990).

59. The Republic of Cyprus, including its occupied territory, became a member of the EU. However, the application of the *acquis communautaire* in the occupied areas has been suspended. In the landmark *Orams* case, the CJEU held that the suspension of the application of the acquis in the occupied areas should be interpreted restrictively and must be limited to what is absolutely necessary to attain its objectives. The suspension is therefore limited to the application of the *acquis* in the northern area of the Republic of Cyprus, which is currently not under the effective control of the Government of the Republic. Such suspension, however, does not apply with respect to judgments of courts sitting in the government-controlled area, the recognition of which is sought, even if such judgments concern land situated in the occupied areas.[72] It was therefore considered that the British Courts had the obligation to recognise and enforce, by virtue of Brussels I Regulation,[73] a judgment of the District Court of Nicosia according to which a British couple were ordered to demolish the villa which they had erected in an area not under the effective control of the Republic of Cyprus, and deliver to the rightful owner of the property free occupation of the land and damages for trespass.[74] The *Orams* judgment confirms that the occupied areas continue to form part of the Republic of Cyprus whose government is the sole internationally recognised government, a position that has been reinforced following the accession of the Republic of Cyprus to the EU.

60. The CPC may further exercise no powers in the British SBAs. According to Article 1 of the Treaty of Establishment of the Republic of Cyprus, the areas referred to as the Akrotiri SBA and the Dhekelia SBA, which cover 250 sq. km of the land area of the island of Cyprus would 'remain under the sovereignty of the United Kingdom'. A further thirteen sites were retained for use by the United Kingdom under provision made in the Treaty of Establishment. According to Article 2, section 2, of the Treaty of Establishment, the Republic of Cyprus shall cooperate fully with the United Kingdom, in order to ensure the security and effective operation of such military Bases, as well as the full enjoyment by the United Kingdom of the rights conferred by the Treaty. The legal status of the SBAs was confirmed by Protocol 3 of the Treaty of Accession of the Republic of Cyprus in the EU, entitled 'on the Base Areas of the United Kingdom of Great Britain and Northern Ireland in Cyprus', where it was provided that the TEU shall not apply to the United Kingdom SBAs of Akrotiri and Dhekelia, except to the extent necessary to ensure the implementation of the agreements set out in the Protocol.

61. The SBAs are not a state, since they do not have autonomous powers and are completely dependent on the United Kingdom. Any authority exercised by the authorities of the SBAs derives exclusively from the United Kingdom sovereignty

72. Case C-420/07, *Orams v. Apostolides*, ECLI:EU:C:2009:271.
73. Council Regulation (EC) No. 44/2001 of 22 December 2000 on jurisdiction and the recognition and enforcement of judgments in civil and commercial matters. This has now been repealed and substituted by Regulation (EU) 1215/2012 of the European Parliament and of the Council of 12 December 2012 on jurisdiction and enforcement of judgments in civil and commercial matters.
74. *Apostolides v. Orams* [2010] EWCA Civ 9.

and the relevant provisions of the Treaty of Establishment. Article 2(ii) of the Declaration by Her Majesty's Government, Regarding the Administration of the Sovereign Base Areas (Appendix O), provides that the Government does not intend to develop the SBAs for purposes other than military and does not intend to set up and administer colonies. Despite such declaration, however, the position under British constitutional law seems to be that the SBAs constitute a colony, in the sense that in 1960 the whole of Cyprus, apart from the SBAs, became independent. Therefore, the SBAs are what remains of the former Colony of Cyprus and are to be regarded as constituting a colony acquired by consent or cession, as from 5 November 1914, which was the date of annexation of Cyprus by the United Kingdom.[75] Concluding, however, that the SBAs are a colony is not so simple, since the United Kingdom has never considered that the SBAs are a colony in the sense of Article 73 of the UN Charter and has refrained from transmitting reports to the UN on the SBAs, as it did for other of its colonies. If it is accepted that the presence of the Base Areas in Cyprus is a form of colonisation, then it should be concluded that such presence cannot be justified according to international law, which prohibits the continuation of colonisation in whichever form.[76] According to another view, prevailing among the Cypriots, 'sovereignty' over the SBAs merely equals to effective control over military base areas.[77]

§2. Special Sectors

A. Electronic Communications

62. The Regulation of Electronic Communications and Postal Services Law 112(I)/04 ('OCECPR Law'), as amended,[78] establishes the office of a Commissioner of Electronic Communications and Postal Regulation (CECPR). The OCECPR Law has harmonised Cypriot domestic law with several EU instruments, mainly Directive 2002/77/EC,[79] Directive 97/67/EC,[80] Directive 2002/58/EC,[81]

---

75. This position was adopted in Halsbury's, *Laws of England* Vol. 6, para. 1074 (3d ed.). *See* more recently *R (on the application of Tag Eldin Ramadan Bashir & Others) v. Secretary of State for the Home Department and Sovereign Base Area Authority* [2018] UKSC 45.
76. *See also* 2019/2, *Legal Consequences of the Separation of the Chagos Archipelago from Mauritius in 1965*, Advisory Opinion ICJ 25 Feb. 2019.
77. *See* A. Pellet, *The British Sovereign Areas,* Cyprus Y.B. Intl. L. 57–72 (2012). *See also* S. Laulhe Shaelou, *Focus on Territorial Exclusion and Sui Generis Territories in the EU: The British Bases in Cyprus. A Special Case*, Cyprus Y.B. Intl. L. 73–110 (2012). *See also Preece v. Estia Insurance and Reinsurance Company Ltd* [1991] 1 CLR 568 (in Greek), *Chimonas*, Civil App. 190/2015, 10 Feb. 2016 (in Greek).
78. By Laws 51(I)/12, 112(I)/16, and 90(I)/20.
79. Commission Directive 2002/77/EC of 16 Sep. 2002 on competition in the markets for electronic communications networks and services.
80. Directive 97/67/EC of the European Parliament and of the Council of 15 December 1997 on common rules for the development of the internal market of Community postal services and the improvement of quality of service, as amended.
81. Directive 2002/58/EC of the European Parliament and of the Council of 12 July 2002 concerning the processing of personal data and the protection of privacy in the electronic communications sector, as amended.

Directive 2002/19/EC,[82] Directive 2002/20/EC,[83] Directive 2002/21/EC,[84] Directive 2002/22/EC,[85] Directive 2015/1535,[86] Directive 2014/53/EU,[87] and Directive 2009/140/EC.[88] The regulatory framework has the objective to, *inter alia*, create a transparent regulatory and procedural framework which encourages innovative technologies and facilitates the transition of the market to full competition, and promote effective competition and ensures that positions of market power are not abused.

63. The CECPR is an independent regulatory authority of the Republic of Cyprus in matters of electronic communications and postal services. Pursuant to section 18 of the OCECPR Law, the CECPR shall act in such manner as to promote: (a) the provision in Cyprus of electronic communications services and networks, associated facilities and postal services for the public as a whole; (b) the interests of consumers, with particular reference to the price and quality of electronic communications and postal services provided in Cyprus; (c) the introduction of effective competition in the provision of electronic communications networks and services and postal services; and (d) the capability to provide or dispose of a wide range of electronic communications equipment and services.

64. The CECPR shall aim, *inter alia*, to ensure that there is no distortion or restriction of competition in the electronic communications sector, including the transmission of content. In this respect, the CECPR shall implement, objective, transparent, non-discriminatory and proportionate arrangements, designed, among others, to promote: (a) regulatory certainty, ensuring a consistent and uniform regulatory approach; (b) non-discrimination in the treatment of providers of electronic communications networks and services; (c) competition to the benefit of consumers and, where applicable, infrastructure-based competition; (d) efficient investment and innovation in new and enhanced infrastructure, taking account, where the access

82. Directive 2002/19/EC of the European Parliament and of the Council of 7 March 2002 on access to, and interconnection of, electronic communications networks and associated facilities, as amended.
83. Directive 2002/20/EC of the European Parliament and of the Council of 7 March 2002 on the authorisation of electronic communications networks and services, as amended.
84. Directive 2002/21/EC of the European Parliament and of the Council of 7 March 2002 on a common regulatory framework for electronic communications networks and services, as amended.
85. Directive 2002/22/EC of the European Parliament and of the Council of 7 March 2002 on universal service and users' rights relating to electronic communications networks and services, as amended.
86. Directive (EU) 2015/1535 of the European Parliament and of the Council of 9 September 2015 laying down a procedure for the provision of information in the field of technical regulations and of rules on Information Society services.
87. Directive 2014/53/EU of the European Parliament and of the Council of 16 April 2014 on the harmonisation of the laws of the Member States relating to the making available on the market of radio equipment and repealing Directive 1999/5/EC.
88. Directive 2009/140/EC of the European Parliament and of the Council of 25 November 2009 amending Directives 2002/21/EC on a common regulatory framework for electronic communications networks and services, 2002/19/EC on access to, and interconnection of, electronic communications networks and associated facilities, and 2002/20/EC on the authorisation of electronic communications networks and services, as amended.

obligation is imposed, the risks taken by the investing undertakings and by permitting various cooperative arrangements between investors and operators seeking access to share the investment risk, while safeguarding competition in the market and the principle of non-discrimination; (e) the inclusion of conditions relating to competition and consumers in the various geographic areas of the same Member State; and (f) the imposition of ex-ante regulatory obligations only where there is no effective and sustainable competition and removing these obligations when that condition is fulfilled.

65. The CECPR shall further, pursuant to section 20 of the OCECPR Law, be competent to designate operators with significant power in a specific electronic communications market and impose regulatory obligations for the enhancement of competition, in cases where it is deemed that competition in that relevant market is not effective. For this purpose, the CECPR shall issue an order specifying the procedure to be followed by his office for the designation of operators with significant market power and the subsequent imposition of regulatory measures. He shall also regulate by order or decision, the access and interconnection, in accordance with the principle of proportionality, ensuring that appropriate levels of access and interconnection are available and that interoperability of services is achieved, in a manner that is in line with the aims of economic efficiency and functional competition and provides maximum benefit to end users. To this end, the CECPR may: (a) prescribe the terms for the interconnection and access of electronic communications networks; (b) prescribe and regulate by decision the framework of charges, including the minimum and/or maximum price levels required to ensure legitimate and healthy competition, and the principles of transparency and cost-orientation of any electronic communications networks provider and/or public electronic communications services provider, which has been designated by the CECPR as universal service provider, including providers of fixed voice telephony services, or those designated by him as holding a position of significant market power in the relevant market, in the exercise of his competence; (c) prescribe and regulate by decision, the appropriate framework of fees, including the minimum and/or maximum price levels required to ensure legitimate and healthy competition for each provider of universal postal service in Cyprus.

66. Section 22 of the OCECPR Law provides for the interrelationship between the CECPR competences and the competition law rules. It is provided that in the exercise of his competences with respect to the providers of electronic communications networks and services and postal services, the CECPR has the authority and the right to exercise competition law powers of fact-finding as provided in the CPC Law, following consultation with the CPC. To this end, he may audit books, information and other documents of electronic communications and postal services undertakings, as well as order research in the offices and other establishments of the latter. The relevant provisions and penalties of the CPC Law shall apply *mutatis mutandis*, and in parallel to the relevant provisions of the OCECPR Law in those cases where a person or an undertaking refuses to provide evidence or obstructs the work of the OCECPR. The CECPR may further, for the effective implementation of this provision, hire independent experts with specialised financial and/or technical and/or legal knowledge. However, the OCECPR shall issue decisions regarding competition law rules, only following consultations with the CPC.

67. The CECPR may impose regulatory obligations, by virtue of section 46 of the OCECPR Law, only on persons designated by him as having significant market power in a relevant market. The determination that a person has significant market power in a relevant market presupposes a finding by the CECPR that there is lack of effective competition in the relevant market as defined by him. The relevant markets, as well as the process of defining further relevant markets and of analysis of the competition regime in a relevant market, shall be prescribed by the CECPR in relevant orders. Where the CECPR decides that there is effective competition in a defined market, he shall not impose regulatory obligations and where regulatory measures apply, he shall withdraw the same after a reasonable period of warning given to affected parties. Reversely, where the CECPR decides that there is no effective competition in the defined market, he shall proceed to designate one or more persons as having significant market power and shall impose on such persons at least a proportionate regulatory obligation.

68. On completion of the review process of a relevant market, the CECPR shall consult with the interested parties and the CPC regarding the draft notification. Such consultation process shall provide all parties the opportunity to comment on the draft notification and lead to a decision within a prescribed period, which shall, in no case, be less than fifteen days. The CECPR shall ensure the existence of a central information point, through which access to all consultations shall be possible, and that the results of such consultation process are published on his website subject to the right of the interested parties to protect their confidential information. In exercising the functions referred to above, the CECPR shall have the power to request from all persons providing electronic communications networks and services in Cyprus all the information considered necessary to allow him to fulfil his obligations when adopting a decision. The CECPR shall carry out for every relevant market, a market review process, which includes the definition of relevant markets, the carrying-out of market analyses regarding the level of competition on each market and the identification of appropriate and proportionate remedies.

69. In exceptional cases, where the CECPR considers this to be necessary in order to ensure healthy competition and safeguard the rights of end users, he may issue an interim decision by which he may take proportionate and interim measures without conducting a public consultation, or without consulting with the regulatory authorities in the other Member States, the Body of European Regulators for Electronic Communicators (BEREC), or the European Commission. Where emergency measures are taken, the CECPR shall inform the European Commission, BEREC, and the regulatory authorities in the other Member States accordingly, regarding the measures taken. In the case of transnational markets defined by decision of the European Commission, the affected regulatory authorities shall carry out a joint market review, taking into utmost account the European Commission guidelines, and shall jointly decide whether to impose, maintain, amend or withdraw regulatory obligations, where such obligations apply.

70. The CECPR shall, pursuant to section 47 of the OCECPR Law, and taking the utmost account of EU Law, define, by order, the relevant markets as well as the procedure for defining additional relevant markets, in accordance with the principles of competition law, as appropriate to the circumstances of Cyprus. It is important to note, however, that the definition of markets for the purposes of imposing regulatory obligations under the OCECPR Law shall be without prejudice to markets defined under the CPC Law. Having completed the definition of the relevant markets, the CECPR shall conduct an analysis of the competition regime. Where, as a result of the analysis of competition in a specific market, the CECPR finds that market to not be effectively competitive, he shall designate, by virtue of section 48 of the OCECPR Law, a person or persons as possessing significant power in that market. A person shall be deemed to have significant market power if, either individually or jointly with others, it enjoys a position equivalent to dominance, which is understood to be a position of economic strength affording a person or persons the power to behave, to an appreciable extent, independently of competitors, customers, and, ultimately, consumers.

71. Where a person has significant market power on a specific market (first market), it may also be deemed to have significant market power on a closely related market (second market), where the links between the two markets in question are such as to allow the market power held in the first market to be leveraged into the second market, thereby strengthening the market power of the person in question. Consequently, remedies aimed at preventing such leverage may be applied in the second market. Where such remedies prove to be insufficient, other remedies may be imposed. Where, as a result of the analysis of the level of competition in a specific market, the CECPR concludes that the market is effectively competitive, he must not impose or maintain any of the regulatory obligations, and shall withdraw existing obligations imposed by prior relevant decision, ensuring that an appropriate period of notice is given to parties affected by any such withdrawal. The market review performed by the CECPR shall be forward-looking, with a view to him taking into account expected or foreseeable technological or economic developments over the period until the next review of the relevant market.

72. The identification of a person or persons as having significant market power in a relevant market shall, individually or collectively, result in the selection by the CECPR of a reasonable remedial measure or measures, pursuant to section 49 of the OCECPR Law. The measure should be proportionate to the objective of promoting competition in the provision of electronic communications networks and services and associated facilities and services by: (a) ensuring that users, including disadvantaged users, derive maximum benefit in terms of choice, price and quality; (b) ensuring that there is no distortion or restriction of competition in the electronic communications sector; (c) encouraging efficient investment in infrastructure and promoting innovation; and (d) encouraging efficient use and ensuring the effective management of the numbering resources. Furthermore, it should be proportionate to the objective of contributing to the development of the internal market, *inter alia*, by: (i) removing remaining obstacles to the provision of electronic communications networks and services, associated facilities and services and electronic communications services at European level; (ii) encouraging the establishment and development of trans-European networks and the interoperability of pan-European services, and end-to-end connectivity; (iii) ensuring that, in similar circumstances, there is no discrimination in the treatment of persons providing electronic communications networks and services; and (iv) cooperating with each other and with the European Commission and BEREC in a transparent manner, such as to ensure the development of consistent regulatory practice and the consistent application of legal obligations under EU Law. In selecting an appropriate regulatory measure or measures to address the maintenance of effective competition, the CECPR shall take the utmost account of the desirability of such measures being technologically neutral in their effect.

73. In the performance of his obligations, the CECPR shall consult, pursuant with section 50 of the OCECPR Law, with all interested parties in the context of a public consultation, as well as with the CPC. In the performance of his obligations, the CECPR shall consult with interested parties, at an appropriate stage of the review of each relevant market and at an appropriate time period, prior to finalising the document of notification of the market review results to the European Commission, BEREC and the regulatory authorities of the other Member States. The terms and procedures to be followed by the CECPR shall be prescribed by relevant order. In the performance of his obligations, the CECPR shall cooperate and consult with the European Commission with a view to providing the European Commission with sufficient information so that it can effectively perform the supervisory role required of it under EU law, including: (a) the communication of regulatory measures to the European Commission, allowing it sufficient time in which to make its views on the draft measures known to the CECPR; (b) the communication of information to the European Commission in the event that the European Commission has serious doubts as to the compatibility of the draft measure with EU Law; (c) the communication of information to the European Commission in the event that the European Commission requests clarifications on the market data or the analyses carried out by the CECPR in the performance of his functions; (d) the notification to the European Commission of a final decision taken in connection with any of the functions performed by the CECPR, including the names of the persons designated as having significant market power and the obligations imposed on them. The manner and form of cooperation and consultation under this section shall be prescribed by relevant order. The CECPR shall follow the notification mechanism prescribed by relevant order wherever he seeks to exercise his right to adopt interim measures. In the performance of his obligations, the CECPR shall be obliged to consult with interested parties at an appropriate stage during the review and for an appropriate period of time prior to adopting measures in connection with market definition, market analysis or the selection of regulatory obligations.

B. Energy

74. The Law Regulating the Electricity Market 122(I)/03 ('Electricity Market Law'), as amended,[89] establishes the Cyprus Energy Regulatory Authority ('CERA'). The Electricity Market Law has harmonised the Cypriot domestic law with Directive 2009/72/EC,[90] Directive 2012/27/EU,[91] and Regulation 1227/11.[92] Pursuant to section 3 of the Electricity Market Law, its objective is to provide for the regulation of the electricity market in the Republic, and to enact common rules concerning the generation, transmission, distribution and supply of electricity, as well as the protection of consumers aimed at improving and integrating competitive electricity markets in the EU. It sets out the rules for the organisation and operation of the electricity sector, the open access to the market, the criteria and the procedures in force for the invitations to tender and the granting for the invitation to tender and the granting of authorisations, as well for the exploitation of networks. It also enacts universal service requirements and the rights of consumers of electricity and clarifies competition requirements.

75. Relevant to competition law is the power of CERA, by virtue of section 25 of the Electricity Market Law, to monitor the level and effectiveness of market opening and competition at wholesale and retail levels, including cross-border electricity exchanges, their prices for household customers, including prepayment systems, supplier switching rates, disconnection rates, charges for and the execution of maintenance services, and complaints by household customers, as well as any distortion or restriction of competition, including the provision of any relevant information, and bring any relevant cases before the CPR. Moreover, CERA has the power to monitor the occurrence of restrictive contractual practices, including exclusivity clauses, which may prevent large non-household customers from contracting simultaneously with more than one suppliers or restricting their choice to do so. Where applicable, CERA shall inform the CPC of such practices. It further has the power to investigate the functioning of the electricity markets and decide upon and impose any appropriate, necessary and proportionate measures to promote effective competition and ensure the proper functioning of the market. Where required, CERA may also cooperate with the CPC and the financial market regulators or the European Commission in conducting an investigation relating to the competition law.

---

89. By Laws 239(I)/04, 143(I)/05, 173(I)/06, 92(I)/08, 211(I)/12, 206(I)/15, 18(I)/17, and 145(I)/18.
90. Directive 2009/72/EC of the European Parliament and of the Council of 13 July 2009 concerning common rules for the internal market in electricity and repealing Directive 2003/54/EC. When the Electricity Markets Law was enacted, the Directive in force was Directive 96/92/EC of the European Parliament and of the Council of 19 December 1996 concerning common rules for the internal market in electricity.
91. Directive 2012/27/EU of the European Parliament and of the Council of 25 October 2012 on energy efficiency, amending Directives 2009/125/EC and 2010/30/EU and repealing Directives 2004/8/EC and 2006/32/EC.
92. Regulation (EU) No. 1227/2011 of the European Parliament and of the Council of 25 October 2011 on wholesale energy market integrity and transparency.

76. Pursuant to section 29 of the Electricity Market Law, CERA may take the appropriate measures: (a) to prevent the abusive exploitation of a dominant position by an authorisation holder or (b) to prohibit or declare invalid, as the case may be, the intentional conclusion of, or attempt to conclude, an agreement by any authorisation holder, which aims at, or results, in limiting, obstructing or falsifying competition in the electricity market. CERA shall not, however prohibit or declare invalid any agreement exempted from the category of prohibited agreements by virtue of the CPC Law, by an order of the Council of Ministers or by publication of a relevant notice by the CPC, or which has been exempted from the said prohibited agreements, by a decision of the CPC, or in relation to which the CPC is examining an application for exemption. CERA may further issue an order only following consultations and deliberations with the CPC; however, it may not prohibit by such an order acts of abusive exploitation of a dominant position, which are prohibited by the CPC Law, or agreements which have been concluded or carried out for purposes of obstructing, limiting or falsifying competition within the meaning of the CPC Law.

77. CERA may, however, prohibit the intended carrying-out of acts of abusive exploitation of a dominant position, or the intended conclusion or carrying-out of agreements whose object is, or whose result shall be, the obstruction, limitation or falsification of competition, provided that these have not been decided in any manner by the CPC, and are not pending for the taking of a decision before it. It may also declare as invalid, acts of abusive exploitation of a dominant position that have already been committed, or agreements which have already been concluded or carried out and whose object is or whose result is the obstruction, limitation or falsification of competition, provided that the CPC has not already decided that there is no abusive exploitation of dominant position or obstruction, limitation or falsification of competition, and that the relevant matter is not pending for examination before it.

78. Pursuant to section 114 of the Electricity Market Law, all measures CERA could take in order to ensure a level playing field must comply with the TEU and EU law, and should be proportional, transparent and non-discriminatory. CERA shall monitor, control and supervise the Distribution System Operator, pursuant with section 54 of the Electricity Market Law, in order to prevent the exploitation of vertical integration, which may cause distortion of competition. Moreover, section 67 §4 of the Electricity Marker Law provides that for the purposes of exercising its power to approve the Transmission System Protocol, CERA may consult with the CPC.

§3. State-Owned Enterprises and Public Utilities

79. The CPC Law applies to all agreements or concerted practices between undertakings or abuse of dominant position of an undertaking. The original definition of an 'undertaking' in section 2 of the CPC Law referred to any natural or legal person which exercised financial or trade activities irrespective of whether such activities are profitable or not. Moreover, it included any undertaking governed by private or public law where the State might exercise, directly or indirectly, due to ownership, financial participation or pursuant to the provisions governing it, decisive influence. The State was presumed to exercise decisive influence when it directly or indirectly owned the majority of the paid capital of the undertaking, or owned the majority in voting rights connected to shares of the undertaking, or might control over more than half the number of members of the administration, management or supervision of the undertaking. The definition of an 'undertaking' has since been amended, pursuant to an amendment of section 2 of the CPC Law, effected by Law 41(I)/14. An 'undertaking' currently includes every entity engaged in economic activities, regardless of its legal status and the way with which it is funded. Consequently, the CPC Law applies to, and the CPC may exercise its powers over undertakings of state-owned enterprises and public utilities.

80. Section 7 of the CPC Law introduces an important exemption to the application of competition law rules in state-owned enterprises and public utilities, in a manner compatible with the TFEU. It is provided that the provisions of the CPC Law shall not apply to agreements relating to wages, terms of employment and working conditions, and to undertakings entrusted with the operation of services of general economic interest or having the character of revenue-producing state monopoly, in so far as the application of these provisions obstructs the performance in law or in fact, of the particular tasks assigned to them by the State. The notion of 'state monopoly' refers to an undertaking that occupies a monopoly position in the market due to the exclusive rights granted to it by the State in order to increase the profit of the State. The notion of the 'State' includes the municipalities and local communities.

81. There is a presumption that the application of the provisions of the CPC Law obstructs the performance in law or in fact of the particular tasks of the said undertakings, when there is no financial or technical way in the disposal of these undertakings, which is compatible with the provisions of the CPC Law and allows the implementation of the particular tasks assigned to these undertakings by the State. The burden of proof that agreements or undertakings do not fall within the scope of the CPC Law, as per the above, shall lie upon the undertakings or associations of undertakings concerned. The CPC may decide that an agreement or undertaking does not fulfil the conditions provided for exemption.

82. In *Stylianou*,[93] the complainant was operating a licensed private employment agency. He alleged that the Ministry of Labour and Social Security (as it then was) was abusing its dominant position in the market, by providing free services of employment agency. The CPC accepted that the Ministry of Labour and Social Security, although funded by the State and not pursuing profit, was engaged in an economic activity. However, the exercise of control over the private employment agencies amounted to the exercise of public authority pursuant to the law, and not

93. Case 1782/12, *Stylianou v. Commission for the Protection of Competition*, 30 Jun. 2014 (in Greek).

to an economic activity. The CPC further considered that the various departments of labour of the Ministry fulfil a public mission, in order to seek employment for persons who are disabled, or otherwise face difficulties, and who, without the contribution of the Ministry would not have access to the labour market. These kinds of services cannot be left solely to the private sector or to for profit companies. The Supreme Court concluded that the function of the departments of labour had not affected the establishment and function of private employment agencies, and there had been no abuse of dominant position.

83. In the *KIE* case,[94] the complainants, who were offering private tutorials to students, alleged that the respective state institute of education (KIE) was abusing its dominant position. The CPC noted that KIE indeed held a dominant position in certain markets of courses, which they were abusing by imposing unfair costs and different terms for equivalent transactions. However, it was concluded that KIE were in essence supplementary public education offered by the State and could not be considered as an economic activity. The State funded the courses from the state budget, in order to exercise its social functions for the public benefit. The Supreme Court upheld the decision of the CPC and noted that even if the courses offered by KIE were not part of the curriculum of the state educational system, they amounted to supplementary public education which served the same objective as public education.

§4. Sensible Effect and De Minimis

84. The CJEU has consistently held that the prohibition of anticompetitive agreements or concerted practices in Article 101 TFEU is not applicable, where the impact of an agreement on competition is not appreciable. The De Minimis Notice[95] issued by the European Commission explains how it can be determined which agreements have no appreciable effect on competition and accordingly fall outside the scope of Article 101 TFEU. The De Minimis Notice uses market share thresholds, so that agreements between companies which fall below those market share thresholds will not be considered as important by the European Commission for the purposes of Article 101 TFEU. Where an agreement falls below the market share thresholds of the De Minimis Notice, the European Commission will not proceed to an antitrust investigation. Moreover, if in a pending proceeding, the companies can demonstrate that they had assumed in good faith that the market shares thresholds were not exceeded, the European Commission will not impose fines. This does not exclude that agreements between companies which exceed the market share thresholds set out in the De Minimis Notice, might still only have a negligible

94. Case 988/09, *Cyprus Private Tutorials Association v. Commission for the Protection of Competition*, 14 Jan. 2011 (in Greek).
95. Commission Notice on agreements of minor importance which do not appreciably restrict competition under Article 101(1) of the Treaty on the Functioning of the European Union, OJEU C 291, 30 Aug. 2014.

effect on competition so as to not be prohibited by Article 101 TFEU. However, the underlying notion is that such agreements would need to be assessed individually.

85. Agreements between actual or potential competitors will thus not caught by the general prohibition of anticompetitive agreements under Article 101 TFEU, provided that the aggregate market share held by the parties to the agreement does not exceed 10% on any of the markets affected by the agreement. For agreements between companies that operate at different levels of the supply chain (as with most distribution agreements), the market share should not exceed 15%. If in a relevant market competition is restricted by the cumulative effect of agreements entered into by different suppliers or distributors, the market share threshold is reduced to 5%, both for agreements between competitors and for agreements between non-competitors. In both types of agreements, the agreement must also not have an anti-competitive object and thus, in particular, not contain any so-called 'hardcore restrictions' of competition, such as price-fixing and market allocation.[96]

86. Hardcore restrictions mainly relate to market partitioning by territory and/or customer group, or to limitations on the buyer's ability to determine its resale price. The first category can be further divided into restrictions limiting the buyer's freedom to sell and restrictions limiting the supplier's freedom to sell. Moreover, the restrictions by object differ depending on whether they are agreed between a supplier and a buyer or between a licensor and a licensee. A restriction on a buyer as to the territory, or to the customers they can sell their products or service is a hardcore restriction and generally considered a restriction by object. Such a restriction may result not only from direct obligations on the buyer but also from indirect measures aimed at inducing the buyer not to sell to particular customers or territories, such as refusal or reduction of bonuses or discounts, termination of supply, reduction of supplied volumes, requiring a higher price for products to be exported, limiting the proportion of sales that can be exported, and so on. However, restrictions which restrict the buyer's place of establishment are not hardcore restrictions.

87. Whereas, the De Minimis Notice has no binding effect on national competition authorities and national courts, the CPC has long accepted that the De Minimis case law of the CJEU, and the De Minimis Notice provides guidance in the application of national competition law rules. Whereas, however, the CPC may typically refer to the need to refrain from dealing with cases which have negligible effect on competition, the CPC has not so far codified national guidelines or exempt thresholds for the application of the De Minimis rules in the Cypriot legal order. It could be argued that due to the relatively small size of the Cypriot market, introducing specific thresholds for De Minimis criteria might not be necessary, although such a guidance would definitely enhance legal certainty.[97]

96. Guidance on restrictions of competition 'by object' for the purpose of defining which agreements may benefit from the De Minimis Notice, SWD (2014) 198 final, rev. 3 Jun. 2015.

97. *See also* P. Agisilaou et al., *Competition Policy in Cyprus 1989-2009* 133 (Nomiki Vivliothiki 2011, in Greek).

Chapter 3. Overview of Substantive Provisions

§1. Restrictive Agreements

88. Section 3 of the CPC Law, which mirrors Article 101 TFEU, provides that all agreements between undertakings, all decisions by associations of undertakings and any concerted practices, which have as their object or effect the prevention, restriction or distortion of competition within the Republic of Cyprus, shall be prohibited,[98] and in particular those which: (a) directly or indirectly fix purchase or selling prices or any other trading conditions; (b) limit or control production, markets, technical development or investments; (c) share markets, geographically or otherwise, or sources of supply; (d) apply dissimilar conditions to equivalent transactions thereby placing certain undertakings at a competitive disadvantage; (e) make the conclusion of contracts subject to acceptance by other parties of supplementary obligations which, by their nature or according to commercial usage, have no connection with the subject of such contracts. Such agreements, decisions and concerted practices shall be *void ab initio*, with no prior relevant decision by the CPC being required.

89. There are two major exceptions to the prohibition introduced by section 3. Section 4 of the CPC Law provides that the agreement, decision and concerted practice shall be permissible and valid, with no prior relevant decision by the CPC being required, if the following requirements apply: (a) it contributes to improving the production or distribution of goods, or to promoting technical or economic progress, while allowing consumers a fair share of the resulting benefit; (b) it does not impose on the undertakings concerned restrictions which are not indispensable to the attainment of these objectives; and (c) it does not afford such undertakings the possibility of eliminating competition in respect of a substantial part of the product in question. The other major exemption to the main prohibitive rule is provided by section 5 of the CPC Law. The Council of Ministers may, following a reasoned opinion of the CPC, publish orders in the Official Gazette of the Republic, which declare section 3 of the CPC Law as inapplicable to certain categories of collusions. These are called block exemptions. The provisions of the EU Regulations made pursuant to subsection 3 of Article 101 TFEU shall apply, *mutatis mutandis*, to national collusions, as long as there is no contradictory provision in an order made by the Council of Ministers pursuant to the above. Accordingly, the collusion may be deemed to be permissible and valid pursuant to the EU Regulation, exempting the said category of collusions in the context of EU competition law. The burden of proof that a collusion does not fall within the scope of section 3 of the CPC Law remains on the undertaking, or association of undertakings, invoking the exemption. If the CPC decides that the said agreement, decision or concerted practice does not meet the conditions provided for its exemption, then the said agreement, decision or concerted practice shall be subject to the prohibition and invalidity.

98. *Commission for the Protection of Competition v. Pancyprian Dentist Association and others* [2006] 3 CLR 285 (in Greek).

§2. Dominant Undertakings

90. Section 6 of the CPC Law, which mirrors Article 102 TFEU, provides that any abuse by one or more undertakings, of a dominant position within the internal market or in a substantial part of it in respect of a product, shall be prohibited, in particular, if this practice results or may result in: (a) direct or indirect fixing of unfair purchase or selling prices or any other unfair, under the circumstances, trading conditions; (b) limiting production, distribution or technical development to the prejudice of consumers; (c) applying dissimilar conditions to equivalent transactions, thereby placing certain undertakings at a competitive disadvantage; (d) making the conclusion of contracts subject to acceptance by the other parties of supplementary obligations which, by their nature or according to commercial usage, have no connection with the subject of such contracts. Any abuse by one or more undertakings, of a relationship of economic dependence where an undertaking stands compared to that or those undertakings, which is either a customer, supplier, producer, representative, distributor or trading partner, shall be prohibited, even as far as a specific kind of products or services is concerned, and so long as there is no equivalent alternative solution. This abuse of a relationship of economic dependence may, in particular, be constituted of the imposition of unfair trading conditions, the application of discretionary treatment, or of sudden and inexcusable interruption of long-term trade relationships.

§3. Concentrations

91. The Concentrations Law applies to all concentrations of major importance, where two or more firms combine by means of a merger or acquisition. In principle, an intra-EU merger need not be notified to several competition authorities in the EU, but on the basis of the principle of subsidiary, it may be examined by the authority best placed to do so. The Concentrations Law introduces the general rule that the party or parties, who will acquire control following the concentration, have an obligation to notify the CPC prior to its implementation. Strict time limits are introduced for the examination of the concentration by the Service and the CPC, in order to determine whether it complies with national and European competition law, and the common market. If the concentration raises serious doubts as to its compatibility, the CPC might proceed to a full investigation. It is a cardinal rule of the system introduced by the Concentrations Law that no concentration may be implemented, without a declaration of compatibility, either interim or final, by the CPC.

§4. Tests of Illegality

I. Per Se Prohibitions

92. Section 3 of the CPC Law, similarly to Article 101 TFEU, prohibits agreements and concerted practices which have as their object or effect to restrict competition. Agreements or concerted practices having the object of restricting competition might lead to agreements which are per se illegal, especially if they refer to hardcore restrictions of competition law, in the sense that the competition authority need not prove that the agreement or concerted practice in question actually has an adverse effect on competition, but only that its object is anticompetitive. Once an agreement or concerted practice has as its object the prevention, restriction or distortion of competition, there is no need to also prove that there has been anticompetitive effect; indeed, the agreement or concerted practice will be caught even if there had been no effect at all.[99] To the extent that the object of the agreement or concerted practice was to restrict competition, it should be immaterial whether the subsequent conduct of the undertakings produces the specific effect of distorting, restricting, or preventing competition. It should, however, be noted that the prohibition of an agreement or concerted practice as having the object to restrict competition, does not preclude that this is exempted pursuant to section 4 or 5 of the CPC Law.

93. It has further been held that abuse is an objective concept relating to the behaviour of a dominant undertaking which is such as to influence the structure of a market where, as a result of the very presence of that undertaking, the degree of competition is weakened. *Fissler* is an interesting application of the above considerations in determining that there has been abuse of dominant position infringing section 6 of the CPC Law. The Supreme Court noted that the criterion for establishing abuse of position of economic dependence is objective, and it is established if it is found that the contractual terms imposed were arbitrary. There is no need to establish that this was also the intention or conduct of the parties. It was accordingly held that the fact that the agreement had not been signed by the parties, and had not entered into force, did not imply that there could be no infringement. The more powerful party had proposed a new framework for agreement, which, if not accepted, would have terminated the partnership between the parties. This was sufficient, since the new framework included arbitrary terms.[100]

II. Balancing Tests

94. Balancing tests are of particular importance. The exemptions applicable in otherwise anticompetitive agreements which are held to be permissible, pursuant to section 4 of the CPC Law, have statutorily set the limits of applying balancing tests to anticompetitive agreements or concerted practices. The exemption shall apply to the extent that the agreement or concerted practice is deemed to be overall beneficial. The language used and the reference to improving the production of distribution of goods, promoting technical or economic progress, allowing consumers a fair

99. Cases 56 & 58/64, *Establissments Consten SA & Grundig-Verkaufs-GmbH v. Commission*, ECLI-:EU:C:1966:41, C-199/92, *Hüls AG v. Commission (Polypropylene Cartel)* ECLI:EU:C:1999:358.
100. Case 2056/12, *Fissler GmbH v. Commission for the Protection of Competition*, 12.9.2016 (in Greek).

share of the resulting benefits on the one hand as positive contributions of the anti-competitive agreements or restrictive practices, and on the other hand the requirement that the restrictions imposed are indispensable to the attainment of the objectives and that the undertakings are not afforded the possibility of eliminating competition in respect of a substantial part of the product in question as negative obligations, mirror the language used when the principle of proportionality is applied. The existence of the 'public interest' objectives does not suffice, unless it is also shown that the restrictions to competition are absolutely necessary and that the negative consequences do not outweigh the positive, on the basis of the statutory criteria.

III. Merger Tests

95. The CPC shall determine whether there is compatibility of the concentration with the functioning of competition in the market, by taking into account a number of factors, and balancing them accordingly. The potential implications of the concentration for the effective competition within the relevant markets, should be determined at their fullest extent, by weighing various parameters, such as the economic and financial power of the undertakings involved, the alternative supply sources of the products and services which are the commercial object in the affected markets, the supply and demand trends for all the products and services, any barriers to entry, the interests of the intermediate and ultimate consumers of the relevant products and services, and the contribution on the development of technical and economic progress provided that it is to consumers' advantage and does not form an obstacle to competition. The main question to be determined is whether the concentration would eliminate or seriously impede competition in the relevant market.

96. The CPC should always apply a test of proportionality so as to safeguard that any measures imposed should not exceed those which are reasonably necessary for the maintenance or restoration of the functioning of competition in the market. An interesting application of the above principles is *Petrolina.*[101] The CPC noted that the concentration might negatively affect thc oil market due to the existing oligopoly and the extent of the influence of the remaining undertakings. It was held that any concentration leading to, or enhancing a dominant position in the affected market, should be held to be incompatible with the requirements of free competition. Accordingly, the conditions imposed by the Council of Ministers, for the approval of the concentration, namely that the applicants should concede a number of gas stations to an undertaking not previously operating in the Republic of Cyprus, were lawful since they were absolutely necessary under the circumstances in order to safeguard free competition.

101. *Petrolina (Holdings) Ltd v. Republic* [2006] 3 CLR 333 (in Greek).

Chapter 4. Overview of Main Notions

§1. UNDERTAKING

97. The notion of an 'undertaking' includes, by virtue of section 2 of the CPC Law, every entity engaged in economic activities, regardless of its legal status and the way with which it is funded. There are accordingly no limitations to the definition of the term. An 'association of undertakings' is defined as any company, partnership, association, society, institution or body of persons having legal personality or not, which represents the trade interests of autonomous undertakings and takes decisions or enters into contracts for the promotion of those interests. Mergers between related companies are not, however, included in the definition of collusion. Hence, 'collusion' is defined as any formal or informal, written or oral, legally enforceable or not, agreement of two or more undertakings or associations of undertakings or concerted practice of two or more undertakings, or the decision of an association of undertakings, but it does not include agreement or concerted practice of the holding and subsidiary company, if: (a) they constitute a single economic entity within which the subsidiary has no real freedom to prescribe its own manner of acting and (b) the agreement or concerted practice relates exclusively to the allocation of activities between the holding and subsidiary company. Moreover, it does not include agreement or concerted practice of two or more subsidiary companies provided they constitute a single economic entity with the holding company.

98. In *Charilaou*,[102] the CPC determined that the Association of Licensed Port Porters of Limassol (LLPA) had abused their dominant position in the market, by refusing to admit the complainants, who were also licensed porters, to the profession, and imposed to LLPA an administrative fine. The members of the board of LLPA filed a recourse against the decision of the CPC. They argued that they were self-employed persons, and that LLPA did not have legal personality and could not therefore be subject to the CPC law, or to be treated as an undertaking. It was a common ground that LLPA did not have legal personality. The Court noted that section 2 of the CPC Law includes in the definition of an association of undertakings a body of persons with, or without legal personality which represents the trade interests of autonomous undertakings and takes decisions or enters into contracts for the promotion of those interests. Accordingly, the Court held that the fact that LLPA did not have a legal personality did not exclude it from the ambit of the CPC law, since it represented the trade interests of its members, i.e., the licensed porters. All activities of the licensed porters, members of LLPA, had taken place within the framework of LLPA, which provided services to its members and exercised activities of an economic and commercial nature. Accordingly, CPC had lawfully treated LLPA as a group of undertakings for the purposes of the CPC law. There was further no obligation for the CPC to distinguish between members of the undertaking who had themselves acted in the prohibited conduct, and members who did not. It was the

102. Case 259/13, *Charilaou and others v. Commission for the Protection of Competition*, 7.12.2015 (in Greek).

undertaking as a collective body that had been held liable for infringement and for abuse of dominant position, and not any individual member in their personal capacity.

99. Pursuant to section 2 of the Concentrations Law an 'undertaking' may include a group of undertakings or a part of an undertaking. 'Group of undertakings' means two or more undertakings the commercial activities of which are under joint control. 'Subsidiary undertaking' means an undertaking the commercial activity of which is under the control of another undertaking. 'Participating undertakings' means the undertakings involved in a concentration, i.e., a merger, acquisition of control or joint venture. In a merger, participating undertakings are all the merging entities. In the case of acquisition of control, participating undertakings is the acquiring undertaking and the target undertaking. In the case of a joint venture, participating undertakings are deemed to be all the undertakings acquiring joint control of the joint venture. An 'investment company' is defined as a company having as its exclusive object the acquisition of participation in other undertakings and the management and exploitation of this participation, without direct or indirect involvement in the management of these undertakings, but subject to the rights it has as a shareholder or partner.

§2. RELEVANT MARKET

100. The determination of the relevant market is one of the most fundamental stages of applying competition law. The European Commission has issued a notice which provides guidance as to how it applies the concept of a relevant product and geographic market.[103] The notice has the objective to increase transparency of its policy and decision-making in the field of EU competition law, by making public the procedures, criteria and evidence on which it relies to reach a decision for the determination of the relevant market. The CJEU has also issued a number of judgments defining the criteria to be used for assessing the relevant market.[104] The CPC has not issued any similar general guidance on how it shall determine the relevant market; it typically, however, applies the criteria adopted in the notice of the European Commission and the case law of the CJEU. A relevant product market comprises all those products and/or services, which are regarded as interchangeable or substitutable by the consumer by reason of the products' characteristics, their prices and their intended use. A relevant geographic market comprises the area in which the firms concerned are involved in the supply of products or services and in which the conditions of competition are sufficiently homogeneous.

---

103. Commission Notice on the definition of relevant market for the purposes of Community competition law, OJ C 372/5, 9 Dec. 1997.

104. For example, Case 27/76, *United Brands & Co and United Brands Continental BV v. Commission*, ECLI:EU:C:1978:22; Case 322/81, *Nederlandsche Banden-Industrie Michelin v. Commission*, ECLI:EU:C:1983:313; Case 6/72, *Europemballage Corp & Continental Can Co Inc v. Commission*, ECLI:EU:C:1973:22.

101. In its preliminary analysis, the CPC attempts to define the product market by investigating whether the products concerned belong to the same market. It also tries to determine the geographic market by producing an overview of the breakdown of the market shares held by the parties in question and by their competitors, the prices charged and any price differentials. Once the product market and the geographic market have been defined, the CPC carries out a more detailed analysis based on the concept of substitutability, by taking into account demand substitution and supply substitution. A market is competitive if customers can choose between a range of products with similar characteristics and if the supplier does not face obstacles to supplying products or services on a given market. The substitutability criterion enables the CPC to target any substitute products, so as to define the relevant product market and geographic market with a greater degree of certainty.

102. The assessment of the demand-side and supply-side substitutability, i.e., of customers and supplies respectively, involves respectively an assessment whether the customers of the product in question can switch readily to a similar product in response to a small but permanent price increase (between 5% and 10%), and whether other suppliers can readily switch production to the relevant products and sell them on the relevant market. Several factors may be taken of account in this respect, such as: (a) the condition of access to the market; (b) the analysis of evidence relating to recent price variations, for example, in terms of substitution between two products or in terms of the customer response; (c) the assessment of the elasticity of demand for a product by conducting econometric and statistic tests; (d) the views of customers and competitors, and any factual evidence collected estimating their reaction in the event of price variations; (e) specific factors relevant to the geographic market in question, such as culture or language, which impact on local preferences; (f) consumer preferences and purchasing habits; (g) barriers to entry and costs associated with switching demand to other products or areas; (h) different categories of customer and price discrimination: a distinct group of customers may constitute a narrower, distinct market when such a group could be subject to price discrimination. The CPC should consult the main actors in the sector on the limits of the market, and where appropriate, it may also carry an on-the-spot inspection.

§3. Market Power/Dominant Position

103. Dominant position, in relation to an undertaking, is defined by section 2 of the CPC Law, as the position of economic strength enjoyed by the undertaking which enables it to prevent the preservation of effective competition in the relevant market and which affords it to behave to a substantial extent, independently from its competitors, customers and ultimately from the consumers. The CPC has not developed specific guidelines on determining market power, and typically adheres to the principles deriving from the case law of the CJEU, and the guidance of the European Commission.[105] The market size of an undertaking can be calculated on the basis of sales of the relevant products in the relevant area, as derived from market sources, such as estimates, studies, etc. The CPC may request suppliers in the relevant market to provide their own sales, in order to calculate total market size and market shares. There are other indications to be taken into account, depending on the industry in question, such as capacity and number of players, but sales (both volume and value sales) are the main reference point for determining dominance. The CJEU has held that a large number of market share is in itself, and save in exceptional circumstances, evidence of the existence of the dominant position.[106]

104. In general, a market share of over 75% would be considered as sufficiently large as to form evidence of a dominant position by itself, and anything over 85% would be sufficient to prove the existence of a dominant position. A market share of over 93% would amount to a monopoly. However, dominance may be found in lower shares as well. When the market share exceeds 50% there is essentially a presumption of dominance, and the undertaking shall have a high burden to prove otherwise. Even lower market share might also suffice, depending on the peculiarities of the market in question; a market, for instance, where the dominant competitor holds 50% of the market share and two other competitors hold 25% each, leads to very different considerations from a market where the dominant competitor holds 50% of the market share, but no other competitor holds more than 1%. In general, a market share of between 40% and 50% might be considered as sufficient for establishing dominance.[107]

§4. Agreements and Concerted Practices

105. Pursuant to section 2 of the CPC Law, an 'agreement' means any arrangement between at least two undertakings or associations of undertakings, by virtue of which one of the parties has willingly undertaken the obligation to constrain its freedom to act in respect of the other party. The CPC has typically adhered to the interpretation of concerted practices adopted by the CJEU. The concept of agreement has been broadly interpreted by the CJEU as not being confined to legally binding contracts, but to also extend to a gentlemen's agreement, or an informal or oral agreement. Such an agreement may be inferred from all the circumstances of the case. However, despite this broad interpretation, the existence of agreement is difficult to prove, in cases where all external evidence of the collusion had been destroyed, or where the parties relied on verbal exchanges. If the prohibition only referred to agreements between undertakings, it would be impossible for the CPC

105. Commission Notice on the definition of relevant market for the purposes of Community competition law, OJ C 372/5, 9 Dec. 1997.
106. Case 85/76, *Hoffmann-la-Roche & Co AG v. Commission*, ECLI:EU:C:1979:36.
107. Case 27/76, *United Brands & Co and United Brands Continental BV v. Commission*, ECLI-:EU:C:1978:22.

to establish collusions between undertakings in oligopolistic markets; in such markets, effective concentration could be achieved without the need for formal agreement, and it would, therefore, be impossible to identify the precise moment at which consensus was reached. The introduction of a more flexible term was necessary in order to avoid distortion of competition by more cunning undertakings; 'concerted practices' was such a concept.

106. Concerted practice means the coordination between undertakings which, without having reached the stage of conclusion of an agreement, knowingly substituted the risks of competition by establishing practices of cooperation between them.[108] The concept of a concerted practice requires some form of coordination and cooperation between the undertakings. The CJEU has repeatedly stressed that the criteria of coordination and cooperation must be understood in the context of the principle that economic operators must determine independently the policy, which they intend to adopt on the common market.[109] Therefore, coordination, though not the result of an agreement, must derive from some positive contact between undertakings, either direct or indirect, which would usually consist of meetings, disclosure of information, or discussions. The requirement that the undertaking must determine its policy independently should not, however, be defined in a manner which would deprive undertakings of the right to adapt themselves in an intelligent manner to the existing and anticipated conduct of their competitors.

107. The undertaking can therefore, determine its policy by examining all relevant factors of the market, so long as this policy is not the result of any direct or indirect contact between undertakings, which have as object or effect to influence the conduct on the market of an actual or potential competitor, or to disclose to such competitor the course of conduct which they themselves have decided to adopt, or consider to adopt on the market. These criteria do not require the working out of an actual plan on behalf of the undertakings. The participation of an undertaking in a particular concerted practice must be adequately proved. When the proof of concerted action is based on documents, the burden is on the undertakings to refute the facts established by the CPC; while when the evidence is circumstantial, the undertakings only have to put forward a convincing alternative explanation for the facts found by the CPC. In practice, the concepts of 'agreement' and 'concerted practice' may overlap, since both concepts aim to catch forms of collusion, which have the same nature. Thus, the distinguishing element between the two concepts is the intensity and the forms in which the two concepts manifest themselves.[110]

108. Section 2 of the CPC Law. *See also* Joined Cases 48, 49, 51–57/69, *ICI v. Commission* (Dyestuffs) [1972] ECR 619.
109. Joined Cases 40/73 and others, *Cooperatiëve Vereniging Suiker Unie UA v. Commission (European Sugar Cartel)*, ECLI:EU:C:1975:174.
110. Case C-49/92, *Commission v. Anic Participazioni*, ECLI:EU:C:1999:356.

§5. Restriction of Competition

108. Section 3 of the CPC Law includes specific instances of agreements or concerted practices which might have as their object or effect the restriction of competition. Defining, however, when there actually is restriction of competition is more complex. If an agreement has as its effect the restriction of competition, this entails that the market would have been more competitive in the absence of the specific prohibited agreement. The position that the undertakings would have in the market in the absence of such an agreement or concerted practice should therefore be taken into account in order to determine the effect of the agreement in competition. This would need to be established by analysing the market in question *in concreto*, and by taking into account the competition between similar products. The CPC is therefore expected to compare between two market situations, the existing, and one in which there would have been no agreement; the latter being a hypothetical market.

109. The CPC has typically adopted the CJEU case law, so that restrictions in conduct would not necessarily amount to restrictions in competition, especially if they are necessary or ancillary to an agreement that as a whole does not restrict competition, such as when they provide incentives to a distributor to risk distribution of a particular product in a particular market, or when they are necessary to the successful operation of a selective distribution system. Particular restraints might be needed to persuade one of the parties in the agreement to be willing to take on the commercial risk inherent in the agreement. However, this does not imply that the protection of commercial risk may justify absolute protection, and the CPC has refused to hold exclusivity agreements as necessary in a number of cases. It would seem that the CPC would need to examine the specific characteristics of the agreement in question, in order to determine its actual or potential economic impact on the market, and whether it might have as its object or effect the restriction of competition. A rigorous economic analysis on behalf of the CPC is therefore required.

§6. Monopolisation and Abuse of Dominance

110. The objective of section 6 of the CPC Law is to prohibit the abusive conduct of dominant undertakings. The CJEU, whose case law the CPC has adopted, determined that the objective of the prohibition is not merely to safeguard the interests of the dominant undertakings' customers (i.e., the consumers) from the exploitation of its market power, but to protect the competitive process itself. Accordingly, abusive behaviour will be prohibited, if it threatens to weaken the competitive structure of the market. In *Continental Can*, the ECJ (as it then was) accepted that a dominant undertaking could strengthen its position by absorbing its rival, thereby eliminating competition.[111] The dominant undertaking may act in a manner which is anticompetitive, or exploitative, such as by purchasing or selling in unfair trading

111. Case 6/72, *Europemballage Corp & Continental Can Co Inc v. Commission*, ECLI:EU:C:1973:22.

conditions, limiting production, distribution or technical development, applying dissimilar conditions to equivalent transactions, or imposing unrelated contractual terms as a precondition for the conclusion of a contract.

111. The dominant undertaking has a special responsibility towards its competitors and the competitive process, to not allow its conduct to impair genuine undistorted competition.[112] In determining whether there has been an abuse of dominant position, infringing section 6 of the CPC Law, the fulfilment of the criteria of a relation of economic dependence and the absence of an equivalent alternative solution, do not suffice for the behaviour of the undertaking to be caught under section 6 of the CPC Law. There is also a requirement to prove that the said behaviour or decisions were abusive, and if this is not proved, then there can be no infringement.[113] It has been held that the role of the CPC in applying the relevant provision is to safeguard that there is free competition in the market; not to administratively supervise undertakings to the extent that competition law is not hindered.[114] It has been similarly held that the CPC does not exercise the role of a mediator. It is not its role to determine whether a contract has been terminated in a manner approved by both parties, but to examine whether certain conduct has infringed competition law.[115] Private interests are accordingly taken into account, only to the extent that they safeguard freedom of competition.[116]

112. A special case is the provision of essential facilities. In a case concerning the Cyprus Telecommunications Authority (CYTA), the semi-governmental provider of electronic communications, the CPC held that CYTA was liable for abuse of dominant position, because it had denied the opportunity to alternative service providers, such as the complainants, to offer to consumers the service of premium SMS, where the charge would be made at the termination of the SMS. The complainants had requested for access to facilities of CYTA in order to be in a position to offer the service of premium SMS to consumers, but CYTA failed to respond. The Court noted that the essential facilities doctrine requires that an undertaking, who is the owner of facilities which are essential for providing a service, should provide access to its competitors when such access is necessary for the exercise of the activity. CYTA had accordingly violated its obligations pursuant to section 6 of the CPC Law.[117] Whether the conduct of the undertaking restricts the technological development and distribution of the market to the detriment of consumers, is accordingly taken into account.[118]

---

112. Case 322/81, *Nederlandsche Banden-Industrie Michelin v. Commission*, ECLI:EU:C:1983:313.
113. Case 1401/12, *Tengerakis v. Commission for the Protection of Competition*, 3 Mar. 2015 (in Greek); Case 612/09, *Ioannou v. Commission for the Protection of Competition*, 23 Sep. 2010 (in Greek).
114. *Cyprus Milk Industry Organization v. Republic* [2005] 4 CLR 795 (in Greek).
115. Case 12/14, *Balenco Ltd v. Commission for the Protection of Competition*, 5 Feb. 2018 (in Greek).
116. Case 919/13, *Koutroupi v. Commission for the Protection of Competition*, 11 Jun. 2018 (in Greek).
117. Case 2004/12, *Cyprus Telecommunications Authority v. Commission for the Protection of Competition and another*, 29 Sep. 2015 (in Greek).
118. Case 1/09, *Cyprus Telecommunications Authority v. Commission for the Protection of Competition and another*, 18 Feb. 2011 (in Greek).

§7. CONCENTRATIONS

113. A concentration of undertakings shall be deemed to arise, by virtue of section 6 of the Concentrations Law, where a change of control on a lasting basis results from: (a) the merger of two or more previously independent undertakings or parts of undertakings, or b) the acquisition, by one or more persons already controlling at least one undertaking, or by one or more undertakings, whether by purchase of securities or assets, by contract or by any other means, of direct or indirect control of the whole or parts of one or more other undertakings. Control shall be constituted by rights, contracts or any other means which, either separately or in combination and having regard to the considerations of fact or law involved, confer the possibility of exercising decisive influence on an undertaking, in particular by: (a) ownership or the usufruct of all or part of the assets of an undertaking; and/or (b) rights or contracts which confer decisive influence on the composition, voting or decisions of the organs of an undertaking. Control is acquired by persons or undertakings which: (a) are holders of the rights or entitled to rights under the contracts concerned, or (b) while not being holders of such rights or entitled to rights under such contracts, have the power to exercise the rights deriving therefrom.

114. A concentration shall not be deemed to arise where: (a) credit institutions or other financial institutions or insurance companies, the normal activities of which include transactions and dealing in securities for their own account or for the account of third parties, hold on a temporary basis securities which they have acquired in an undertaking with a view to reselling them; provided that they do not exercise voting rights in respect of those securities with a view to determining the competitive behaviour of that undertaking, or provided that they exercise such voting rights only with a view to preparing the disposal of all or part of that undertaking or of its assets or the disposal of those securities; and that any such disposal takes place within one year of the date of acquisition, a period which may be extended by the CPC on request where such institutions or companies can show that the disposal was not reasonably possible within the period set; (b) control is acquired by an office-holder, according to the law relating to liquidation, bankruptcy or other analogous proceedings; (c) the acquisition of direct or indirect control of the whole or parts of one or more other undertakings are carried out by investment companies, provided however that the voting rights in respect of the holding are exercised, in particular in relation to the appointment of members of the management and supervisory bodies of the undertakings in which they have holdings, only to maintain the full value of those investments and not to determine directly or indirectly the competitive conduct of those undertakings; or (d) property is devolved due to death by will or intestate succession.

115. Two or more legal acts constitute only one concentration, by virtue of section 7 of the Concentrations Law, if they result in the acquisition of a direct or indirect control on the activities of one or more other undertakings. Moreover, pursuant to section 8 of the Concentrations Law, a concentration of undertakings which took place by stages, within a period of time not exceeding four years, and which resulted in the acquisition of the control of an undertaking from another, shall be considered to fall within the scope of application of the Concentrations Law and deemed to have occurred on the occurrence of the final event as a result of which the said control was acquired. The Concentrations Law shall not apply to a concentration of two or more undertakings, each of which is a subsidiary of the same undertaking. It should be noted that the provisions of the Concentrations Law effectively apply only to concentrations of major importance, which meet the applicable turnover thresholds. This will be analysed in the appropriate sections.

§8. Joint Ventures

116. Section 6 §1(b) of the Concentrations Law provides that the creation of a joint venture performing on a lasting basis all functions of an autonomous economic entity shall also constitute a concentration. The application of the Concentrations Law to joint ventures depends also on the notion of control. An acquisition of sole control will mean that only one party will be able to exercise decisive influence over the target, while an acquisition of joint control means that two or more parties will each be able to exercise decisive influence over the joint venture resulting from the transaction. A concentration will also arise if there is a change from sole control to joint control, in the structure of joint control, such as an increase in the number of shareholders exercising joint control, or from joint control to sole control, including where this is a return to an earlier situation. The CJEU has confirmed that the transfer of an existing undertaking or part of an undertaking from sole control by one company to joint control by the same company and another company unrelated to it constitutes a concentration only where the joint venture resulting from that transaction performs, on a lasting basis, all of the functions of an autonomous economic entity.[119]

119. Case C-248/16, *Austria Asphalt GmbH & Co OG v. Bundeskartellanwalt*, EU:C:2017:643.

Chapter 5. Consequences of Violations and Enforcement Institutions

§1. Administrative Enforcement

I. Antitrust Authorities

A. Formation and Composition

117. The CPC was established as an independent organ by the CPC Law. It is composed of five members, the Chair and four other members, pursuant to section 9 of the CPC Law. All members are appointed by a decision of the Council of Ministers, on a proposal of the Minister of Energy, Commerce and Industry. The Council of Ministers also appoints four substitute members of the CPC. The Chair of the CPC should be a person of a high standing and probity, possessing specialised knowledge and experience in law and being capable to contribute to the carrying into effect of the purposes of the CPC Law. The four other members of the CPC should possess specialised knowledge and experience in law, or economics, or competition, or accounting, or trade, or industry, capable to contribute to the carrying into effect of the purposes of the CPC Law. The Chair and the other four members of the CPC shall serve under full-time employment contract, and shall not be allowed to have any financial or other interest likely to affect the impartiality of their judgment in the exercise of the competences, powers and duties of the CPC.

118. In *Exxon Mobil*,[120] the full Bench of the Supreme Court held that the decision of the Council of Ministers to appoint the Chair of the CPC had not included any mention that the Chair fulfilled the qualifications required by the CPC law. The CPC law required specialised knowledge and experience in law, and the ability to contribute to the realisation of the objectives of the CPC Law. It was accordingly held that the constitution of the CPC was unlawful and that any decision taken with the participation of the Chair was void. In another case, the Plenary of the Supreme Court held that a mayor or member of a municipal board could not lawfully be appointed as a member of the CPC.[121] As a result, it was held that the constitution of the CPC was unlawful, because of the appointment and participation of a member of the municipal board of Latsia as a member of the CPC. Neither the Municipalities Law, nor the CPC Law, precluded such appointment, not established incompatibility due to the position of a member of the CPC. However, the Plenary held that the CPC has competencies over undertakings of private or public law, to which the state might exercise decisive influence. The definition of the state

120. *Exxon Mobil Ltd and others* v. *Commission for the Protection of Competition* [2011] 3 CLR 449 (in Greek).

121. *Cyprus Telecommunications Authority v. Republic* [2007] 3 CLR 560 (in Greek).

included municipalities. As a result, the participation of municipal councillors and majors in the CPC was held to be unlawful. This view was ratified by the Full Bench of the Supreme Court.[122]

119. More recently, the First Instance Court held that the appointment and participation to the CPC of a member, who was concurrently member of the central committee of a political party, violated the principle of separation of powers. It accordingly declared that the CPC had been unlawfully constituted, and that its decisions were void. The public interest dictated that the CPC should carry out its obligations independently of political parties and interventions. The Supreme Court reversed and held by majority 7-4 that this was not a correct approach.[123] The exercise of political power, to which the principle of separation of powers refers to, does not extend to a person who is merely a member of a political party. A 'political office' is therefore not the same as membership in a political party or even office in a political party. In the particular case, there had been no intervention by the House of Representatives, or of the political party as such. The Council of Ministers, which exercises the executive power in accordance with the Constitution, was the organ that lawfully decided to appoint the member. If in a specific case the member could not participate in the composition of the CPC, this would have to be decided ad hoc and the member could be excused for the specific case. The appointment of the member, however, could not be precluded in advance for all cases.

120. The Court stressed that the CPC should be politically independent and should exercise its duties in an impartial manner. However, the requirement for impartiality does not imply that members of political parties cannot be appointed as members of the CPC. The CPC law had expressly introduced incompatibilities, and there was no incompatibility for members because of their participation in political parties. It was held that the previous case law should be distinguished as it referred to the appointment of a mayor or municipal councillors, and accordingly to persons holding a political office and who could exercise political power. A different conclusion would effectively preclude any person who participates in the public affairs from becoming a member to the CPC, since their objectivity and impartiality might be questioned. If the member had a conflict of interest in a specific case, then this should be examined within the framework of such case only.

121. The dissenting judgment held that the CPC should be independent, impartial and free from any outside influence, or political intervention. It should further be insulated from political and business interests, and independent from ministries, and reach their decisions solely on the basis of legal and economic considerations. It was accordingly held that section 9 §3 of the CPC law, which precludes any financial or other interest of the members of the CPC, during the exercise of their competencies, does not merely refer to the composition of the organ, but to its

122. *Cyprus Telecommunications Authority v. Commission for the Protection of Competition* [2009] 3 CLR 258 (in Greek).

123. *Commission for the Protection of Competition v. Cyprus Telecommunications Authority*, Apps 2/16 and 7/16, 3 Mar. 2017 (in Greek).

constitution. Impartiality should not be determined ad hoc, but in advance. It was accordingly held that the appointment of the member of the central committee of a political party hindered the independence of the decisions taken by the CPC in all cases. The dissenting judgment declared that it would be impossible for an objective external actor to separate the capacity of the appointed member of the CPC as member of a political party from his personal capacity. Especially since a political party is funded by the state. The Council of Ministers itself had referred to the member's experience and contribution to public affairs, which derived to a large extent from his prior participation to the public affairs as a member of the political party concerned.

122. A member of the CPC is further precluded from participating in the composition of the CPC in a given case, if it has any financial or other interest, or bias. It has accordingly been held that the participation of a member of the CPC in a case, despite the fact that it had adversarial relations with the undertaking, banking institution, in question, amounted to a violation of the rules of natural justice. The undertaking had terminated the overdue loan of the member of the CPC and had filed judicial proceedings against him.[124] In another case the Court held that a private conversation between the Mayor of Paphos, who was the complainant, and the Chair of the CPC, regarding the pending investigation and proceedings before the CPC, had objectively raised concerns about the impartiality of the CPC.[125]

123. Section 9 §8 of the CPC Law explicitly provides that a defect in the appointment of the Chair, other member or substitute member of the CPC shall not affect its legal constitution and the fulfilment of its competences, powers and duties. Although a literal interpretation of the statutory provision would imply that deficiencies relating to the appointment of a member of the CPC would not invalidate the latter's decisions, the Supreme Court disagreed. It held that such an interpretation would lead to absurd results.[126] It would not make sense for the legislator to expressly provide for the qualifications of the president and members of the CPC, only to then reverse the effect of such requirement. It was accordingly held that the true meaning of the said provision was to provide that the CPC could continue to operate despite the deficiency to the appointment of the member, without the participation of such a member; but the CPC was not allowed to operate with the participation of the member who had been unlawfully appointed. Accordingly, any decision taken with the participation of the unlawfully appointed Chairman or member of the CPC was held to be void. This unavoidably led to a decision by the CPC

124. Case 804/17, *Bank of Cyprus and another v. Commission for the Protection of Competition*, 20 Jun. 2018 (in Greek); *Emporiki Bank Cyprus Ltd and others v. Commission for the Protection of Competition*, Cases 843/17 and others, 16 May 2019 (in Greek).

125. Case 1462/17, *SEMIEK v. Commission for the Protection of Competition*, 23 Nov. 2020 (in Greek).

126. *Exxon Mobil Ltd and others v. Commission for the Protection of Competition* [2011] 3 CLR 449 (in Greek), *Demetriades and others v. Polynikis and others* [2008] 3 CLR 1 (in Greek), Case 846/13, *Salamis Shipping Services Ltd v. Commission for the Protection of Competition*, 13 Jul. 2016 (in Greek).

to revoke all its decisions which had been judicially contested, and to also revoke all procedures in pending cases which had been taken by it while unlawfully constituted.

B. Term and Working Conditions

124. The term of office of the Chair and the other four members of the CPC shall be for five years and may be renewed only once. Where the office of the Chair or other member of the CPC becomes vacant before the expiry of his term of office, the Council of Ministers, shall on a proposal of the Minister, appoint a new Chair or other member for the remainder of the term of office. The term of office of the Chair or other member of the CPC who shall be appointed pursuant to the above, shall be renewable twice, provided that at his first appointment he was summoned to serve for a period less than two years and six months. Any vacancy in the office of the Chair or other member of the CPC shall not affect the legal composition of the CPC and the fulfilment of its competences, powers and duties. Where the office of a member of the CPC, besides the Chair, becomes vacant before the expiry of his term of office, until the appointment of a new member, the substitute member shall participate in the CPC, in the place of the member whose office became vacant. Where the office of the Chair becomes vacant before the expiry of his term of office, the CPC shall continue to operate with the rest of its members until the appointment of a new Chair.

125. Where the Chair is temporarily precluded from exercising his duties for any reason, or the office of the Chair becomes vacant until the appointment of a new Chair, the Chair shall be replaced by a member of the CPC elected among the members participating in the meeting. In case of an equality of votes, the eldest member shall serve as the Chair. The Council of Ministers shall, on a proposal of the Minister, appoint as a substitute member for every member of the CPC, besides the Chair, persons possessing specialised knowledge and experience in law, or economics, or competition, or accounting, or trade, or industry, capable to contribute to the carrying into effect of the purposes of the CPC Law. The substitute member shall replace, in the exercise of his duties, the member of the CPC, when the member is temporarily hampered for any reason. The term of office of the substitute members of the CPC shall be of five years and may be renewed. Where the CPC is dealing with a matter that was dealt with in a previous meeting to which the substitute member had not participated, the discussion that has already been made in the previous meeting shall not be repeated, on condition that the substitute member is informed on the minutes and the rest of the data of the previous meeting.

126. The Council of Ministers may, by its decision, and pursuant to section 10 of the CPC Law, determine the working conditions, remuneration and other benefits of the Chair, the other members of the CPC and the substitute members thereof. It should not, however, adversely modify the working conditions, remuneration and the other benefits, after the appointment of the said member. At any event, by virtue of section 11 of the CPC Law, the Chair and the other members of the CPC should work during the working hours set for other public officers. They shall not be allowed, by virtue of section 12 of the CPC Law, to practice any profession or occupation or to employ themselves in a business of any nature or to accept payment for any kind of employment besides their duties, except with the permission of the Council of Ministers. The Chair, other member or substitute member of the CPC, may submit to the Council of Ministers their resignation from such office in writing, pursuant to section 13 of the CPC Law. Such resignation shall become effective immediately, no prior approval from the Council of Ministers being required, and shall not be subject to withdrawal.

127. The Council of Ministers may further remove from office the Chair, other member or substitute member of the CPC, if: (a) he has been declared bankrupt, or if an order for the appointment of a receiver has been made against him; (b) if he has been declared insane or mentally incapable; c) if he has been convicted for a criminal offence which entails dishonesty or moral turpitude; (d) if he is incapable, by reason of physical incapacity or disease, to perform his duties; (e) if he has maintained or acquired a financial or other interest which may affect the impartiality of his judgment and yet he did not submit his resignation; (f) if he has so abused his tenure of office as to render the continuance of his term of office prejudicial to the public interest; or (g) upon recommendation of the CPC, in case of an unjustified abstention from the exercise of his duties, and in particular in case of an unjustified absence from three consecutive meetings of the CPC. The Council of Ministers, before removing anyone from office shall give him the opportunity to submit his views.

128. The Chair shall preside over the CPC, shall convene meetings, and shall sign the minutes and any other important documents, by virtue of section 15 of the CPC Law. The Chair shall convene the CPC to a meeting whenever he deems it necessary; however he shall be bound, by virtue of section 16 of the CPC Law, to convene a meeting as soon as possible and, in any case, within a period of seven days, if requested so to do by notice in writing by at least three members of the CPC, who shall also, at the same time, specify the matters to be discussed. The summons of a meeting shall be in writing and shall be addressed to the members of the CPC at least twenty-four hours prior to the date appointed for the meeting; as an exemption, in extraordinary cases, a meeting of the CPC shall be convened by a summons circulated among the members immediately prior to the meeting. The agenda shall be drawn up by the Chair and shall be communicated along with the summons to a meeting. As an exemption, if the CPC so decides, in extraordinary and justified cases, a matter outside the agenda may be introduced for discussion, both by the Chair and by another member of the CPC. The quorum required for the CPC to be lawfully in session, pursuant to section 16 of the CPC Law, shall be at least three members present. The decisions of the CPC shall be taken by majority of those present, and in case of an equality of votes, the presiding member shall have a casting vote.

129. Pursuant to section 49 of the CPC Law, and the equivalent section 49 of the Concentrations Law, the Chair, other members, and substitute members of the

CPC, members of staff and persons working under the supervision of the CPC shall not have any liability for anything done or omitted to be done or said, or for any opinion stated, or any report or other document prepared in the bona fide exercise of their duties, competences or powers pursuant to the CPC and/or the Concentrations Law and/or the regulations made thereunder

C. *Investigating Powers*

130. Pursuant to section 26 of the CPC Law, the proceedings before the CPC, in the exercise of its competences and powers, shall be of an examining and/or exploratory nature and the CPC may submit questions, request clarifications and explanations from the parties concerned, order the adducing of evidence, call witnesses and determine matters in contestation. Accordingly, the CPC has wide investigating powers. These include the power to hold general sector inquiries, ex-officio investigations, and to investigate complaints submitted to it. The CPC may collect information that is necessary for the exercise of its competences, powers and duties under the CPC Law, both on its behalf as well as on behalf of other competition authorities, by addressing to that effect a written request to undertakings, associations of undertakings or other natural person or public or private entity. It further has far-reaching powers to carry out investigations and searches.

D. *Adjudicating Powers (Ascertaining and Sanctioning)*

131. The CPC has the following powers relating to adjudication, by virtue of section 23 of the CPC Law: (a) to investigate and decide regarding infringements of sections 3 and/or 6 of the CPC Law, either on its own initiative or on a complaint; (b) to decide whether the illegal collusions fulfil the conditions required for exemption to be granted; (c) to decide whether a collusion falls within a category of collusions for which an order declares section 3 of the CPC Law inapplicable; (d) to decide whether a collusion, in respect of which an EU Regulation is being invoked, falls within the category of collusions regulated by the said EU Regulation in the context of European Union competition law; (e) to decide whether a collusion or undertaking does not fulfil the conditions provided in section 7 of the CPC Law; (f) to investigate and decide regarding infringements of Articles 101 and/or 102 TFEU, either on a complaint, or on its own initiative, or as otherwise determined by the Modernisation Regulation; (g) to decide whether the collusions falling within the provisions of paragraph 1 of Article 101 TFEU may be allowed and considered valid, as defined in paragraph 3 of Article 101 TFEU, or pursuant to EU secondary legislation for the application of paragraph 3 of Article 101 TFEU in a category of collusions; (h) to impose administrative fines and administrative sanctions; (i) to take interim measures; (j) to withdraw the benefit of the application of an exemption Regulation issued by the European Commission in respect of a specific collusion, when the distinct geographic market is the Cypriot market, pursuant to Article 29 of the Modernisation Regulation; (k) to decide on undertaking of commitments;

and (l) to set, by a decision, the criteria for examination of cases in priority, for infringements of sections 3 and/or 6 and/or Articles 101 TFEU and/or Article 102 TFEU.

E. Other Institutional Tasks (Consultancy to Parliament/Government)

132. The CPC has the power to submit an opinion on issues within its competence to any public entity, provided that the opinion submitted shall not bind the CPC as to the context of a subsequent decision, nor affect the validity of such a decision. The said power of the CPC is, however, rarely applied. On a related note, a question has arisen as to a potential conflict of interest due to the fact that the CPC receives legal counsel from the Attorney-General of the Republic, who is also the legal advisor of the State, in cases where the complaint is directed against the State or state-owned undertakings. The Court held that this did not in any way undermine the independence of the CPC to assess a complaint against the State.[127]

F. The Service

133. The Service of the CPC is composed, pursuant to section 19 of the CPC Law, by staff, which are members of the Public Service, who are appointed by the Public Service Commission, as the typical appointment of public servants. The Director of the Service shall be the head of the administration and shall be responsible for the Service. The Director of the Service shall further designate a member of the staff of the Service to be the Secretary of the CPC. The Secretary of the CPC shall be present in the meetings and/or the proceedings before the CPC and keep the minutes. Staff of the Service enjoy permanent employment until their age of retirement. The CPC Law explicitly provides that even in case of abolition of the Service, members of its staff shall be placed among the personnel of the Ministry of Energy, Commerce, and Industry or any other Ministry or independent authority, without any change in their conditions of service, being understood that their duties may be differentiated. The members of the staff of the Service shall be allowed to be present in the meetings and/or the proceedings before the CPC, including the consultations of the CPC, for the taking of decision, and to inform and/or express their opinion to the CPC on issues entrusted to them, while their presence shall not affect the validity of the decisions of the CPC.

134. The competences of the Service shall be, by virtue of section 20 of the CPC Law, to: (a) carry out the secretarial work of the CPC; (b) keep the Registers referred to in section 22 of the CPC Law, namely a Register of Complaints and Ex-Officio Investigations of the CPC, in which all the complaints submitted and all

127. Case 1782/12, *Stylianou v. Commission for the Protection of Competition*, 30 Jun. 2014 (in Greek).

the ex-officio investigations of the CPC shall be recorded, and a Register of Decisions on collusions or practices. The Registers shall be public, subject to the obligation of safeguarding business secrets and/or confidential information of the undertakings and/or of the persons who submitted a complaint. The Service shall further keep a Register of Concentrations, pursuant to section 51 of the Concentrations Law; (c) collect and examine the information necessary for the exercise of the competences, powers and duties of the CPC; (d) introduce complaints and submit recommendations to the CPC; (e) make the necessary communications and publications; (f) grant to the CPC every possible facilitation in order to fulfil its competences, powers and duties.

135. In *Salamis Shipping*,[128] the applicants argued that there was no separation of competencies between the CPC and its Service, and that accordingly the principle of impartiality had been infringed. The Court held that the investigation of a complaint fell within the competencies of the Service and its role to assist the CPC. The Court dismissed the suggestion of the applicants that it should have been reasonably expected that the CPC would have given written instructions to the Service, prior to sending a mere written letter to the parties. The Service should undertake the investigation of the complaint and then submit a relevant memo to the CPC; the latter should then decide whether to proceed with the preparation of a statement of objections. The Service was therefore acting within the limit of its competencies.

II. Government Direct Enforcement Activities

136. The Consumer Protection Service was named until 2016, as the Competition and Consumer Protection Service. This caused some confusion, since the said department of the Ministry of Energy, Commerce and Industry had no authority on the application of domestic competition law, a fact which led to the decision to rename it by the Renaming of the Competition and Consumer Protection Service Law 108(I)/16. The Consumer Protection Service has the responsibility of monitoring the market and – when needed – to propose to the relevant Minister specific policy and legal measures which will restore conditions of effective competition. The implementation, however, of the domestic competition legislation is the responsibility of the CPC, and not of any governmental authority. Section 34 of the CPC Law imposes a duty upon the officers of the Consumer Protection Service to communicate to the CPC any possible infringements of the CPC Law, which come to their knowledge by reason of their post, or in the performance of their official duties. Any omission to act accordingly shall constitute a disciplinary offence.

128. Case 846/13, *Salamis Shipping Services Ltd v. Commission for the Protection of Competition*, 13 Jul. 2016 (in Greek).

III. Other Administrative Agencies Applying Antitrust Rules

137. In addition to what has already mentioned about CERA and the CECPR, reference should also be made to the office of the State Aid Commissioner. State aid is important for competition law, since a company which receives government support may gain an advantage over its competitors. Therefore, Article 107 TEU generally prohibits state aid, unless it is justified by reasons of general economic development. To ensure that this prohibition is respected and exemptions are applied equally across the EU, the European Commission is in charge of ensuring that state aid complies with EU rules. State aid is defined as aid granted by a Member State, or through State resources in any form, which distorts or threatens to distort competition by favouring certain undertakings or the production of certain goods. Despite the general prohibition, Article 107 TEU allows for state aid to be compatible with a number of policy objectives. There are a number of EU legislative instruments in the field of state aid. These include Regulation 794/04,[129] Regulation 1407/13,[130] Regulation 1408/13,[131] Regulation 717/04,[132] Regulation 360/12,[133] and Regulation 2015/1588.[134] The Control of State Aid Law 30(I)/01 aims to supplement EU law in the field of state aid, by establishing the office of Commissioner for State Aid Control. The provisions on state aid will not be considered further for the purposes of this monograph.

138. It is noted that the CPC may, pursuant to section 23B of the CPC Law,[135] cooperate with regulatory or other authorities that exercise control in specific sectors of the economy of the Republic and offer its assistance, upon their request. The CPC may further request the assistance of the above regulatory or other authorities, when exercising its powers to set criteria for the examination of complaints in priority. The CPC may conclude Memoranda of Cooperation with other national competition authorities.

129. Commission Regulation (EC) No. 794/2004 of 21 April 2004 implementing Council Regulation (EC) No. 659/1999 laying down detailed rules for the application of Article 93 of the EC Treaty.
130. Commission Regulation (EU) No. 1407/2013 of 18 December 2013 on the application of Articles 107 and 108 of the Treaty on the Functioning of the European Union to de minimis aid.
131. Commission Regulation (EU) No. 1408/2013 of 18 December 2013 on the application of Articles 107 and 108 of the Treaty on the Functioning of the European Union to de minimis aid in the agriculture sector.
132. Commission Regulation (EU) No. 717/2014 of 27 June 2014 on the application of Articles 107 and 108 of the Treaty on the Functioning of the European Union to de minimis aid in the fishery and aquaculture sector.
133. Commission Regulation (EU) No. 360/2012 of 25 April 2012 on the application of Articles 107 and 108 of the Treaty on the Functioning of the European Union to de minimis aid granted to undertakings providing services of general economic interest.
134. Council Regulation (EU) No. 2015/1588 of 13 July 2015 on the application of Articles 107 and 108 of the Treaty on the Functioning of the European Union to certain categories of horizontal State aid.
135. Introduced by the amending Law 41(I)/14.

IV. Administrative Fines

A. Infringements

139. For every infringement of sections 3 and/or 6 of the CPC Law and or Articles 101 and/or 102 TFEU, the CPC may, by virtue of section 24 of the CPC Law, impose administrative fines, depending on the gravity and duration of the infringement. The administrative fines should not exceed 10% of either the total turnover of the undertaking or of the sum of the total turnover of every undertaking which is a member of the infringing association of undertakings. The turnover corresponds to the preceding financial year. The CPC may further impose administrative fines in case of other violations of the CPC Law, such as: (a) failure to comply with the CPCs decision, or a decision imposing interim measures, pursuant to section 24(d) and 28 §5 respectively of the CPC Law (an administrative fine up to 5% of the average daily turnover during the preceding financial year for each day during which the infringement continues); (b) failure to provide the required information and/or comply with the CPC request for inspection within the time limit fixed and/or of intentional or negligent provision of false, incomplete, inaccurate or misleading information, or provision of the required records, books, accounts or other business records in incomplete or falsified manner, pursuant to sections 30 §8, and 31 §7 and §8 of the CPC Law (an administrative fine of up to 1% of their turnover in the preceding financial year, and in case of omission to provide the required information within the time limit fixed, an additional administrative fine up to 5% of the average daily turnover during the preceding financial year for each day during which the infringement continue); or (c) failure to comply with the commitments they undertook, and which have been deemed binding according to the CPC decision, pursuant to section 25 §2 of the CPC Law (an administrative fine of up to 10% on the turnover of the preceding financial year).

140. The imposition of an administrative fine by the CPC is not equivalent to criminal sanctions.[136] However, its effect has grave consequences, not only for the undertaking itself, but potentially also for the members of the managerial or administrative board or committee arranging the affairs, as well as the general manager or director or managing director, of the legal person. The said officers of the legal person will be liable, in addition to the legal person, for the payment of the administrative fine. Moreover, pursuant to section 44 of the CPC Law, when an administrative fine is imposed on an association of undertakings taking account of the turnover of its members, and the association is not solvent, the association shall be obliged to call for contributions from its members to cover the amount of the administrative fine. Where such contributions have not been made to the association within a time limit fixed by the CPC, the CPC may require payment of the

136. Case 1130/13, *Fereos Ltd v. Republic*, 7 Feb. 2019 (in Greek); *Pfizer Hellas-Cyprus Branch and another v. Commission for the Protection of Competition*, Cases 5669–5670/13, 12 Sep. 2016 (in Greek). *See also Jupiwind Ltd and others v. Governor of the Central Bank*, Rev. App. 91/12, 18 Jan. 2018 (in Greek)

administrative fine directly by any of the undertakings whose representatives were members of the decision-making bodies involved of the association of undertakings.

141. The CPC may also impose administrative sanctions to the participants in a concentration, or to undertakings or associations of undertakings, natural or legal persons or private entities, infringing or omitting to comply with the CPC Law, pursuant to section 40 of the Concentrations Law. In particular, the CPC may impose an administrative fine: (a) not exceeding 10% of the total turnover of the undertaking which has the obligation for notification in the financial year immediately preceding the concentration, in case the concentration is partially or completely implemented by infringement of the obligation for notification, or without the fulfilment of a condition imposed by the CPC, or in case of omission to comply within the time limit with any measure ordered by the CPC, and in addition an administrative fine not exceeding EUR 8,000 for every day during which the infringement continue; (b) not exceeding EUR 50,000 for the supply of false or misleading information in the course of compliance with an obligation imposed by any provision of the Concentrations Law, or in case of omission to provide information pursuant to an obligation imposed by any provision of the Concentrations Law, or in case of refusal to comply with an order of the CPC for an inspection, or intentional or negligent provision of incomplete or altered evidence. Moreover, the CPC may impose on the undertaking an administrative fine not exceeding EUR 17,000 for each day of its omission to comply with an order of the CPC for conducting an inspection. The administrative sanctions shall be imposed by a duly reasoned decision and after taking into account the gravity and the duration of the infringement, and after the party affected is given the opportunity to be heard.

B. Procedure and Guidelines

142. Pursuant to section 42 of the CPC Law the administrative fines for infringements of the provisions of the CPC Law and/or Articles 101 and/or 102 TFEU are imposed by the CPC, in a fully reasoned decision, following the conduct of a proper investigation, and taking into consideration the gravity and the duration of the infringement in each case. Before the imposition of an administrative fine, the CPC shall inform the undertaking or association of undertakings or person affected, of its intention to impose the administrative fine, informing the said undertaking or association of undertakings or person, on the reasons for which it intends to act in this way, and granting the said undertaking or association of undertakings or person the right to submit objections, within a strictly limited period of thirty days. All administrative fines may be collected as civil debts owed to the Republic, and judicial measures may be taken for this purpose, pursuant to section 43 of the CPC Law, and section 41 of the Concentrations Law.

143. Whereas, the CPC has not issued general guidelines on the methodology adopted when imposing administrative fines, it typically adheres to the methodology and general guidelines issued by the European Commission.[137] The CPC has a duty to take properly into account all the material facts, and whether there are mitigating factors in their overall assessment for the imposition of an administrative fine. In *Fissler*,[138] the decision of the CPC to impose an administrative fine was annulled, because the CPC had failed to take into account that the infringement did not have any effect in competition, since the agreement had never entered into force. This factor, as well as the lack of intention by the undertaking to infringe competition law, should have been taken into account by the CPC, when imposing an administrative fine.

144. The European Commission adopts a two-step methodology for imposing an administrative fine. It first determines a basic amount for each undertaking or association of undertakings, and it may then adjust that basic amount upwards or downwards. The basic amount is set by reference to the value of the sales of goods or services, to which the infringement directly or indirectly relates. This will typically refer to the sales made during the last full business year of its participation in the infringement, on the basis of the best available figures it can collect. The basic amount will be related to a proportion of the value of sales, depending on the degree of gravity of the infringement, multiplied by the number of years of infringement. The assessment of gravity will be made on a case-by-case basis for all types of infringement, taking account of all the relevant circumstances of the case. As a general rule, the proportion of the value of sales taken into account will be set at a level of up to 30% of the value of sales. In order to decide whether the proportion of the value of sales to be considered in a given case should be at the lower end or at the higher end of that scale, the European Commission will have regard to a number of factors, such as the nature of the infringement, the combined market share of all the undertakings concerned, the geographic scope of the infringement and whether or not the infringement has been implemented.

145. In setting the fine, the European Commission may then take into account circumstances that result in an increase or decrease in the basic amount, on the basis of an overall assessment. The basic amount may thus be increased where there are aggravating circumstances, such as: (a) where an undertaking continues or repeats the same or a similar infringement after the European Commission or a national competition authority has made a finding that the undertaking has infringed Article 101 or 102 TFEU; in such a case, the basic amount will be increased by up to 100% for each such infringement established; (b) where there is refusal to cooperate with, or obstruction of the European Commission in carrying out its investigations; (c) where the undertaking was the leader or instigator of the infringement, or where

137. Guidelines on the method of setting fines imposed pursuant to Article 23(2)(a) of Regulation No. 1/2003, OJ C 210, 1 Sep. 2006.

138. Case 2056/12, *Fissler GmbH v. Commission for the Protection of Competition*, 12 Sep. 2016 (in Greek).

steps had been taken to coerce other undertakings to participate in the infringement,, and/or retaliatory measures taken against them. The basic amount may be reduced where there are mitigated circumstances, such as: (a) where the undertaking concerned provides evidence that it terminated the infringement as soon as the European Commission intervened: this will not apply to secret agreements or practices, and in particular cartels; (b) where the undertaking provides evidence that the infringement has been committed as a result of negligence; (c) where the undertaking provides evidence that its involvement in the infringement is substantially limited and thus demonstrates that, during the period in which it was party to the offending agreement, it actually avoided applying it by adopting competitive conduct in the market. However, the mere fact that an undertaking participated in an infringement for a shorter duration than others will not be regarded as a mitigating circumstance since this will already be reflected in the basic amount; (d) where the undertaking concerned has effectively cooperated with the European Commission outside the scope of the Leniency Notice and beyond its legal obligation to do so; or (e) where the anticompetitive conduct of the undertaking has been authorised or encouraged by public authorities or by legislation.

146. The European Commission will pay particular attention to the need to ensure that fines have a sufficiently deterrent effect; to that end, it may increase the fine to be imposed on undertakings which have a particularly large turnover beyond the sales of goods or services to which the infringement relates. It will also take into account the need to increase the fine in order to exceed the amount of gains improperly made as a result of the infringement where it is possible to estimate that amount. In exceptional cases, the European Commission may, upon request, take account of the undertaking's inability to pay in a specific social and economic context. It will not base any reduction granted for this reason in the fine on the mere finding of an adverse or loss-making financial situation. A reduction could be granted solely on the basis of objective evidence that imposition of the fine as provided for in these Guidelines would irretrievably jeopardise the economic viability of the undertaking concerned and cause its assets to lose all their value. In certain cases, a symbolic fine only may be imposed.

147. Section 41 of the CPC Law provides for limitation periods. The CPC is deprived of the power to impose administrative fines for infringements of the provisions of the CPC Law and/or of the EU competition law, unless it exercises its power within the following limitation periods: (a) within three years in the case of infringements of provisions concerning requests for information or the conduct of inspections; and (b) within five years, in the case of all other infringements. Time shall begin to run on the day on which the infringement is committed, whereas in the case of continuing or repeated infringement time shall begin to run on the day on which the infringement ceases. The limitation period shall be interrupted by any act of the CPC, aiming at the conduct of preliminary investigation or at the examination of a possible infringement of this Law. These acts mainly include initiation of examination procedure on behalf of the CPC, a written request by the CPC to provide information, or a written order by the CPC for inspection. The limitation period shall re-commence, from the beginning, after every interruption. The limitation period for the imposition of administrative fines shall be suspended for as long as the CPC decision is the subject of an ongoing review procedure before the competent court.

148. Cypriot courts have dismissed several allegations that the power of the CPC to impose an administrative fine had been subject to limitation. It has been held that in continuous violations, the prescription period is calculated from the date when the infringement ceased; so long as the undertaking had continued to infringe the CPC law, the infringement in question was a continuous one, and not subject to limitation.[139] It has further been held that the prescription period is interrupted whenever the CPC initiates proceedings to examine an infringement pursuant to a preliminary investigation that found potential infringement.[140] In another case it was held that the imposition of the administrative fine was not subject to the statute of limitations, since the prescription period had began, not from the time that the complaint was filed before the CPC, but from the time that the infringement had been terminated. Furthermore, pursuant the prescription period had been interrupted after the decision of the CPC to prepare a statement of objections.[141]

149. The reconsideration of an administrative act that has been annulled by the Supreme Court does not violate the principle of *non bis in idem.*[142] In *Pfizer*, however, a distinction was made between cases where the decision of the CPC has been annulled on procedural grounds, and cases where it had been annulled on substantive grounds, i.e., due to lack of proof of the infringement. It was held that where in the former case there is no violation of the principle of *non bis in idem*, in the latter case, the application of the principle precludes the new assessment of the existence of the infringement, which would lead to the imposition of a new administrative fine.[143] It has been further confirmed that during the re-examination of the case by the CPC, after annulment or revocation of the initial decision, the CPC could lawfully use the material collected by their Service, and which mainly consisted of replies given by the parties to questionnaires. The material had been evaluated de novo by the Service and by the CPC, and accordingly there was no violation of the rule of material time.[144]

139. Case 259/13, *Charilaou and others v. Commission for the Protection of Competition*, 7 Dec. 2015 (in Greek), Case 1130/13, *Fereos Ltd v. Republic*, 7 Feb. 2019 (in Greek).
140. , Case 1927/12, *Cyprus Telecommunications Authority v. Commission for the Protection of Competition* 31 May 2017 (in Greek).
141. Case 2004/12, *Cyprus Telecommunications Authority v. Commission for the Protection of Competition and another*, 29 Sep. 2015 (in Greek).
142. Case 2003/12, *Cyprus Telecommunications Authority v. Commission for the Protection of Competition*, 29 Aug. 2016 (in Greek).
143. *Pfizer Hellas-Cyprus Branch and another v. Commission for the Protection of Competition*, Cases 5669–5670/13, 12 Sep. 2016 (in Greek).
144. Case 259/13, *Charilaou and others v. Commission for the Protection of Competition*, 7 Dec. 2015 (in Greek), Case 846/13, *Salamis Shipping Services Ltd v. Commission for the Protection of Competition*, 13 Jul. 2016 (in Greek).

C. Leniency Programme

150. The CPC reserves the power to exempt and/or reduce the amount of the administrative fine which would have otherwise been imposed on an undertaking or association of undertakings, if the said undertaking or association of undertakings cooperates and/or gives such assistance or proof which will assist the CPC to prove the infringement. The CPC has indeed adopted a Leniency Programme in the form of secondary legislation, which defines the leniency or full exemption from administrative fines of an undertaking and/or associations of undertakings wishing to cooperate with the CPC to uncover illegal cartels.[145] Pursuant to the Leniency Programme, the CPC shall grant immunity from administrative fines which would have otherwise been imposed to an undertaking disclosing its participation in an alleged restrictive collusion if the undertaking is the first to submit evidence which is sufficient to initiate the inspection procedure, or to find an infringement of section 3 of the CPC Law and/or Article 101 TFEU. The CPC shall not, however, grant immunity, if, at the time of the submission, it had at its disposal sufficient evidence in order to adopt a decision to carry out an inspection of the Law for alleged infringements of section 3 of the CPC Law and/or Article 101 of the TFEU, or had already carried out such an inspection. The aim is therefore to grant immunity only when at the time of submission, the CPC did not have sufficient evidence at its disposal.

151. In order to qualify for immunity, the undertaking has to: (a) cooperate fully, actively and on a continuous basis with the CPC, from the date of submission up until the completion of the procedure and in particular to provide the CPC, willingly and promptly, with all relevant information and evidence it possesses or is available to it, or that came to its possession later on, in relation to the alleged collusion; (b) remain at the CPC's disposal to answer, willingly and promptly, to any request that may contribute to the establishment of the relevant facts; (c) make current (and, if possible, former) employees and directors available for interviews with the CPC or any member of the Service; (d) not destroy, falsify or conceal relevant information or evidence relating to the alleged restrictive collusion; and (e) not disclose the fact or any of the contents of its application before the CPC has issued a statement of objections in the case, unless otherwise agreed, and unless the disclosure is made to other national competition authorities which may be affected by the alleged infringement and/or to the European Commission. The undertaking must further terminate its involvement in the alleged infringement, the latest at the time it submits the evidence, except for what would, in the CPC's view, be reasonably necessary to act otherwise to preserve the integrity of the inspection being carried out. Moreover, the undertaking must not have incited other undertakings to participate in the infringement; in such a case, the undertaking may apply for a reduction from the imposition of administrative fines.

152. Before submitting the application for immunity from administrative fines, the undertaking may informally and/or anonymously, contact the CPC, via its Chair,

145. *See also* the European Commission Notice on Immunity from fines and reduction of fines in cartel cases, OJ C 298 and OJ C 144.

in order to receive informal guidance in relation to the immunity application. The Chair shall promptly inform the other members of the CPC. The undertaking may either: (a) apply for a marker, on the basis of which an immunity applicant shall secure its place in the priority, for a period to be specified by the CPC, on a case-by-case basis, in order to allow for the gathering of the necessary information and evidence, or (b) submit a formal application providing all necessary information. The undertaking may initially present this information and evidence in hypothetical terms, in which case the undertaking must present a detailed descriptive list of the evidence it proposes to disclose at a later date which is agreed together with the CPC. This list must accurately reflect the nature and content of the evidence, while safeguarding the hypothetical nature of its disclosure. Copies of documents, from which sensitive parts have been removed, may be used to illustrate the nature and content of the evidence. When receiving the application for immunity from administrative fines, the Service shall provide the applicant undertaking with an acknowledgement of receipt, confirming the date and time of the submission of application.

153. Upon receiving the application, the CPC shall give instructions to the Service to examine, within no later than seven working days, whether the conditions are met, and to submit a relevant recommendation. If the undertaking meets the conditions for immunity, then the CPC shall grant the undertaking conditional immunity from an administrative fine, and communicate this decision to the undertaking in writing, no later than the date the statement of objections is notified. If the undertaking had submitted the evidence in hypothetical terms, the conditional immunity shall be granted once the evidence is submitted and verified. If the conditions for granting immunity are not fulfilled, the CPC shall inform the applicant accordingly that their application has not been accepted. In the latter case, the undertaking may either request the CPC to examine the information and evidence submitted in order to be granted a reduction of the administrative fine, or to withdraw the evidence; this does not prevent the CPC from using its powers to investigate and collect evidence in order to obtain the information itself. The CPC shall not consider any other applications for immunity before deciding on a pending application in relation the same alleged infringement. If the undertaking has submitted a complete immunity application before the European Commission, or before a national competition authority of a Member State that is prima facie competent to deal with the case, the CPC may accept a summary application for immunity. Once the CPC has established that the undertaking has fully cooperated, as per the requirements of the Leniency Programme, it may grant immunity.

154. Other than immunity, the Leniency Programme provides for the possibility of reduction of the fine that would have otherwise been imposed. This may occur, if the undertaking has provided the CPC with evidence of the alleged infringement, which represents significant added value with respect to the evidence already in the CPC possession, and subject to the general requirements for full cooperation. 'Significant added value' is dependent upon the extent to which the evidence provided has strengthened, by its very nature and/or its level of detail, the ability of the CPC to prove the alleged restrictive collusion, such as if there is written evidence originating from the period of time to which the facts occurred, evidence directly relevant to the facts in question, or corroboration from other sources. An undertaking wishing to benefit from a reduction of an administrative fine must submit an application to the CPC, accompanied by sufficient evidence of the collusion. The procedure for submitting the application and evidence is equivalent to the respective procedure for submitting an application for immunity.

155. If the applicant meets the conditions for reduction of a fine, the CPC shall inform them accordingly in writing of its intention to reduce the fine. Otherwise, it will inform the applicant that it does not meet the conditions for reduction of a fine. The CPC shall take its final decision on the application for granting a reduction of an administrative fine, and if the conditions are met, it may grant a reduction between 30% and 50% for the first undertaking which complied with the conditions, a reduction of 20–30% for the second undertaking, and a reduction of up to 20% for subsequent undertakings. In order to determine the level of reduction of the administrative fine within the above bands the CPC shall take into account the time at which the evidence was submitted and the extent to which it represents added value. The CPC may also take into account the extent and consistency of cooperation of the undertaking after submitting the evidence. If an undertaking is the first to submit evidence, which has added value, which the CPC uses to establish additional facts increasing the gravity or the duration of the infringement, the CPC shall not take into account this additional evidence when determining the administrative fine to be imposed on the undertaking that submitted this evidence.

156. Joint applications for immunity from, or reduction of an administrative fine by two or more undertakings, shall not be accepted. False, inaccurate or misleading declarations by an applicant undertaking, as well as failure to comply with any term or obligation of the CPC decision at any stage of the process, may result in the loss of the benefit of immunity from an administrative fine or any other favourable treatment. The granting of immunity from an administrative fine or reduction of a fine, by way of a CPC decision, shall not exclude the undertaking's civil liability arising from its participation in an infringement of section 3 of the CPC Law and/or Article 101 of the TFEU. If the application by an undertaking in order to be granted immunity from, or reduction of, an administrative fine, was rejected, the CPC shall not use the data and/or information submitted to it, unless the undertaking gave its consent or, the said data and/or information came to the knowledge of the CPC in a different way. The CPC shall further protect the identity of the undertaking that applies for immunity from or reduction of an administrative fine, the content of the application and its cooperation with the CPC, until the compilation of the statement of objections, unless the CPC is bound by another legal obligation or it has the consent of the applicant undertaking.

V. Administrative Injunctions and Other Restrictive Orders

157. The CPC has the power, by virtue of section 24 of the CPC Law, to force the undertakings or associations of undertakings concerned, to bring to an end within a fixed time limit the infringement ascertained and avoid any repetition of it in the future. In case the infringement is brought to an end before the issuing of the decision of the CPC, the CPC may condemn the infringement by a declaratory decision. The CPC may impose any terms and measures whether behavioural and/or structural, depending on the infringement ascertained, which are necessary for the bringing to an end of the said infringement. In case that the undertakings or associations of undertakings concerned do not comply with the CPC decision pursuant to the above, the CPC may impose an administrative fine up to 5% of the average daily turnover during the preceding financial year for each day during which the infringement continues.

158. In case the CPC intends to issue a decision demanding that an infringement of the provisions in sections 3 and/or 6 of the Law and/or Articles 101 and/or 102 TFEU be brought to an end, and the undertakings or associations of undertakings concerned offer to undertake commitments to meet with the CPC concerns in its preliminary assessment, the CPC may decide to make these commitments binding on the undertakings or associations of undertakings concerned, pursuant to section 25 of the CPC Law. The CPC decision may be issued for a specified period and has to conclude that there are no longer grounds for further action. In case where the undertakings or associations of undertakings concerned, do not comply with the commitments they undertook to comply with, and which have been deemed binding according to the CPC decision pursuant, the CPC may impose an administrative fine of up to 10% on the turnover of the preceding financial year.

VI. Interim Measures

159. The CPC may order interim measures and impose such terms as it deems necessary under the circumstances. Such measures, whether mandatory or prohibitory, must be of temporary and conservative nature and their extent must not exceed what is absolutely necessary under the circumstances. The CPC shall, either act on its own initiative or on the application of the interested parties, which may be submitted either ex parte or by service of a summons on all the undertakings or associations of undertakings concerned, as long as: (a) there is a reasonably strong prima facie case of infringement of section 3 and/or 6 of the CPC Law and/or Articles 101 and/or 102 TFEU, and (b) there is urgency due to the serious risk of irreparable damage on competition. An application for interim measures by an interested party shall be accepted only as long as it is accompanied by a complaint, or follows the complaint, or as long as it is lodged during the proceedings before the CPC for infringement of section 3 and/or 6 of the CPC Law and/or Articles 101 and/or 102 TFEU.

160. The application should prescribe the required interim measures and the applicant should pay, upon request of the CPC, a guarantee for damages that may be caused to the undertaking or association of undertakings against which the interim measures are ordered in case no infringement is found. The CPC may impose to an undertaking or an association of undertakings an administrative fine up to 5% on the average daily turnover of the preceding financial year for each day during which it omits to fully comply with a decision of the CPC imposing interim measures. Moreover, in case where the interested undertakings or associations of undertakings act in a way which is contrary to the decision imposing interim measures, the CPC may impose an administrative fine of up to 5% of the turnover of the preceding financial year.

§2. Civil Enforcement

I. Competent Civil Courts

161. Competition law cases fall under the jurisdiction of the District Courts, which are the general courts of the Republic. Section 3 of the Courts of Justice Law 14/60 has established six District Courts, one for each administrative district of the Republic of Cyprus (Nicosia, Famagusta, Limassol, Larnaca, Paphos and Kyrenia). Since the 1974 Turkish Invasion, the District Court of Famagusta is located at Paralimni (at Larnaca for civil cases) and the District Court of Kyrenia is located at Nicosia. The Supreme Court has jurisdiction with regard to all civil appeals. Cases before the District Courts are heard by a single judge, who may be, depending on the amount of the dispute, a District Court Judge, a Senior District Court Judge, or a President of a District Court.

II. Sanctions

A. *Nullity*

162. If the terms of a contract are in contravention of sections 3 and/or 6 of the CPC, and/or Articles 101 and/or 102 TFEU, the said contractual provisions shall be void and shall have no effect.[146] A contract cannot be enforceable, if it violates public policy, pursuant to the rule that *ex dolo malo non oritur actio*. Accordingly, courts will not entertain a cause of action which is based on an unlawful contractual term, i.e., which violates provisions of Cypriot or EU competition law. Section 40 §2 of the CPC Law further provides that the person who has suffered any damage due to an act or omission of an undertaking or association of undertakings done in contravention of sections 3 and/or 6 of the CPC, and/or Articles 101 and/or 102 TFEU, shall have the right to apply to the Court for an injunction, in order to prohibit the continuation of the infringement.

146. *See also* P. Polyviou, *Law of Contract*, Vol. II, 621 (Chrysafinis and Polyviou, 2014, in Greek).

B. Damages

163. The objective of the Antitrust Damages Law is to safeguard that any person who has suffered damages because of an infringement of competition law by an undertaking or an association of undertakings, may effectively exercise his right to obtain full compensation for the harm suffered. Section 4 of the Antitrust Damages Law provides that any natural or public person or public authority has a right to obtain full compensation for the harm suffered due to an infringement of the provisions of competition law. Full compensation should place the person who has suffered harm in the position in which that person would have been, had the infringement of competition law not been committed. It shall therefore cover the right to compensation for actual loss and for loss of profit, plus the payment of interest, but shall not include punitive damages.

164. In actions for damages, the Court may order, and following a relevant application, that any party or third person should disclose evidence under his control (section 5 of the Antitrust Damages Law). The evidence requested to be disclosed must be precisely and narrowly determined by the applicant, on the basis of reasonably available facts. The Court should apply the principle of proportionality, in order to determine whether the disclosure request should be granted, taking into account the legitimate interests of all parties and third parties concerned, and in particular: (a) the extent to which the claim or defence is supported by available facts and evidence justifying the request to disclose evidence; (b) the scope and cost of disclosure, especially for any third parties concerned, including preventing non-specific searches for information which is unlikely to be of relevance for the parties in the procedure; and (c) whether the evidence the disclosure of which is sought contains confidential information, especially concerning any third parties, and what arrangements are in place for protecting such confidential information. The interest of undertakings to avoid actions for damages following an infringement of competition law shall not constitute an interest that warrants protection.

165. The Court should order the disclosure of evidence containing confidential information, where it consider it necessary, provided that it shall ensure that, when ordering the disclosure of such information, it shall also impose effective measures to protect such information, including: (a) keeping the confidential information in secured and sealed files to which only the Court, or the parties designated by the Court, have access; (b) keeping the confidential information in a specifically designed place under the responsibility of the Registrar of the Court; (c) appointing experts to prepare a summary of the information in a non-confidential version. The Court should further give full effect to applicable legal professional privilege under EU or national law, when ordering the disclosure of evidence. Before disclosure, the Court should give the affected parties, the opportunity to be heard.

166. Pursuant to section 6 of the Antitrust Damages Law, when assessing, the proportionality of an order to disclose information, the Court shall, in addition to what was previously mentioned, consider the following: (a) whether the request has been formulated specifically with regard to the nature, subject matter or contents of documents submitted to a competition authority or held in the file thereof, rather than by a non-specific application concerning documents submitted to a competition authority; (b) whether the party requesting disclosure is doing so in relation to an action for damages before a national court; and the need to safeguard the effectiveness of the public enforcement of competition law. With regard to certain categories of evidence, it is provided that the Court may order their disclosure only if the national competition authority or the European Commission has closed their proceedings, by adopting a decision or otherwise. These categories of evidence are the following: (a) information that was prepared by a natural or legal person specifically for the proceedings of a competition authority; (b) information that the competition authority has drawn up and sent to the parties in the course of its proceedings; or (c) settlement submissions that have been withdrawn. The Court may not order a defendant or a third party to disclose leniency statements or settlement submissions.

167. A claimant may request that the Court should access the evidence referred to above, in order to ensure that their content should properly be excluded. In that assessment, the Court courts may request assistance only from the competent competition authority or the European Commission, and the authors of the evidence in question may also have the possibility to be heard. In no case shall the national court permit other parties or third parties access to that evidence. If only part of the evidence requested is excluded, then the remaining parts thereof shall, depending on the category under which they fall, be released. The disclosure of evidence in the file of a competition authority that does not fall into any of the above-mentioned categories may be ordered. If a party or a third person is reasonably not able to produce the evidence, the Court may request such from the national competition authority or the European Commission. It is further provided that the national competition authority or the European Commission may, on their own initiative, submit observations on the proportionality of a disclosure request.

168. Evidence obtained by a natural or legal person solely through access to the file of a competition authority is deemed to be inadmissible in actions for damages, if they refer to leniency statements or settlement submissions (section 7 of the Antitrust Damages Law). The categories of evidence referred to in section 6 of the Antitrust Damages Law, which is obtained by a natural or legal person solely through access to the file of that competition authority, i.e., information prepared specifically for the proceedings of a competition authority, or that the competition authority has drawn up and sent to the parties in the course of its proceedings, or settlement submissions that have been withdrawn, shall also be inadmissible until the competition authority in question, or the European Commission, has closed its proceedings by adopting a decision or otherwise. Evidence obtained by a natural or legal person solely through access to the file of a competition authority, can be used in an action for damages only by that person or by a natural or legal person that succeeded to that person's rights, including a person that acquired that person's claim.

169. The Court may impose penalties on parties, third parties or their legal representatives, in the event of: (a) failure or refusal to comply with the disclosure order of any national court; (b) destruction of relevant evidence; (c) failure or refusal to comply with the obligations imposed by an order of the Court protecting confidential information; or (d) breach of the limits on the use of evidence. The Court may, in particular, impose an administrative fine not exceeding EUR 250,000 and/or imprisonment not exceeding six months. It may also draw adverse inferences, such as presuming the relevant issue to be proven or dismissing claims and defences in whole or in part, and the possibility to order the payment of costs (section 8 of the Antitrust Damages Law).

170. Section 40 §1 of the CPC Law provides that in case of an action for damages brought by any person who has suffered loss and/or financial injury from any acts or omissions of an undertaking or associations of undertakings done in contravention of sections 3 and/or 6 of the CPC Law and/or Articles 101 and/or 102 TFEU, a final decision of the CPC or of other competition authority or of the European Commission, ascertaining the said infringement shall constitute a rebuttable presumption about the truth of its context. However, section 9 of the Antitrust Damages Law overrules this by providing that a final decision of the CPC ascertaining an infringement of competition law shall be deemed to be an irrefutable (and not simply a rebuttable as provided in section 40 of the CPC Law) presumption, for the purposes of an action for damages. Moreover, a final decision issued in another Member State, may be presented before the Court as prima facie evidence that an infringement of competition law has occurred and, as appropriate, may be assessed along with any other evidence adduced by the parties.

171. The limitation period of an action for damages for infringement of competition law rules is six years, by virtue of section 10 of the Antitrust Damages Law. The limitation period shall not begin to run before the infringement of competition law has ceased and the claimant knows, or can reasonably be expected to know: (a) of the behaviour and the fact that it constitutes an infringement of competition law; (b) of the fact that the infringement of competition law has caused harm to him; and (c) the identity of the infringer. The limitation period is suspended if a national competition authority or the European Commission takes action for the purpose of the investigation or proceedings in respect of an infringement of competition law to which the action for damages relates. The suspension shall end at the earliest one year after the infringement decision has become final or after the proceedings are otherwise terminated.

172. Undertakings which have infringed competition law through joint behaviour are jointly and severally liable for the harm caused by the infringement, pursuant to section 11 of the Antitrust Damages Law. By way of derogation, where the infringer is a small or medium-sized enterprise (SME),[147] the infringer is liable only to its own direct and indirect purchasers where: (a) its market share in the relevant market was below 5% at any time during the infringement of competition law; and

147. As defined in Commission Recommendation 2003/361/EC.

(b) the application of the normal rules of joint and several liability would irretrievably jeopardise its economic viability and cause its assets to lose all their value. The derogation shall not, however, apply where: (a) the SME has led the infringement of competition law, or has coerced other undertakings to participate therein; or (b) the SME has previously been found to have infringed competition law. It is further provided that an immunity recipient is jointly and severally liable as follows: (a) to its direct or indirect purchasers or providers; and (b) to other injured parties only where full compensation cannot be obtained from the other undertakings that were involved in the same infringement of competition law.

173. An infringer may recover a contribution from any other infringer, the amount of which shall be determined in the light of their relative responsibility for the harm caused by the infringement of competition law. The amount of contribution of an infringer which has been granted immunity from fines under a leniency programme shall not exceed the amount of the harm it caused to its own direct or indirect purchasers or providers. To the extent the infringement of competition law caused harm to injured parties other than the direct or indirect purchasers or providers of the infringers, the amount of any contribution from an immunity recipient to other infringers shall be determined in the light of its relative responsibility for that harm.

174. Section 12 of the Antitrust Damages Law provides that compensation can be claimed by anyone who suffered harm because of the infringement of competition law, irrespective of whether they are direct or indirect purchasers from the infringer. The compensation awarded should not exceed that caused by the infringement of competition law to the claimant, and should take into account the liability of the infringer. Compensation for actual loss at any level of the supply chain shall not exceed the overcharge harm suffered at that level. It is further provided that an injured party has the right to obtain compensation for any loss of profits due to a full or partial passing-on of that overcharge. The Court shall take into account nay share of the overcharge passed on to the indirect purchasers. In this respect, the defendant can invoke as a defence the fact that the claimant passed on the whole or part of the overcharge resulting from the infringement of competition law. The burden of proving that the overcharge was passed on shall be on the defendant, who may reasonably require disclosure from the claimant or from third parties (section 13 of the Antitrust Damages Law).

175. Section 14 of the Antitrust Damages Law further provides that where in an action for damages, the existence of a claim for damages or the amount of compensation to be awarded depends on whether, or to what degree, an overcharge was passed on to the claimant, taking into account the commercial practice that price increases are passed on down the supply chain, the burden of proving the existence and scope of such a passing-on shall rest with the claimant, who may reasonably require disclosure from the defendant or from third parties. The indirect purchaser shall be deemed to have proven that a passing-on to that indirect purchaser has occurred where that indirect purchaser has shown that: (a) the defendant has committed an infringement of competition law; (b) the infringement of competition law has resulted in an overcharge for the direct purchaser of the defendant; and (c) the indirect purchaser has purchased the goods or services that were the object of the infringement of competition law, or has purchased goods or services derived from or containing them. The above do not apply where the defendant may convincingly prove that the overcharge was not, or was not entirely passed on to the indirect purchaser.

176. In order to avoid that actions for damages by claimants from different levels in the supply chain lead to a multiple liability or to an absence of liability of the infringer, the Court, in assessing whether the burden of proof is satisfied, shall take due account of any of the following, pursuant to section 15 of the Antitrust Damages Law: (a) actions for damages that are related to the same infringement of competition law, but that are brought by claimants from other levels in the supply chain, as well as judgments resulting from actions for damages as above; and (b) relevant information in the public domain resulting from the public enforcement of competition law. Moreover, and with regard to the quantification of damages, the Court may, if it establishes that a claimant suffered harm but it is practically impossible or excessively difficult precisely to quantify the harm suffered on the basis of the evidence available, request the assistance of the CPC (section 16 of the Antitrust Damages Law). It shall be reputably presumed that cartel infringements cause harm.

177. The limitation period is suspended for the duration of any consensual dispute resolution process, by virtue of section 17 of the Antitrust Damages Law. Such suspension shall only apply to the parties involved, or represented, in the consensual dispute resolution process. The Court before which an action for compensation for infringement of competition law is pending may suspend proceedings for up to two years, if the parties thereto are involved in consensual dispute resolution concerning the claim covered by that action for damages. The CPC may consider compensation paid as a result of a consensual settlement, prior to the imposing of an administrative fine, as a mitigating factor. Following a consensual settlement, the claim of the settling injured party is reduced by the co-infringer's share of the harm that the infringement of competition law inflicted upon the injured party, pursuant to section 18 of the Antitrust Damages Law. Any remaining claim of the settling injured party shall be exercised only against non-settling co-infringers. Non-settling co-infringers shall not be permitted to recover contribution for the remaining claim from the settling co-infringer. By way of derogation, where the non-settling co-infringers cannot pay the damages that correspond to the remaining claim of the settling injured party, the settling injured party may exercise the remaining claim against the settling co-infringer. When determining the amount of contribution that a co-infringer may recover from any other co-infringer in accordance with their relative responsibility for the harm caused by the infringement of competition law, the Court shall take due account of any damages paid pursuant to a prior consensual settlement involving the relevant co-infringer.

C. Interim Measures

178. The Court may exercise its powers to grant interlocutory orders by virtue of section 32 of Law 14/60.[148] The three-stage test that an applicant has to satisfy for interim protection to be granted is the following that: (1) there is a serious issue to be tried; (2) there is a possibility that the plaintiff shall be entitled to the relief he seeks; and (3) it would be impossible or difficult for justice to be achieved at any subsequent stage, unless the interim order is issued. If the three requirements are fulfilled, the Court should further consider whether it would be on the balance of convenience fair and just to grant the interim order.[149] At the interim stage, the Court should not attempt to resolve conflicts of evidence as to the material facts, or to decide difficult questions of law which call for detailed argument. Nor is the Court ordinarily expected at this stage to determine whether an affiant is a reliable witness or not.[150] However, this should not mean that the Court should not evaluate, at least prima facie, the concrete allegations and facts, as well as the accompanying exhibits and the provisions of the relevant legislation, in order to determine whether there are preliminary good chances for the application to succeed at its substance.[151] Vague allegations do not suffice to establish probability.

179. Considering that the parties are asserting inconsistent claims, the Court should contemplate the possibility that either party may succeed at trial and should accordingly compare between on the one hand the plaintiff being granted an interim injunction in his favour and against the defendant but subsequently having his action dismissed, and on the other hand the plaintiff not being granted an interim injunction but subsequently being granted relief at trial. In the first instance the defendant will have suffered injustice in the wider sense of the term, whereas in the second the plaintiff. Accordingly, the Court should contemplate which course of action would lead to comparatively less injustice. In this sense what is sought is a balance of justice, not convenience.[152] The Court may thus decide that even if the three requirements are fulfilled, it would not be just on the balance to grant the interim order. Usually the aim of the Court would be to safeguard the *status quo ante*, i.e., the existing state of affairs, in the sense of the position prevailing before the defendant engaged on the activities sought to be restrained.[153]

148. *See*, in detail, A. Emilianides, *Civil Procedure in Cyprus* (Kluwer, 2020).

149. *Odysseos v. A. Pieris Estates Ltd and others* [1982] 1 CLR 557; *T.A. Micrologic Computer Consultants Ltd v. Microsoft Corporation* [2002] 1 CLR 1802 (in Greek).

150. *Reckendorfer v. Reckendorfer* [2004] 1 CLR 1132 (in Greek); *Kouppas v. Poullas Tsadiotis Ltd and another,* Civil App. 312/2010, Judgment of 17 Jul. 2014 (in Greek).

151. *Skordis v. Lantou and others* [2008] 1 CLR 844 (in Greek), *Kytala and others v. Chrysanthou and others* [1996] 1 CLR 253; *Lawford and others v. Hatzigabriel* [2004] 1 CLR 818 (in Greek).

152. *Antonis and Foulis Michael Ltd v. Ioannides*, Civil App. E44/14, Judgment of 16 Jul. 2019 (in Greek); *Francome v. Mirror Group Newspaper* [1984] 1 WLR 892.

153. *Kosma v. Hatzikypri and others* [2000] 1 CLR 169 (in Greek), *Bacardi & Co Ltd v. Vinco Ltd* [1996] 1 CLR 788 (in Greek); *Zena Co Ltd v. Demenian Catering Ltd* [2011] 1 CLR 1848 (in Greek); *Polyford Holdings Ltd and others v. Rosestage Enterprises Ltd* [2007] 1 CLR 1042 (in Greek).

§3. Criminal Enforcement

I. Criminal Sanctions for Antitrust Violations

180. Pursuant to sections 36 and 37 of the CPC Law, any person who omits to comply with, or acts in contravention of a final decision of the CPC, or a decision ordering interim measures, shall commit a criminal offence punishable with a sentence of imprisonment not exceeding two years, and/or with a fine not exceeding EUR 340,000. Failure to comply with the power of the CPC to carry searches, concealment, falsification or destruction of material, also constitute criminal offences by virtue of section 31 §11 of the CPC Law, and/or section 43 §9 of the Concentrations Law, punishable with a sentence of imprisonment not exceeding one year and/or with a fine not exceeding EUR 85,000. Where a legal person commits a criminal offence pursuant to the above sections, the members of the managerial or administrative board or committee arranging the affairs of the legal person, and the general manager or director or managing director of the legal, may also be held liable, by virtue of section 39 of the CPC Law.

181. The Chair, other members, and substitute members of the CPC, the persons employed by the CPC or working under its supervision, and other public officers who by reason of their post or in the performance of their official duties obtain information on business secrets and information of a confidential nature, shall have a duty to secrecy, by virtue of section 33 of the CPC Law, and shall be bound not to communicate and/or publicize such information, except in so far as this proves necessary to prove an infringement of sections 3 and/or 6 of the CPC Law and/or Articles 101 and/or 102 TFEU, or to implement the provisions of the CPC Law, or for the purposes of applying EU competition law. The same duty to secrecy shall be also owed by any other natural or legal person who obtains such information in the application of the CPC Law. The violation of the duty to secrecy shall constitute, in the case of public officers, a serious disciplinary offence. Any person who contravenes the duty to secrecy shall commit a criminal offence, by virtue of section 38 of the CPC Law, punishable with imprisonment not exceeding one year, and/or with a fine not exceeding EUR 3,500. An equivalent provision may be found in section 48 of the Concentrations Law. However, the criminal offence under section 48 of the Concentrations Law is punishable with imprisonment not exceeding six months, and/or with a fine not exceeding EUR 1,500.

II. Role of Prosecutors

182. The Attorney-General is the general prosecutor of the State. The Attorney-General of the Republic is, by virtue of Article 112 of the Constitution, the Head of the Law Office of the Republic; the Law Office is an independent office of the Republic, which shall not be under any Ministry. The Deputy Attorney-General acts as the Deputy Head of the Law Office. One of the most important powers of the Attorney-General is the power to institute, conduct, take over, continue or discontinue any proceedings for an offence against any person in the Republic; such power may be exercised by him in person or by officers subordinate to him acting under and in accordance with his instructions.[154] The Attorney-General has the power to direct the police, oversee the investigation of any offence and decide whether there is a case justifying prosecution. Furthermore, such power shall be exercised in accordance with his discretion at the public interest, by virtue of Article 113 of the Constitution. In the exercise of his powers the Attorney-General is not subject to control from any executive or judicial authority; his decision to prosecute or discontinue, or suspend any prosecution by a *nolle prosequi* are absolute and not subject to judicial control.[155]

III. Competent Criminal Courts

183. Competition law offences fall within the jurisdiction of the District Courts. District Courts have jurisdiction to hear and determine at first instance all criminal offences for which the accused is liable to imprisonment not exceeding five years and/or a fine of 85,000 euro. However, the District Court may, as an exception and with the consent of the Attorney-General, hear and determine at first instance an offence for which the accused is liable to imprisonment exceeding five years if it is satisfied that this would be in the interests of justice on the basis of the circumstances of the case and provided that the sentence imposed by the District Court judge may not exceed five years of imprisonment (such as when the particular facts of the case do not disclose a serious offence). Assize Courts normally have jurisdiction hear criminal offences for which the accused is liable to imprisonment exceeding five years. The Supreme Court has jurisdiction with regard to all criminal appeals. Cases before the District Courts are heard by a single judge, whereas the Assize Courts are constituted by three judges, one of whom has the rank of a President of the District Court and the other two having the rank of a Senior District Court Judge and a District Court Judge respectively.

---

154. D. Kyprianou, *The Role of the Cyprus Attorney-General's Office in Prosecutions: Rhetoric, Ideology and Practice* (Heidelberg 2010); C. Tornaritis, *The Constitutional Power of the Attorney-General to Institute, Conduct or Discontinue any Criminal Proceedings*, 2 Cyprus L. Rev. 203–224 (1983) (in Greek).

155. *Police v. Athienitis* [1983] 2 CLR 194, *Chomatenos v. Police* [1979] 2 CLR 119, *Ellinas v. Republic* [1989] 1 CLR 17.

Part II. Application of the Prohibitions

Chapter 1. Restrictive Agreements

§1. Horizontal Agreements

I. Cartels

A. Introduction

184. Adam Smith observed as far back as 1776 that: 'People of the same trade seldom meet together, even for merriment and diversion, but the conversation ends in a conspiracy against the public, or in some contrivance to raise prices.'[156] There is considerable literature on the origin of the term 'cartel'.[157] Cartels manifest in several ways, making it challenging to arrive at an all-encompassing definition. 'Hardcore cartels' have been defined as 'anticompetitive agreements, concerted practices or arrangements by actual or potential competitors to agree on prices, make rigged bids (collusive tenders), establish output restrictions or quotas, or share or divide markets by, for example, allocating customers, suppliers, territories, or lines of commerce'.[158] At the level of EU law, cartels are addressed under Article 101 TFEU. The European Commission investigates potential infringements of the provisions of Article 101 TFEU under the Modernisation Regulation. In the Cypriot legal order, while 'cartels' are not defined per se, they are nevertheless caught under the definition of 'collusion' pursuant to section 2 of the CPC Law.

B. Price-Fixing

185. Price-fixing is one of the most flagrant types of horizontal collusion and is unsurprisingly at the core of 'hardcore cartels'. Agreements, decisions and concerted practices which directly or indirectly fix purchase or selling prices, or any other terms of trade, are expressly caught by 3 §1 of the CPC Law, which mirrors

156. A. Smith, *An Inquiry into the Nature and Causes of the Wealth of Nations* (University of Chicago Press 1977 [1776]: 144.
157. *See, inter alia,* D.J. Gerber, *Law and Competition in Twentieth Century Europe: Protecting Prometheus* (OUP 1998); C. Harding & J. Joshua, *Regulating Cartels in Europe: A Study of Legal Control of Corporate Delinquency* (OUP 2003).
158. OECD, *Recommendation of the Council concerning Effective Action against Hard Core Cartels* (2 July 2019).

the language of Article 101 §1 TFEU. It is evident from the case law of the CJEU that certain types of coordination between undertakings reveal a sufficient degree of harm to competition so that there may be no need to examine their effects.[159] Price-fixing is one of such types of coordination, which may be considered so likely to have negative effects, in particular on the price, quantity or quality of the goods and services, that it may be considered redundant, for the purposes of applying Article 101 §1 TFEU, to prove that they have actual effects on the market.[160] Price-fixing conduct can be seen to result in falls in production and price increases, therefore leading to poor allocation of resources to the detriment of consumers.

186. The CPC and Cypriot courts have typically referred to EU case law in order to assess infringements of the CPC Law. In the absence of an extensive body of Cypriot case law on price-fixing, it becomes imperative that we refer in this chapter to the main interpretative principles laid down by the courts of the EU in price-fixing cases. To begin with, it is irrelevant how the price-fixing takes place. On a non-exhaustive basis, prices may be fixed by means of: (a) an agreement;[161] (b) a trade association directing its members or setting prices;[162] (c) a concerted practice;[163] and (d) price-fixing meetings,[164] or information exchange regarding trading strategies. On the concept of 'concerted practice' in particular, the CJEU ruled in *T-Mobile Netherlands*[165] that depending on the structure of the market, a concerted practice could even arise from a single meeting.[166] The key question was whether the meeting allowed the undertakings concerned to take account of the information exchanged with their competitors in determining their conduct on the market in question, and knowingly to substitute practical cooperation between them for the risks of competition.[167]

187. Second, it is not necessary that the agreement expressly or directly fixes the actual selling or purchasing prices. The prohibition applies to 'prices' in its broadest sense. Price-fixing may involve an agreement to set minimum or target prices for particular customers or sales in general. Collusive behaviour may entail coordination of the timing and the level of price increases, while price 'ceilings' may also be fixed to prevent competition between the undertakings concerned in terms of price.

159. Case 56/65, *Société Technique Minière (L.T.M.) v. Maschinenbau Ulm GmbH (M.B.U.)*, EU:C:1966:38, paras 359 and 360; Case C-32/11, *Allianz Hungária Biztosító and Others*, C-32/11, EU:C:2013:160.
160. *See, inter alia*, Case C-67/13 P, *Groupement des cartes bancaires (CB) v. European Commission*, ECLI:EU:C:2014:2204, para. 51; Case 123/83, *Bureau national interprofessionnel du cognac v. Guy Clair*, ECLI:EU:C:1985:33, para. 22.
161. European Commission Decision IV/30.717 – *Uniform Eurocheques*, 10 December 1984, ELI: http://data.europa.eu/eli/dec/1985/77/oj.
162. *See, inter alia*, Joined Cases C-427/16 and C-428/16, *CHEZ Elektro Bulgaria AD v. Yordan Kotsev*, ECLI:EU:C:2017:890; *Case 246/86*, Belasco v. Commission, ECLI:EU:C:1989:301.
163. Case 48/69, *Imperial Chemical Industries v. Commission*, ECLI:EU:C:1972:70, para. 118.
164. European Commission Decision IV/31.149 – *Polypropylene,* 23 April 1986 ELI: http://data.europa.eu/eli/dec/1986/398/oj.
165. Case C-8/08, *T-Mobile Netherlands BV, KPN Mobile NV, Orange Nederland NV and Vodafone Libertel NV v. Raad van bestuur van de Nederlandse Mededingingsautoriteit*; ECLI:EU:C:2009:343.
166. *Ibid.*, para. 59.
167. *Ibid.*, para. 61.

Setting levels of discounts or rebates, purchase prices or deploying a common strategy to raise retail prices may all be caught as illegal collusion. The CJEU has held that although a producer was free to change their prices, taking into account the present or foreseeable conduct of their competitors, it was a breach of competition law for a producer to 'co-operate with his competitors … in order to determine a coordinated course of action relating to a price increase and to ensure its success by prior elimination of all uncertainty as to each other's conduct regarding the essential elements of that action, such as the amount, subject-matter, date and place of the increases'.[168]

188. Over the past years, the CPC has found several price-fixing arrangements which infringed section 3 of the CPC Law, as a result of both ex-officio investigations and complaints made to the CPC. In *CYTA/Forthnet,*[169] the CPC found CYTA and Forthnet to have infringed, *inter alia*, section 3 §1(a) of the CPC Law. The said decision resulted from an ex-officio investigation of the CPC into an agreement concluded between CYTA and Forthnet Media Holdings S.A. concerning the distribution of satellite television platform 'NOVA' through CYTA's cable subscription platform, 'Cytavision'. Among the CPC's findings in *CYTA/Forthnet* were that the agreement between the undertakings concerned contained provisions for indirect price-fixing and the sharing of confidential information between the parties on their potential trade policies, thereby seeking to limit the competitive conditions between them. The CPC found that the terms of the agreement between the undertakings concerned by nature constituted a violation of section 3 of CPC Law, as these terms removed from the parties their ability to act independently on the market and lead them to align their behaviour in the retail market of paid television. The agreement was further found to confer CYTA with the ability to be informed of ranges of prices by Forthnet (and in particular Multichoice, Forthnet's subsidiary) and in turn, the ability for CYTA to predict with certainty Forthnet's pricing policy in the retail market for the provision of subscription television services, in which the undertakings concerned were competitors. This aspect, together with other terms of the agreement (which are redacted in the public version of the decision), were found to afford each undertaking concerned the ability to become aware of the pricing policies of one another.[170] The CPC held that 'price-fixing is one of the typical cases of prohibited collusion and an agreement to fix prices by nature constitutes a restriction of competition and indeed the primary case of distortion of competition by object, since pricing forms the main field of competition'.[171]

189. The *Oil companies case*[172] concerned information exchange and price-fixing. The first decision of the CPC on the conduct of the undertakings concerned

168. Case 48/69, *Imperial Chemical Industries v. Commission of the European Communities*, ECLI:EU:C:1972:70, para. 118.
169. CPC Decision 13/2015, *Ex officio investigation against CYTA, Forthnet AE and Multichoice Hellas S.A.*, 13 May 2015 (in Greek).
170. *Ibid.*, para. 125.
171. *Ibid.*, para. 120.
172. CPC Decision 51/2017, *Ex officio investigation on ExxonMobil Cyprus Ltd, Petrolina (Holdings) Public Ltd, Hellenic Petroleum Cyprus Ltd and Lukoil Cyprus Ltd*, 30 Oct. 2017 (in Greek).

was annulled by the Supreme Court in the exercise of its administrative review jurisdiction,[173] due to an irregularity in the composition of the CPC at the time of issuing of the decision. The CPC reassessed the same factual circumstances under a new composition in 2017 and arrived at a new decision. ExxonMobil Cyprus Ltd, Petrolina (Holdings) Public Ltd, Hellenic Petroleum Cyprus Ltd and Lukoil Cyprus Ltd were the major undertakings active in the retail sale of fuel (gasoline and petroleum) in Cyprus. The CPC embarked on examining whether these undertakings adjusted their product prices homogenously to each other and at a rate which indicated that such conduct constituted a concerted practice. The CPC scrutinised commercial relationships between the undertakings concerned and their respective distributors, to assess whether the market conditions did not correspond to the natural conditions that should have prevailed in the relevant market. The CPC's investigation and assessment were directed at establishing whether the undertakings had infringed section 3 §1(a) of the CPC Law.

190. The CPC noted that when parallel behaviour which would otherwise be legal cannot be attributed to the market conditions, consequently leaving no other grounds to explain such conduct, then this behaviour would constitute a concerted practice. To address the evidential difficulties faced in assessing whether a concerted practice existed, the CPC evaluated the characteristics of the relevant market. The CPC found the following as the main characteristics of the relevant market under investigation: i) a small number of competing undertakings; ii) an analogy in market shares (save for Lukoil); iii) a high rate of concentration in a relevant market; iv) similar cost structures; v) the absence of unpredictability in demand; vi) the existence of structural bonds between the undertakings concerned; vii) an absence of innovation; viii) the high frequency of interaction between the undertakings concerned; ix) the capability of the undertakings concerned for regular and low-cost adjustments of recommended prices of the relevant products; and x) the exchange of confidential information.

191. The CPC identified the existence of artificial transparency conditions in the relevant market, mainly through the constant dissemination of prices by the undertakings concerned. This dissemination took place through the media and was aimed at informing each of the competitors of the other's future pricing. That the dissemination of confidential information was carried out publicly through the media did not relieve the undertakings concerned of culpability. This artificial transparency had the result of relieving the undertakings concerned from the reasonable insecurity that should have prevailed as to each other's future behaviour and also supported a mechanism which complemented the implementation of the concerted practice under discussion and the practice itself. This practice offended the ideal of free competition and operated to restrict the freedom of market participants to responsibly set their prices and take on a business risk independently. Fuel prices in the relevant product market were parallel and these undertakings were indeed

173. *ExxonMobil Cyprus Ltd, Petrolina (Holdings) Public Ltd, Hellenic Petroleum Cyprus Ltd and Lukoil Cyprus* Ltd *v. Commission for the Protection of Competition* [2011] 3 CLR 449 (in Greek).

adjusting their products' prices homogenously to each other's and at a rate which indicated that it was not a matter of intelligent business activity but rather a coordinated activity, namely a concerted practice.

192. The commercial relationship between the undertakings concerned and their respective distributors (gas stations) was also part of the price-fixing and emanated from the concerted practice between the undertakings themselves. This relationship, within the context where the supplier undertakings exercised economic pressure concerning their retailers, was one of economic dependence of the retailers on the supplier. The conduct of the oil companies had created market conditions that did not correspond to the natural conditions that should exist in the relevant market, also taking into account the size and number of undertakings active in the said market. The parallel adjustment of pricing and their simultaneous announcement to the public at the material time was found to be an unequivocal indication of the existence of a concerted practice among the undertakings concerned. The CPC found the undertakings concerned to be engaged in a concerted practice having as its object the fixing of prices and the consequent distortion of competition. It was not necessary to establish the effect of the said behaviour. Without having concluded any express agreement, the undertakings concerned artificially fixed stable fuel prices in the relevant market through their concerted practice. As such, they were found to consciously substitute the risks of competition, which had the result of eliminating competition between themselves. As a result of their concerted practice, it was held that the four undertakings infringed section 3 §1(a) of the CPC Law, both due to their engagement in a concerted practice between them having their object the fixing of fuel prices as well as due to the conclusion of agreements with their distributors (gas stations) on that basis and with the same object.

C. Market/Client Allocation

193. Among the agreements specifically prohibited by section 3 §1 of the CPC Law and Article 101(1) TFEU are those which 'limit or control' markets, and those which 'share' markets. Agreements between competitors that divide markets by geographical territory, and those that allocate market sectors or customers as between competitors, are considered below. It has been argued that collusion resulting in geographical market sharing may be more efficient to achieve than price-fixing for colluding undertakings, as it can avoid the cost of fixing common prices.[174] From the consumer's perspective, geographical market sharing is particularly restrictive, because it reduces choice. In the case of price-fixing, the choice to select a product remains and the restriction of price competition might coerce the parties to compete in other ways.[175]

174. R. Whish & D. Bailey, *Competition Law* 541 (9th ed., OUP 2018).
175. *Ibid.*

194. The Courts of the EU consider market-sharing agreements as having the restriction of competition as their object.[176] This can be justified for the two following reasons. It is first argued that in the EU context it is relatively simple to achieve geographical market allocation because there are many ways of separating national markets from one another. Until the establishment of a single market, the factual, legal and economic inconsistencies among national markets will be ongoing barriers to inter-state trade. Second, one of the European Commission's priorities is to take action to prevent any collusive activity that could hinder the process of integration of the single market. Horizontal market-sharing may be expected to be heavily punished.[177] Market sharing or market allocation agreements, which are caught by section 3 §1 of the CPC Law and Article 101 §1 TFEU), may be divided into: (a) geographical market sharing; (b) customer or market allocation; (c) market control; or (d) limitations of supply to the market.

195. Another manifestation of market sharing is bid-rigging. Bid-rigging occurs when two or more undertakings agree that one or more of them will not submit a bid, withdraw a bid or submit a bid at pre-agreed high prices in relation to a tender. Bid-rigging is generally considered to restrict competition by object. It is a form of price-fixing and market allocation which may, for example, take place in the case of public procurement contracts. Rigging tenders can be seen to draw on consumers and taxpayers' money, destroying public trust in the competitive process and weakening the advantages of a competitive market.[178]

196. Market sharing practices findings are scarce in the CPC's practice to date. One instance of a market sharing finding can be seen in the CPC's *CYTA/Forthnet* case.[179] In that case, the CPC found that the undertakings concerned notified one another of their respective intention to bid for the acquisition of rights to broadcast the football competitions UEFA Champions League and UEFA Europa League for football seasons between 2012 and 2015. While Forthnet did not bid for these rights, CYTA did (and was eventually awarded the rights), a development which the CPC found was a consequence of the understanding between CYTA and Forthnet that they would not compete for the acquisition of sports content they already held prior to their agreement.[180] The CPC held that the conduct of CYTA and Forthnet was by object restrictive of competition in the form of sharing markets or supply sources, irrespective of the fact that such conduct relates solely to content which is already held by the undertakings concerned.[181] The CPC found the undertakings concerned as being engaged in an informal agreement which had as its object the restriction of competition in the market for the acquisition of audiovisual content for subscription television, infringing section 3 §1(c) of the CPC Law and Article 101 §1(c) TFEU.

176. Case C-239/11 P, etc. *Siemens v. European Commission,* EU:C:2013:866, para. 218.
177. R. Whish & D. Bailey, *Competition Law* 542 (9th ed., OUP 2018).
178. OECD, *Guidelines for fighting bid-rigging and manipulation of tenders in public procurement* (2009).
179. CPC Decision 13/2015, *Ex officio investigation against CYTA, Forthnet AE and Multichoice Hellas S.A.*, 13 May 2015 (in Greek).
180. *Ibid.*, paras 146–147.
181. *Ibid.*, para. 148.

197. In *Lalizas/Rementzo,*[182] Lalizas, a Greek company, supplied marine goods, fishing equipment, boat equipment and other items to Rementzo, a Cypriot company, under a franchise agreement which contained restrictions relating to the enforcement of resale price maintenance and the prohibition of cross-supply between other franchisees. Lalizas was also able to track Rementzo's prices through software that Lalizas installed at the Rementzo's store. The CPC found this arrangement to be an abuse of a dominant position on the part of Lalizas. The CPC held that trade between the Member States was impaired in this case, through the discussed restrictive policies, as the goods concerned were not of a nature that could impede cross-border sales. Furthermore, it has been noted that in the case of a franchise agreement which imposes resale price maintenance and covers more than one Member State, it is capable of affecting trade between the Member States by its very nature. As such, Lalizas had infringed section 3 §1 of the CPC Law and Article 101 §1(a) TFEU imposing resale price maintenance through a franchise agreement with Rementzo and had also infringed section 3 §1(c) of the CPC Law and Article 101 §1(c) TFEU as a consequence of the restriction of cross-supply between network members.

198. In the *Ready-mix concrete case,*[183] the CPC found collusion in the form of bid-rigging concerning public tenders procured by the Ministry of Transport, Communications and Works. The undertakings concerned were found to have colluded by bid-rigging a number of public tenders for the supply and transportation of ready-mix concrete for the district of Limassol. The CPC stressed in the *ready-mix concrete case* that such restrictions are considered per se anticompetitive, as they are presumed to have a negative effect on the functioning of competition. Citing the judgment of the CJEU in *Consten and Grundig,*[184] it was held that where an agreement has as its object the restriction of competition, there is no need to demonstrate the effect on competition. With regard to the manipulation of public tenders, the CPC noted that buyers, and in particular public bodies, frequently rely on a competitive bidding mechanism to obtain the best value for money, when it comes to public tenders. Distortion of competition is inconsistent with this practice and can result in higher prices and lower quality of products or services. These secret agreements and coordinated practices have a particularly negative effect on the public works market, the management of state resources and the public interest in general.

D. Production/Innovation Limitation

199. Agreements that limit or control production are among those specifically prohibited by section 3 §1(b) of the CPC Law. Such restrictive practices will often

182. CPC Decision 15/2015, *Complaint of G&G Rementzo Ltd against Lalizas AE* (in Greek).
183. CPC Decision 29/2018, *Ex officio investigation into Mattheos Ioannou Ready Mix Concrete Ltd, C.Kythreotis Skyrodema Ltd, Skyramix Ltd, Athinodorou & Poullas Super Beton Ltd, Top Mix Concrete Ltd, I & S Kritonis Limited, Betoman Limited, Alfa Concrete Public Company Ltd through its financial successor Alfa Beton Ltd and Psaroudis Beton Limited*, 18 Jul. 2018.
184. Joined Cases 57 & 58/64, *Établissements Consten S.à.R.L. and Grundig-Verkaufs-GmbH v. Commission of the European Economic Community,* ECLI:EU:C:1966:41.

be implemented together with other anticompetitive practices, such as price-fixing. In production limitation, colluding members will agree to limit their performance or output. When output is reduced, prices can be expected to rise. Horizontal production-restriction arrangements need to be closely monitored, as overproduction by certain cartel leaders will result in a decline in market price, unless the scheme is run in tandem with a price-fixing mechanism, which is often the case. In the absence of price control, members of the cartel will always agree to a quota scheme under which they will each supply a specified proportion of the entire output of the industry during any given time.[185] There will be costs involved in enforcing these quotas, as in the case of price-fixing, as certain businesses will be larger or more competitive or grow faster than others, so that intense and prolonged negotiations will have to take place. Having fixed the quotas, the cartel will need a mechanism to avoid cheating. For example, this can be achieved by requiring comprehensive production and sales details to be submitted to a trade association or 'cartel consultancy'. The cartel can use a system whereby those who surpass their allotted quotas will make compensation payments to those who fail to dispose of theirs, as a necessary corollary.[186]

200. In the absence of a substantive body of Cypriot case law on production limitation, we must refer to the practice of the European Commission. In *Peroxygen products*, the European Commission found that members of the cartel had entered into a series of comprehensive national agreements dividing markets into negotiated fractions, as well as geographically splitting the markets.[187] The European Commission held in *MELDOC* that a quota and compensation scheme concerning the Dutch dairy sector infringed Article 101 TFEU.[188] An exacerbating factor was that the Dutch milk producers concerned had also agreed to a coordinated response to the threat posed to their market position by imports from other Member States. An arrangement not to increase production without competing firms' permission infringes Article 101 §1 TFEU[189] and would accordingly be expected to infringe section 3 §1 of the CPC Law. It is not permissible to set up a joint venture for the allocation of orders between competitors.[190] Quota agreements not infrequently confer exclusive or priority rights on particular undertakings in supplying their own domestic markets: they undoubtedly will not be tolerated.[191]

185. *Ibid.*
186. *Ibid.*
187. Commission Decision No. 85/74/EEC: Commission Decision of 23 November 1984 relating to a proceeding under Article 85 of the EEC Treaty (IV/30.907 – Peroxygen products), ELI: http://data.europa.eu/eli/dec/1985/74/oj.
188. Commission Decision No. 86/596/EEC: Commission Decision of 26 November 1986 relating to a proceeding under Article 85 of the EEC Treaty (IV/31.204 – MELDOC), ELI: http://data.europa.eu/eli/dec/1986/596/oj.
189. Commission Decision No. 72/474/CEE: Décision de la Commission, du 22 décembre 1972, relative à une procédure d'application de l'article 85 du traité CEE (IV/243, 244, 245 – Cimbel), ELI: http://data.europa.eu/eli/dec/1972/474/oj.
190. European Commission, *XII Report on Competition Policy* (1982), available at https://ec.europa.eu/competition/publications/annual_report/ar_1982_en.pdf, point 85.
191. Case 41/69, *ACF Chemiefarma NV v. Commission of the European Communities*, EU:C:1970:71.

201. In *Cartonboard,* the European Commission considered an elaborate 'price before tonnage scheme' to be anticompetitive, including the 'freezing' of market shares, their continuous tracking and review, and the management of 'system downtime' in an attempt to preserve prices and control supply.[192] In *Europe Asia trades,* the European Commission found that a 'capacity non-utilisation' agreement coupled with the exchange of information on maritime transport infringed Article 101 §1 TFEU.[193] The arrangement was found to unnaturally limit the shipping capacity of liners, thus reducing price competition. In *Compagnie Royale Asturienne des Mines*[194] the CJEU held that the continued sale of goods to rivals was a violation of Article 101 §1 TFEU. Although this could be appropriate for dealing with such situations, it was not permissible for rivals to conclude indeterminate-length agreements and large amounts. It has had the effect of institutionalising mutual assistance instead of competition, creating market dynamics similar to those produced by quota arrangements.[195]

E. Group Boycott

202. A collective boycott that infringes section 3 §1 of the CPC Law would occur when a group of competing undertakings agree to exclude an actual or potential competitor. This practice generally constitutes a restriction by object. In the absence of a substantive body of cases from the CPC on group boycott, we note the CJEU's judgment in *Slovenská sporiteľňa a.s.*[196] In that case, three banks monitored a competitor's activity, conferred with each other and decided, by common agreement, to terminate in a coordinated manner the contracts they had concluded with that competitor. It was irrelevant whether the competitor's alleged illegality for the purposes of determining whether an infringement of competition law was found.[197]

II. Information Exchange Practices

203. When sharing information between them, competing undertakings risk infringing section 3 §1 of the CPC Law and Article 101 TFEU. Information exchange can only be addressed under competition rules if it establishes or is part of an agreement, concerted practice or decision by an association of undertakings.

192. Commission Decision No. 94/601/EC: Commission Decision of 13 July 1994 relating to a proceeding under Article 85 of the EC Treaty (IV/C/33.833 – Cartonboard), ELI: http://data.europa.eu/eli/dec/1994/601/oj.
193. Commission Decision No. 1999/485/EC: Commission Decision of 30 April 1999 relating to a proceeding pursuant to Article 85 of the Treaty (IV/34.250 – Europe Asia Trades Agreement), ELI: http://data.europa.eu/eli/dec/1999/485/oj.
194. Joined Cases 29/83 and 30/83, *Compagnie Royale Asturienne des Mines SA and Rheinzink GmbH v. Commission of the European Communities*, EU:C:1984:130.
195. R. Whish & D. Bailey, *Competition Law* 546 (9th ed., OUP, 2018).
196. Case C-68/12, *Protimonopolný úrad Slovenskej republiky v. Slovenská sporiteľňa a.s.*, ECLI-:EU:C:2013:71.
197. *Ibid.*, paras 18–20.

In 2010, the European Commission issued valuable guidance on information sharing in the context of its guidelines on horizontal cooperation agreements (the 'Horizontal Agreements Guidelines').[198] The Horizontal Agreements Guidelines draw substantially on EU Court case law, including *John Deere*[199] and *T-Mobile.*[200] While information exchange can in certain contexts generate efficiency gains and benefit consumers, it may also lead to restrictions of competition in particular in situations where it is liable to enable undertakings to be aware of market strategies of their competitors.

204. The competitive outcome of information exchange depends on the characteristics of the market in which it takes place as well as on the type of information that is exchanged, which may modify the relevant market environment towards one liable to coordination.[201] As such, the exchange of information can facilitate collusion and result in restrictive effects on competition. Exchange of information can also lead to anticompetitive foreclosure when the exchange of commercially sensitive information places unaffiliated competitors at a significant competitive disadvantage as compared to the undertakings not affiliated with the scheme. As the European Commission notes, this type of foreclosure is only possible if the information concerned is very strategic for competition and covers a significant part of the relevant market.[202] Exchange of information intended to restrict competition on the market will be considered as a restriction by object. Whether an information exchange constitutes a restriction of competition by object requires careful attention to the legal and economic context in which the information exchange takes place.[203]

205. To restrict competition within the meaning of section 3 §1 of the CPC Law, information exchange must be likely to have an appreciable adverse impact on the parameters of competition such as price, output, product quality, product variety or innovation.[204] The *Oil companies case*[205] entailed information exchange. In that case, the CPC identified the existence of artificial transparency conditions in the relevant market, mainly through the constant dissemination of prices by the undertakings concerned. This dissemination took place through the media and was aimed at

198. Guidelines on the applicability of Article 101 of the Treaty on the Functioning of the European Union to horizontal co-operation agreements, OJ C 11, 14 Jan. 2011, pp. 1–72.
199. Case C-7/95 P, John Deere Ltd v. Commission of the European Communities, ECLI:EU:C:1998:256, para. 77.
200. Case C-8/08, T-Mobile Netherlands BV, KPN Mobile NV, Orange Nederland NV and Vodafone Libertel NV v. Raad van bestuur van de Nederlandse Mededingingsautoriteit, ECLI:EU:C:2009:343, paras 29 et seq.
201. *Ibid.*
202. Horizontal Agreements Guidelines, para. 70.
203. Joined Cases C-501/06 P, C-513/06 P, C-515/06 P and C-519/06 P, *GlaxoSmithKline Services Unlimited v. Commission of the European Communities et al*, para. 58; Case C-209/07; *Competition Authority v. Beef Industry Development Society Ltd and Barry Brothers (Carrigmore) Meats Ltd*, ECLI:EU:C:2008:643, paras 15 et seq.
204. Case C-7/95 P, *John Deere Ltd v. Commission of the European Communities*, ECLI:EU:C:1998:256, para. 76.
205. CPC Decision 51/2017, *Ex officio investigation on ExxonMobil Cyprus Ltd, Petrolina (Holdings) Public Ltd, Hellenic Petroleum Cyprus Ltd and Lukoil Cyprus Ltd*, 30 Oct. 2017.

informing each of the competitors of the other's future pricing. That the dissemination of confidential information was carried out publicly through the media did not relieve the undertakings concerned of culpability. The artificial transparency had the result of relieving the undertakings concerned from the reasonable insecurity that should have prevailed as to each other's future behaviour and also supported a mechanism which complemented the implementation of the concerted practice under discussion and the practice itself. This practice offended the ideal of free competition and operated to restrict the freedom of market participants to responsibly set their prices and take on a business risk independently. The CPC found the undertakings concerned to be engaged in a concerted practice having as its object the fixing of prices and the consequent distortion of competition. Without having concluded any express agreement, the undertakings concerned artificially fixed stable fuel prices in the relevant market through their concerted practice.

III. Cooperation Agreements

A. *Research and Development Agreements*

206. Research and development ('R&D') agreements range from outsourcing R&D to cooperation concerning research, development and marketing of either existing technology or offerings to developing new products or services. R&D agreements may restrict competition in a number of ways. Illustratively, R&D agreements may hinder innovation, leading to decreased or delayed offer of products in the market. R&D cooperation may also reduce competition between undertakings which are not part of the cooperation, or render anticompetitive coordination more likely, leading to increased prices. Foreclosure issues may also arise in an R&D cooperation context, where they involve an undertaking with significant market power and the R&D leads to the exclusive exploitation of its results.[206] The CPC has not specifically considered R&D agreements in its practice to date.

207. R&D agreements between competitors are covered by Regulation 1217/2010[207] (the 'R&D Block Exemption Regulation'), which expires on 31 December 2022. The R&D Block Exemption Regulation applies *mutatis mutandis* to the Cypriot legal order pursuant to the R&D Block Exemption Order of 2018 issued by the Council of Ministers.[208] The benefit of the exemption established by the R&D Block Exemption Regulation concerns those R&D agreements for which it can be assumed with sufficient certainty that they satisfy the conditions of Article 101 §3 of the Treaty. The R&D Block Exemption Regulation exempts R&D agreements where the following apply: (a) in the case of a joint R&D agreement, the combined

206. *Ibid.*, para. 127.
207. Commission Regulation (EU) No. 1217/2010 of 14 December 2010 on the application of Article 101 §3 of the Treaty on the Functioning of the European Union to certain categories of research and development agreements, ELI: http://data.europa.eu/eli/reg/2010/1217/oj.
208. 70/2019, OJ III(I) 364, 1 Mar. 2019 (in Greek).

market share of the parties does not exceed 25% on the relevant product and technology markets; (b) in the case of a paid-for R&D agreement, the combined market share of the financing party and all of its contracting parties in the market for the same products or technologies covered by the agreement, does not exceed 25% on the relevant product and technology markets. To be exempted under the R&D Block Exemption Regulation, the R&D agreement concerned must provide that all the parties have full access to the final results of the R&D, including any resulting intellectual property rights and know-how, for further R&D and exploitation. If the parties limit their rights of exploitation, access to the results for exploitation may be limited accordingly.

208. Where the parties to the R&D agreement are not competing undertakings, the exemption provided for by this regulation is applicable for the duration of the R&D. Where the results are jointly exploited, the exemption continues to apply for seven years after the contract products or contract technologies are first put on the EU market. At the end of the seven years, the exemption shall continue to apply as long as the combined market share of the parties does not exceed 25% on the relevant markets. The exemption does not apply to R&D agreements which, directly or indirectly, in isolation or combination with other factors under the control of the parties, have as their object: (a) the restriction of the freedom of the parties to carry out R&D in an unrelated field; (b) the restriction of the freedom of the parties to pursue R&D in a related field after the completion of the R&D agreement concerned; (c) the limitation of output or sales, with certain exceptions. The exemption does not apply to the following obligations contained in R&D agreements: (a) the obligation not to challenge the validity of related intellectual property rights after completion of the R&D, b) the obligation not to grant licences to third parties to manufacture the contract products or to apply to contract technologies, unless the agreement provides for the exploitation of the results by at least one of the parties and such exploitation takes place in the internal market vis-à-vis third parties.

B. Specialisation Agreements

209. Article 101 §1 TFEU does not apply to specialisation agreements (including joint production agreements) provided the agreement does not contain any hardcore restrictions of competition and the parties' combined market share does not exceed 20%. The European Commission adopted Regulation 1218/2010[209] (the 'Specialisation Block Exemption Regulation') to regulate how specialisation agreements are exempted from Article 101 §1 TFEU, which will expire on 31 December 2022. The exemption provided for in the Specialisation Block Exemption Regulation applies to specialisation agreements (including joint production agreements), provided the agreement does not contain any hardcore restrictions of competition and the combined market share of the undertakings concerned does not exceed 20%.

209. Commission Regulation (EU) No. 1218/2010 of 14 December 2010 on the application of Article 101(3) of the Treaty on the Functioning of the European Union to certain categories of specialisation agreements, ELI: http://data.europa.eu/eli/reg/2010/1218/oj.

The hardcore restrictions which, if present, negate the application of the Specialisation Block Exemption Regulation, relate to specialisation agreements aimed, directly or indirectly, at the fixing of prices, the limitation of output or sales and the allocation of markets or customers. The CPC has not specifically considered specialisation agreements to date.

210. Article 1 §2(a) of the Specialisation Block Exemption Regulation defines specialisation agreements as including unilateral agreements on specialisation, reciprocal specialisation agreements and joint production agreements. A unilateral specialisation agreement is, pursuant to Article 1 §1(b) of the Specialisation Block Exemption Regulation, an agreement between two parties active on the same product market whereby one party agrees to cease the production of certain profits in whole or in part or to refrain from producing those products and to buy them from the other party which agrees to produce and supply those products. A reciprocal specialisation agreement means, pursuant to Article 1 §1(c) of the Specialisation Block Exemption Regulation, an agreement between two or more parties active on the same product market whereby, on a reciprocal basis, two or more parties agree in full or in part to cease or refrain from producing certain but different products and to buy those products from the other parties which agree to produce and supply them. Article 2 §3 of the Specialisation Block Exemption Regulation provides that the exemption also applies to specialisation agreements where the parties accept an exclusive purchase or supply obligation and agreements whereby the parties jointly distribute, rather than independently sell, the products which are the subject of the agreement.[210]

C. Standardisation Agreements

211. The primary objective of standardisation agreements is to specify the technological or quality specifications that current or future products, manufacturing processes or methods, including agreements establishing environmental performance standards. As the European Commission notes,[211] standardisation agreements may produce their effects on four possible markets: (a) on the product or service market or markets to which the standard or standards relates; (b) where the standard-setting involves the selection of technology and where the rights to intellectual property are marketed separately from the products to which they relate, the standard can have effects on the relevant technology market; (c) the market for standard-setting may be affected if different standard-setting bodies or agreements exist; and (d) where relevant, a distinct market for testing and certification may be affected by standard-setting.

212. The Horizontal Agreements Guidelines recognise that standardisation agreements typically have substantial positive economic effects, especially by fostering innovation and ensuring interoperability. However, standardisation can affect

210. R. Whish & D. Bailey, *Competition Law* 614 (9th ed., OUP, 2018).
211. Horizontal Agreements Guidelines, para. 261.

competition in three ways: price competition reduction following anticompetitive discussions; foreclosure of advanced technologies; and prevention of effective access to the standard.[212] Agreements which use a standard as part of a broader restrictive agreement that aims to exclude current or potential competitors limit competition by object.[213] In the *Pre-insulated pipe cartel*, the use of regulations and specifications to discourage or postpone the introduction into the market of new technologies which would have contributed to price reductions.[214] Agreements to limit competition by using the disclosure of the most stringent licensing terms before implementing a standard as a cover for mutual price-fixing are often known as by object restrictions. Agreements requiring members of a standard association to sell only goods that follow a standard may, under certain circumstances, limit competition by object.[215] The CPC has not specifically considered standardisation agreements to date.

D. *Joint Production Agreements*

213. The Horizontal Agreements Guidelines refer to all types of joint production arrangements, including horizontal subcontracting arrangements, that is, agreements between companies operating in the same market, regardless of whether they are current or perceived competitors.[216] The Horizontal Agreements Guidelines raise three key competitive concerns about production agreements:[217] (a) they can lead to a direct limitation of competition between the parties where they directly align output levels and quality, the price at which the joint venture sells on its products, or other competitively important parameters (even if the parties market the products independently), (b) they can result in the coordination of competitive behaviour as suppliers leading to higher prices or reduced output, product quality, product variety or innovation, subject to the parties having market power and the existence of market characteristics conducive to such coordination; and (c) they can lead to anticompetitive foreclosure of third parties in a related market (e.g., the downstream market relying on inputs from the market in which the production agreement takes place).

214. In evaluating whether Article 101 TFEU – and, therefore, section 3 of the CPC Law – applies to production agreements, the applicable product and regional markets must be defined and the risk of a 'spillover impact' on an upstream, downstream or neighbouring market must also be considered.[218] While the CPC has not

212. Horizontal Agreements Guidelines, paras 263–268.
213. Horizontal Agreements Guidelines, para. 273.
214. 1999/60/EC: Commission Decision of 21 October 1998 relating to a proceeding under Article 85 of the EC Treaty (Case No IV/35.691/E-4: Pre-Insulated Pipe Cartel), ELI: http://data.europa.eu/eli/dec/1999/60(1)/oj.
215. Horizontal Agreements Guidelines, para. 293.
216. *Ibid.*, para. 151.
217. *Ibid.*, paras 157–159.
218. *Ibid.*, para. 156.

to date assessed joint production agreements, the practice of the European Commission demonstrates instances where joint production agreements can have anticompetitive effects. In *Exxon/Shell*,[219] the undertakings concerned agreed to set up a joint venture to construct and operate a plant to manufacture linear low-density polyethylene (LLDPE) on the EU market. The relevant market for LLDPE and its substitutes was oligopolistic, and the undertakings concerned together held 20% of total LLDPE capacity in the EU, while the joint venture represented 17% of their joint capacity. The European Commission found that as a result of the parents of the joint venture coordinating their production with one another, as well as with the joint venture competition will exist in a weaker form only.

E. Joint Purchasing Agreements

215. The Horizontal Agreements Guidelines point out that joint purchasing typically aims at creating buying power: for example, a coalition of retailers that work together to negotiate lower prices with their suppliers, which may, in turn, allow giving customers lower prices.[220] Joint purchasing arrangements are less likely to give rise to competition concerns when the parties do not have market power on the selling market or markets.[221] Joint purchasing must be viewed in the sense of the particular procurement market;[222] in certain situations, the sales market will also need to be looked at, if the parties to the joint purchasing agreement also participate vigorously in that industry.[223]

216. The Horizontal Agreements Guidelines set out three potential issues posed by a joint purchasing agreement: (a) if the undertakings concerned have a large degree of market power (not necessarily dominance) in that market, they will have little motivation to pass on any lower prices from their suppliers to consumers;[224] (b) if the undertakings concerned have considerable market power in their purchasing market, they can compel their suppliers to reduce the variety or quality of the goods they make;[225] and (c) buyers with buying power may be able to keep out competitive buyers by limiting their access to productive suppliers.[226]

217. While the CPC has not to date dealt with joint purchasing agreements, the practice of the European Commission demonstrates how Article 101 TFEU can

219. 94/322/EC: Commission Decision of 18 May 1994 relating to a proceeding pursuant to Article 85 of the EC Treaty (IV/33.640 – Exxon/Shell), ELI: http://data.europa.eu/eli/dec/1994/322/oj.
220. Horizontal Agreements Guidelines, paras 194 and 196.
221. *Ibid.*, para. 203.
222. *Ibid.*, para. 198.
223. *Ibid.*, para. 199.
224. *Ibid.*, para. 201.
225. *Ibid.*, para. 202.
226. *Ibid.*, para. 203.

apply to such agreements.[227] The European Commission has challenged joint purchasing agreements covering a significant part of the market when they include exclusive purchasing obligations.[228] In *Gøttrup-Klim Grovvareforeninger*[229] the CJEU held that a clause in the regulation of a cooperative purchasing organisation, preventing its members from engaging in certain types of cooperation which were in direct competition with the cooperative organisation, did not automatically limit competition and could even have positive effects on competition.[230]

F. Joint Selling Agreements

218. Joint selling agreements concern cooperating in the selling of products or services established by competitors active at the same level of the supply chain. The Horizontal Agreements Guidelines bring joint selling agreements under the heading of commercialisation agreements. At the one end of the spectrum, joint selling agreements may lead to a joint determination of all commercial aspects related to the sale of the product, including price. At the other end, there are more limited agreements that only address one specific commercialisation function, such as distribution, after-sales service, or advertising.[231] The primary competition concern regarding commercialisation agreements is that they can contribute to cartel activity: price-fixing,[232] restriction of production,[233] market division[234] and sharing of strategic information.[235] The purpose of joint selling is likely to be the restriction of competition as it eliminates price competition between the parties on substitute products and may also limit the total volume of products to be delivered by the parties within the framework of an order allocation system.[236]

219. A commercialisation agreement does not necessarily limit competition if it is reasonably appropriate to allow one party to join a market which it would not have been able to enter independently. The Horizontal Agreements Guidelines afford a safe harbour for commercialisation agreements where the combined market share of the parties is below 15% an individual assessment will be needed above

227. Cf., *inter alia*, 80/917/EEC: Commission Decision of 9 July 1980 relating to a proceeding under Article 85 of the EEC Treaty (IV/27.958 National Sulphuric Acid Association) ELI: http://data.europa.eu/eli/dec/1980/917/oj; 89/536/EEC: Commission Decision of 15 September 1989 relating to a proceeding under Article 85 of the EEC Treaty (IV/31.734 – Film purchases by German television stations, ELI: http://data.europa.eu/eli/dec/1989/536/oj.

228. 80/234/EEC: Commission Decision of 5 December 1979 relating to a proceeding under Article 85 of the EEC Treaty (IV/29.011 – Rennet), ELI: http://data.europa.eu/eli/dec/1980/234/oj.

229. Case C-250/92, *Gøttrup-Klim e.a. Grovvareforeninger v. Dansk Landbrugs Grovvareselskab AmbA*, EU:C:1994:413.

230. *Ibid.*, para. 34.

231. Horizontal Agreements Guidelines, para. 225.

232. *Ibid.*, para. 230.

233. *Ibid.*, para. 231.

234. *Ibid.*, para. 232.

235. *Ibid.*, para. 233.

236. *Ibid.*, paras 234–235.

that amount.[237] As the European Commission's decision in *Floral*[238] demonstrates, joint selling arrangements set up by the biggest undertakings in highly concentrated markets are likely to give rise to anticompetitive conduct. In *Floral*, the three leading French manufacturers of fertilisers, accounting for more than two-thirds of total French production of fertilisers, set up a joint selling scheme, through which all sales to Germany were channelled. The European Commission found that the channelling and standardisation of export sales led to the exclusion of competition between them on the German market. The CPC has not dealt with joint selling agreements per se in its decisional practice to date.

§2. Vertical Agreements

I. General

220. Vertical agreements are agreements for the sale and purchase of goods or services, which are entered into between companies operating at different levels of the production or distribution chain, such as a manufacturer and supplier, a distributor and reseller, a franchisor and franchisee or a principal and agent. Agreements between undertakings at different market levels, which simply determine the price and quantity for a specific sale and purchase transaction, do not normally restrict competition. However, a restriction of competition may occur if the agreement contains restraints on the supplier or the buyer, which are called vertical restraints. Vertical agreements normally involve one or both of the parties accepting certain restraints on their freedom of action, such as exclusive dealing requirements and territorial limitations. Whether a vertical agreement actually restricts competition and whether, in that case, the benefits outweigh the anticompetitive effects will depend on the market structure and would need a case-by-case assessment.

221. The European Commission adopted Regulation 330/2010 ('VBER'),[239] which provides a safe harbour for most vertical agreements. Under Article 1 §1(a) VBER, 'vertical agreements' are defined as agreements or concerted practices entered into between two or more undertakings each of which operates, for the purposes of the agreement, at a different level of the production or distribution chain, and which relate to the conditions under which the parties may purchase, sell or resell certain goods or services. To facilitate a consistent application of competition law throughout the EU, Article 3 §1 of the Modernisation Regulation requires EU Member States to ensure that agreements which are permitted under Article 101 TFEU (including agreements covered by the VBER) are not prohibited under national competition laws. As such, a distribution arrangement that complies with the VBER should also be compliant with national competition law in Cyprus.

237. R. Whish & D. Bailey, *Competition Law* 618 (9th ed., OUP 2018).
238. 80/182/EEC: Commission Decision of 28 November 1979 relating to a proceeding under Article 85 of the EEC Treaty (IV/29.672-Floral), ELI: http://data.europa.eu/eli/dec/1980/182/oj.
239. Commission Regulation (EU) No. 330/2010 of 20 April 2010 on the application of Article 101 §3 of the Treaty on the Functioning of the European Union to categories of vertical agreements and concerted practices, OJ L 102.

Indeed, section 5 §2 of the CPC Law provides that in respect of collusions to which the provisions of the CPC Law – and not the provisions of EU competition law – apply, the provisions of EU regulations adopted under subsection 3 of Article 101 TFEU shall apply, *mutatis mutandis*, as long as there is no contradictory provision in an order made pursuant to section 5 §1 of the CPC Law. In such a case, the agreements are deemed to be permissible and valid according to the relevant EU regulation regulating the same category of agreements in the context of EU competition law.

222. At the level of the national legal order, there are three relevant block exemption orders issued by the Council of Ministers pursuant to the provisions of section 5 of the CPC Law. Under these orders, section 3 of the CPC Law is declared inapplicable to the following vertical agreements: (a) vertical agreements between a union of undertakings and its members or between such union and its suppliers, where all members of the union of undertakings are retail sellers of goods and no member of the union together with its affiliated undertakings have a turnover exceeding EUR 2 million;[240] (b) vertical agreements between a union of undertakings and its members or between such union and its suppliers, where all members of the union of undertakings are distributors of cars or car replacement parts or repairers of cars and no member of the union together with its affiliated undertakings have a turnover exceeding EUR 9 million;[241] (c) agreements and practices in the insurance sector, to which Regulation 267/2010 applies *mutatis mutandis*.[242]

223. The VBER applies to vertical agreements concerning the sale of all kinds of goods and services, with the exception of motor vehicles.[243] Although the VBER applies in principle to all vertical agreements, it does not apply to vertical agreements concluded between competitors. The regulation gives a block exemption from Article 101 §1 TFEU to vertical agreements which fulfil certain requirements. The first requirement concerns the 'hardcore restrictions' under Article 4 VBER. Article 4 contains a list of restrictions which lead to the exclusion of the whole vertical agreement from the scope of application of the VBER. Where such a hardcore restriction is included in an agreement, that agreement is presumed to fall within Article 101 §1 TFEU. Second, for the block exemption to apply, the market share of the supplier on the market where it sells the contract products to the buyer, and the market share of the buyer on the market where it purchases the contract products, must each be 30% or less. For the supplier, this concerns its market share on the relevant supply market, i.e., the market on which it sells the goods or services that is decisive for the application of the block exemption. For the buyer, this concerns its market share on the relevant purchase market, i.e., the market on which it purchases the goods or services, which is decisive for the application of the VBER.

240. 141/2014, OJ III(I) 483, 7 Mar. 2014 (in Greek).
241. 140/2014, OJ III(I) 482, 7 Mar. 2014 (in Greek).
242. 139/2014, OJ III(I) 481, 7 Mar. 2014 (in Greek).
243. Commission Regulation (EC) No. 1400/2002 of 31 July 2002 on the application of Article 81(3) of the Treaty to categories of vertical agreements and concerted practices in the motor vehicle sector, as extended by Commission Regulation (EU) No. 461/2010, ELI: http://data.europa.eu/eli/reg/2002/1400/2004-05-01.

224. Third, Article 5 VBER excludes certain obligations from the coverage of the VBER even though the market share threshold is not exceeded. These excluded obligations concern non-compete obligations during the contract; non-compete obligations following termination of the contract; and the exclusion of specific brands in a selective distribution system. When the conditions are not fulfilled, these vertical restraints are excluded from the exemption by the VBER. However, the VBER continues to apply to the remaining part of the vertical agreement if that part is severable from the non-exempted vertical restraints. The European Commission has published the Guidelines on Vertical Restraints.[244] These set out the European Commission's approach towards vertical agreements not covered by the VBER.

II. Distribution

A. *Exclusive Distribution*

225. The main competitive concern concerning exclusive distribution agreements is the reduction of intra-brand competition and the partitioning of the market. A separate concern arises when most or all of the suppliers in a given market adopt exclusive distribution agreements as this may soften competition and facilitate collusion, both at the market level of the suppliers and the distributors; this would be detrimental to inter-brand competition. The European Commission also notes that exclusive distribution could result in other distributors being foreclosed and thus reduce competition at that level.[245] The VBER refers to exclusive distribution agreements, as long as the manufacturer and buyer's market share is less than 30% and there are no 'hardcore' restrictions. In particular, passive sales (sales in response to unsolicited orders) should not be limited to other territories; if there is a mixture of exclusive distribution and selective distribution, sales between approved distributors must not be excluded. The Guidelines provide guidance in those situations where an individual review of the agreements is required because the block exception does not apply.[246]

226. An illustrative case of the CPC's practice concerning exclusive distribution is the *Cattle farmers case.*[247] The CPC had carried out an ex-officio investigation into the practices of the Pancyprian Organisation of Cattle Farmers (POCF) Public Ltd (POCF) for alleged violation of competition law regarding the sale/supply of raw cow milk. Under their exclusive distribution contracts with POCF, its members were required to cede all their production exclusively to POCF under the prices set by the latter, who then resold their milk to pasteurisers, dairies and ice cream companies. POCF determined both the purchasing price of cow milk as well as its sale price to pasteurisers, dairies and ice cream companies. The duration of the contracts

244. Guidelines on Vertical Restraints, OJ C 130, 19.5.2010, pp. 1–46.
245. R. Whish & D. Bailey, *Competition Law* 653 (9th ed., OUP 2018).
246. *Ibid.*
247. CPC Decision 42/2014, *Ex officio investigation against the Pancyprian Organisation of Cattle Farmers (POCF) Public Ltd*, 17 Oct. 2014.

in question was limitless and could only be terminated after twelve months' written notice and three years after its beginning. The contracts also specified that producers should not directly or indirectly participate in activities interfering with POCF or undermining its interests. The CPC acknowledged that this particular provision was a non-compete clause, therefore preventing producers to transfer their goods to other sources of disposal. POCF insisted in the hearings before the CPC that cow breeders should not be able to deal directly with dairies, cheesemakers and other third parties.

227. The CPC found that purchase prices of raw cow milk were determined by POCF. Cow breeders, members of POCF, despite being the producers of cow milk could not determine the prices at which they would sell their product, seeing as POCF determined the product's purchase price. In this way, POCF, taking advantage of its position as the sole recipient of the dairy production of its members under an exclusive distribution contract, fixed the purchasing price of milk at the amount it desired for all cow breeders / POCF members. The CPC held that the object of POCF's decision on the setting of prices was to obstruct, limit and distort competition. The CPC found POCF to have infringed section 3 §1(a) of the CPC Law, by concluding exclusive raw cow milk supply contracts with cattle farmers which included specific terms for the determination of the purchase price of raw cow milk; section 3 §1(b) of the CPC Law by concluding exclusive supply contracts with cattle farmers for raw cow milk which contained exclusivity clauses and non-compete obligations, and by enforcing the 'stable milk production' measure; and section 6 §1(a) of the CPC Law by placing unreasonable and/or unfair prices on raw cow milk as a dominant undertaking on the relevant market.

B. Exclusive Dealing

228. Exclusive dealing can refer to an exclusive supply obligation whereby a supplier is prevented from selling to someone other than a particular downstream customer or to an exclusive buying obligation whereby a downstream customer is prohibited from purchasing goods other than from a particular supplier.[248] The main competition risk in exclusive dealing is the foreclosure of other buyers and the elimination of intra-brand competition.[249] Exclusive supply is exempted by the VBER where both the supplier's and buyer's market share does not exceed 30%, even if combined with other non-hardcore vertical restraints such as non-compete.

C. Selective Distribution

229. Selective distribution agreements restrict the number of authorised distributors on the one hand and the possibilities of resale on the other. They can be distinguished from exclusive distribution in that the restriction of the number of dealers

248. R. Whish & D. Bailey, *Competition Law* 699 (9th ed., OUP 2018).
249. Vertical Restraints Guidelines, para. 194.

does not depend on the number of territories, but on selection criteria linked in the first place to the nature of the product.[250] Another difference with exclusive distribution is that the restriction on resale is not a restriction on active selling to a territory but a restriction on any sales to non-authorised distributors, leaving only appointed dealers and final customers as possible buyers. Selective distribution is almost always used to distribute branded final products.[251] The Guidelines on Vertical Restraints state that selective distribution systems can restrict intra-brand competition, foreclose market access, and weaken competition and/or encourage collusion between suppliers or purchasers.[252]

230. In *Metro SB-Grosmarkte GmbH v. Commission*,[253] the CJEU defined three conditions to be cumulatively met in order to classify a selective distribution system as solely qualitative and therefore falling outside the prohibition of Article 101 TFEU:[254] (a) the properties of the product necessitate a selective distribution system; (b) resellers are chosen on the basis of objective criteria of a qualitative nature which is determined uniformly for all potential resellers and applied in a non-discriminatory manner; and c) the restrictions placed on authorised distributors do not go beyond what is necessary. In *Coty*,[255] the CJEU held that a selective distribution system for luxury goods designed primarily to preserve the luxury image of those goods did not breach competition rules when the system relies on objective, non-discriminatory and necessary criteria for the selection of authorised resellers. A contractual clause which prohibits authorised resellers within a selective distribution network from using third-party platforms for online sales of the goods in question (in a discernible manner by the consumer) is permissible when that clause has the objective of preserving the luxury image of the goods, is non-discriminatory and is proportionate.[256]

231. In *Kapodistrias/Kyros/Daimler/CIC*,[257] a selective distribution arrangement was considered by the CPC. Chr. Kapodistrias & Sons Ltd (Kapodistrias) and Kyros Auto Services Ltd (Kyros) filed a complaint with the CPC against Daimler AG (Daimler) and Cyprus Import Corporation Ltd (CIC). Kapodistrias and Kyros were active in the import, purchase, supply and resale of genuine spare parts for Mercedes-Benz vehicles, which were supplied by dealers and suppliers from abroad. According to Kapodistrias and Kyros, after the introduction of the selective distribution scheme in the supply of spare parts by Daimler, they no longer had the right to buy and import spare parts to Cyprus, as the distribution scheme reserved the sale of original spare parts bearing the Mercedes-Benz logo to members of the network, namely CIC (and its authorised distributors and repairers). The CPC held

250. *Ibid.*, para. 174.
251. Vertical Restraints Guidelines, para. 174.
252. *Ibid.*, para. 175.
253. Case 26/76, *Metro SB-Grosmarkte GmbH v. Commission*, EU:C:1977:167.
254. *Ibid.*, para. 20.
255. Case C-230/16, *Coty Germany GmbH v. Parfümerie Akzente GmbH*, ECLI:EU:C:2017:941.
256. *Ibid.*, para. 58.
257. CPC Decision 11/2015, *Complaint by Chr. Kapodistrias & Sons Ltd and Kyros Auto Service Ltd against Daimler AG and Cyprus Import Corporation Ltd*, 23 Apr. 2015 (in Greek).

that the vertical agreement between Daimler and CIC, by introducing a selective distribution system in the Cypriot market was an agreement prohibited under section 3 §1 of the CPC Law and the relevant Article 101 §1 TFEU.

232. The CPC determined that neither Regulation 461/2010, nor the VBER exempted the selective distribution under assessment, as the market shares of the undertakings concerned exceeded the 30% threshold. As such, the CPC considered the vertical arrangement as being subject to assessment for the potential infringement of Article 3 §1(b) of the CPC Law and Article 101 §1(b) TFEU. The CPC considered the examined arrangement a restriction of competition by effect, seeing as the agreement between Daimler and CIC for the implementation of the selective distribution scheme did not incorporate any of the prescribed hardcore restrictions listed in Regulation 461/2010 or VBER. CIC was found to have very high market shares prior to the introduction of the selective distribution scheme and the introduction of the latter rendered the conditions of the market a monopoly.

233. While CIC as the general distributor of spare parts was aware that it would be the only remaining player on the market as the sole member of the limited distribution network, it did not nominate any other approved dealers. Daimler had failed to adequately enforce the selective distribution scheme on the domestic market, which resulted in a limitation of supply of original spare parts, whereas the selective distribution scheme could be implemented on the domestic market without any limitation or control of production and distribution. The CPC held that the market has all the characteristics of a distinct geographical market, as it is an isolated island industry, where competition between the general distributor (CIC) and independent companies (such as Kapodistrias and Kyros) was eliminated and consumer choices were removed as well as the access to better market prices of the products, due to the selective distribution system's implementation. The CPC found CIC and Daimler to have infringed section 3 §1(b) of the CPC Law and Article 101 §1(b) TFEU and imposed administrative fines of EUR 700,000 and EUR 20,000,000 on CIC and Daimler respectively.

D. Franchising

234. Under a franchise agreement, one party (the franchisor) allows the other party (the franchisee) to exploit the franchisor's intellectual property for the sale and distribution of goods or services. A franchise agreement would be expected to contractually confer control to the franchisor over how the franchisee operates the business under the franchise. The franchisee will usually pay a fee or royalty to the franchisor in return for licence and rights granted under the agreement. A franchise arrangement enables a franchisor to establish, with limited investment, a uniform network for the distribution of its goods or services. From the franchisee's point of view, such a system gives it the opportunity to take advantage of an already well-known name and image, as well as the practical and technical help of the franchisor in setting up the business. While franchises are commonly associated with fast food and fashion outlets, franchising is a method of distribution which has also gained popularity in an increasing number of other sectors.

235. The VBER applies to franchise agreement where these contain intellectual property (IP) rights provisions five conditions are fulfilled:[258] (a) the IP provisions must be part of a vertical agreement, that is, an agreement with conditions under which the parties may purchase, sell or resell certain goods or services; (b) the IP must be assigned to, or licensed for use by, the buyer; (c) the IP must not constitute the primary object of the agreement; (d) the IP provisions must be directly related to the use, sale or resale of goods or services by the buyer or its customers; (e) the IP provisions, in relation to the contract goods or services, must not contain restrictions of competition having the same object as vertical restraints which are not exempted under the VBER.

236. The application of Article 101 TFEU to franchising agreements was first considered by the CJEU in *Pronuptia,*[259] which held that the compatibility of franchise agreements with Article 101 TFEU depends on the provisions of such agreements. Specifically, the CJEU held that two essential elements were required for a franchise agreement to function effectively (and thus fall outside the scope of Article 101 §1 TFEU):[260] (a) the franchisor must be able to communicate their IP rights to the franchisees and provide them with the necessary assistance in order to enable them to apply his methods, without running the risk that that know-how and assistance might benefit competitors, even indirectly; and (b) the franchisor must be able to take the measures necessary for maintaining the identity and reputation of the network bearing their business name.

III. Technology Licensing

A. Patent Licensing

237. Intellectual property laws confer exclusive rights on holders of intellectual property rights to prevent unauthorised use of their intellectual property and to exploit it. Such exploitation includes the right to license the intellectual property rights to third parties. However, exclusive rights of exploitation do not result in immunity from competition law intervention. As per the ECJ (as it then was) held in *Consten and Grundig*,[261] Article 101 TFEU is applicable to agreements whereby the holder licenses another undertaking to exploit its intellectual property right. The European Commission, in its Guidelines on the application of Article 101 of the TFEU to technology transfer agreements (the 'Technology Transfer Guidelines'),[262]

258. VBER, Article 2(3).
259. Case 161/84, *Pronuptia de Paris GmbH v. Pronuptia de Paris Irmgard Schillgallis*, ECLI:EU:C:1986:41.
260. *Ibid.*, paras 16–17.
261. Joined Cases 56/64 and 58/64, *Consten and Grundig*, [1966] ECR 429, ECLI:EU:C:1966:41.
262. *OJ C 89, 28.3.2014, pp. 3–50.*

notes that, in assessing licensing agreements under Article 101 TFEU, the existing analytical framework is sufficiently flexible to take due account of the dynamic aspects of technology rights licensing and that there is no presumption that intellectual property rights and licence agreements as such give rise to competition concerns.

238. Technology licensing agreements (or technology transfer agreements in EU law nomenclature), concern the licensing of intellectual property rights by a rightsholder to licensee, for the latter to exploit the licensed rights for the production of goods or services. Regulation (EU) 316/2014[263] regulates the application of Article 101 TFEU to certain technology transfer agreements (the 'TTBER'). Pursuant to the provisions of Article 1 §1(b) of the TTBER, the concept of 'technology rights' covers know-how, patents, utility models, design rights, topographies of semiconductor products, supplementary protection certificates for medicinal products or other products for which such supplementary protection certificates may be obtained, plant breeder's certificates and software copyrights or a combination thereof, as well as applications for these rights and for registration of these rights. The TTBER only applies in EU Member States where the licensor holds relevant technology rights. The TTBER exempts licensing agreements between companies that have a market share of under 20% if they are competitors and 30% for agreements where the contracting parties are not competitors, subject to certain conditions. Subject to the duration of the TTBER, which expires on 30 April 2026, the block exemption applies for as long as the licensed property right has not lapsed, expired or been declared invalid.

239. In technology and other patent-reliant industries, patent licensing often occurs in order to create design freedom by removing the risk of infringement claims by the licensor. As such, patent licensing may serve the removal of obstacles to the development and exploitation of the licensee's own technology, in a pro-competitive manner. With respect to the licensing of patents, a prevalent practice is that of patent pools. Such pools are essentially arrangements whereby two or more parties assemble a package of technology which is licensed not only to contributors to the pool but also to third parties. Pools can be purely contractual or can employ a separate entity under which the pooled technology is placed. In either case, the pool may allow licensees to operate on the market on the basis of a single licence.

240. Agreements establishing technology pools and setting out the terms and conditions for their operation are not regulated under the TTBER, as these are usually multiparty agreements. Technology pools may prove to restrict competition in some cases. As the Technology Transfers Guidelines note, the creation of a technology pool necessarily implies joint selling of the pooled technologies, which in the case of pools composed solely or predominantly of substitute technologies amounts to a price-fixing cartel.[264] Moreover, in addition to reducing competition between

263. Commission Regulation (EU) No. 316/2014 of 21 March 2014 on the application of Article 101 §3 TFEU to categories of technology transfer agreements.

264. Technology Transfers Guidelines, para. 246.

the parties, technology pools may also, in particular when they support an industry standard or establish a de facto industry standard, result in a reduction of innovation by foreclosing alternative technologies. The existence of the standard and a related technology pool may make it more difficult for new and improved technologies to enter the market.[265]

B. Trademark Licensing

241. Trademark licensing is covered by the TTBER, if it is directly related to the production or sale of the contract products. Where the holder of a trademark licenses use of its trademark on the products incorporating the licensed technology, the Technology Transfers Guidelines note that such licence may allow the licensee to better exploit the licensed technology by allowing consumers to make an immediate link between the product and the characteristics imputed to it by the licensed technology rights.[266] An obligation on the licensee to use the licensor's trademark may also promote the dissemination of technology by allowing the licensor to identify itself as the source of the underlying technology.

242. Discriminatory trademark licensing practices may arise where a dominant licensor unjustifiably applies different terms to equal circumstances. A dominant trademark licensor could abuse its dominance by charging licensees a higher licensing fee when they sourced their trademark-bearing products from a rival of the licensor rather the licensor itself. Another example could be for a dominant licensor to charge royalties regardless of whether or not the products actually implement the dominant licensor's intellectual property rights. Also, where the licensor competes with the licensee in the relevant market, information exchange provisions that may be included in trademark licences in the context of the licensor's exercise of quality control, which could give rise to anticompetitive conduct.

C. Know-How and Trade Secret Licensing

243. 'Know-how' is defined under the TTBER as a package of practical information, resulting from experience and testing, which is: (a) secret, that is to say, not generally known or easily accessible; (b) substantial, that is to say, significant and useful for the production of the contract products; and (c) identified, that is to say, described in a sufficiently comprehensive manner so as to make it possible to verify that it fulfils the criteria of secrecy and substantiality.[267]

244. Know-how is caught under the definition of 'technology rights' in the TTBER.[268] Subject to the duration of the TTBER, which expires on 30 April 2026,

265. *Ibid.*
266. *Ibid.*, para. 47.
267. TTBER, Article 1 §1(i).
268. TTBER, Article 1 §1(b).

the block exemption applies for as long as the licensed property right has not lapsed, expired or been declared invalid. In the case of know-how, the block exemption applies as long as the licensed know-how remains secret, except where the know-how becomes publicly known as a result of action by the licensee, in which case the exemption applies for the duration of the agreement.[269]

245. The Technology Transfers Guidelines note that the European Commission will be favourable where the recovery of the licensed know-how is likely to be impossible or very difficult once it is disclosed.[270] In such cases, an obligation on the licensee not to challenge the licensed know-how promotes dissemination of new technology, by allowing weaker licensors to license stronger licensees without fear of a challenge once the know-how has been absorbed by the licensee.[271] Therefore, non-challenge and termination clauses solely concerning know-how are not excluded from the scope of the TTBER.

246. The block exemption under the TTBER shall not apply to any of the following obligations contained in licensing agreements:[272] (a) any direct or indirect obligation on the licensee to grant an exclusive licence or to assign rights, in whole or in part, to the licensor or to a third party designated by the licensor in respect of its own improvements to, or its own new applications of, the licensed technology (known as a grant-back obligation); (b) any direct or indirect obligation on a party not to challenge the validity of intellectual property rights which the other party holds in the EU, without prejudice to the possibility, in the case of an exclusive licence, of providing for termination of the technology transfer agreement in the event that the licensee challenges the validity of any of the licensed technology rights (known as a non-challenge clauses).

247. The Technology Transfer Guidelines clarify the rationale behind the non-application of the block exemption of the TTBER to grant-back obligations and non-challenge clauses.[273] When grant backs are made against consideration it is less likely that the obligation creates a disincentive for the licensee to innovate. In the assessment of exclusive grant backs outside the scope of the block exemption the market position of the licensor on the technology market is also a relevant factor. The stronger the position of the licensor, the more likely it is that exclusive grant back obligations will have restrictive effects on competition in innovation. The stronger the position of the licensor's technology the more important it is that the licensee can become an important source of innovation and future competition.[274]

269. TTBER, Article 2.
270. Technology Transfers Guidelines, para. 140.
271. *Ibid.*
272. TTBER, Article 5.
273. Technology Transfer Guidelines, paras 129–140.
274. *Ibid.*, para. 130.

248. The Technology Transfer Guidelines also clarify that the reason for excluding non-challenge clauses from the scope of the block exemption is the fact that licensees are normally in the best position to determine whether or not an intellectual property right is invalid.[275] Invalid intellectual property can be seen to stifle innovation rather than promoting it.

249. The TTBER is directly applicable in Cyprus. Moreover, while the CPC has not considered technology licensing per se in its decisional practice to date, it is expected that the CPC will closely adhere to the decisional practice of the European Commission on technology transfers and apply the TTBER and national law in alignment with the Technology Transfers Guidelines.

275. *Ibid.*, para. 134.

Chapter 2. Dominant Undertakings' Prohibited Practices

§1. Introduction

250. In its guidance on abusive exclusionary conduct by dominant undertakings, the European Commission notes that the assessment of dominance will take into account the competitive structure of the market, and in particular the following factors:[276] (a) constraints imposed by the existing supplies from, and the position on the market of, actual competitors (the market position of the dominant undertaking and its competitors); (b) constraints imposed by the credible threat of future expansion by actual competitors or entry by potential competitors (expansion and entry); (c) constraints imposed by the bargaining strength of the undertaking's customers (countervailing buyer power). The CPC has demonstrated an approach to assessing whether a dominant position is identified, which closely adheres to the European Commission's guidance and the case law of the Courts of the EU.

251. In *Demstar Rentals/Hermes Airports*,[277] the CPC clarified that for a dominant position to exist, various criteria are taken into account, among which the market shares of the undertaking concerned. Citing CJEU judgments,[278] the CPC stressed that particularly high market shares, usually those exceeding 50%, indicate the substantial ability of the undertaking to unilaterally influence the conditions of the market concerned, by imposing terms that do not necessarily correspond to those prevailing under competition conditions.[279] In *Antoniadou/Vouros*,[280] the CPC held that for the market share of an undertaking to form sufficient indication of the existence of a dominant position, the relationship of this market share with those of the competitors of the undertaking concerned should be taken into account.[281] The market share of the undertaking concerned must be considerably larger than that of its competitors for the said undertaking to be able to act independently of such competitors. In cases where the market share is lower than 50%, it is possible to establish a dominant position based on the market structure and the market shares of competitors, in relation to which the CPC cited *United Brands*.[282]

252. Dominance is not per se anticompetitive unless it is accompanied by abusive conduct. Infringement of section 6 §1 of the CPC Law can only occur when

276. Communication from the European Commission – Guidance on the European Commission's enforcement priorities in applying Article 82 of the EC Treaty to abusive exclusionary conduct by dominant undertakings (2009/C 45/02) OJ C 45, 24.2.2009, pp. 7–20, para. 12.
277. CPC Decision 20/2015, *Complaint of Demstar Rentals (2005) Ltd against Hermes Airports Ltd*, 23 Jun. 2015 (in Greek).
278. Case 85/76, *Hoffmann-La Roche & Co. AG v. Commission of the European Communities*, ECLI:EU:C:1979:36 and Case C-62/86, *AKZO Chemie BV v. Commission of the European Communities*, ECLI:EU:C:1991:286.
279. CPC Decision 20/2015, *Complaint of Demstar Rentals (2005) Ltd against Hermes Airports Ltd*, 23 Jun. 2015 (in Greek), para. 8.2.
280. CPC Decision 62/2018, *Complaint of Angela Antoniadou against A.J. Vouros Ltd*, 30 Nov. 2018 (in Greek).
281. *Ibid.*, para. 10.
282. *Ibid.*

the undertaking concerned, which must be in a dominant position, abuses its position of dominance. 'Abuse' has been determined by the CPC as an objective concept,[283] reflecting the case of the courts of the EU. The CJEU has held that the conduct of an undertaking in a dominant position may be regarded as abusive even in the absence of any fault.[284] In reflecting the language of Article 102 TFEU, section 6 §1 of the CPC Law must be interpreted as referring not only to practices which may cause damage to consumers directly but also to those which are detrimental to them through their impact on competition. This chapter examines exploitative practices and exclusionary practices. Exploitative practices are those practices deployed by dominant undertakings which reduce the welfare of consumers, while not directly harming competitors in the market. They can take various forms, such as excessive pricing and discrimination. Exclusionary practices relate to the hampering or elimination of effective access of actual or potential competitors to supplies or markets as a result of abuse of a dominant position, which is likely to be in a position to profitably increase prices to the detriment of consumers.

253. Cyprus is one of some EU Member States[285] which feature the concept of economic dependence in their legal orders. EU Member States which provide for abuse of economic dependence can enforce their national antitrust legislation to prevent, *inter alia*, non-dominant firms from adopting anticompetitive conduct. As such, provisions prohibiting the abuse of economic dependence are able to capture conduct that Article 102 TFEU cannot. Such abusive conduct does not require an undertaking to hold a dominant position – it will suffice that third parties are in a position of economic dependence without having an alternative solution. Pursuant to section 6 §2 of the CPC Law, the abuse of a relationship of economic dependence by one or more undertakings in relation to an undertaking that is a customer, supplier, producer, representative, distributor or commercial associate of the first undertaking, is prohibited.

254. The practice of the CPC vis-à-vis the abuse of a relationship of economic dependence[286] has shed ample light on the elements of an infringement of the discussed prohibition under section 6 §2 of the CPC Law. Specifically, the CPC has consistently identified the following requirements as cumulatively necessary for an abuse of a relationship of economic dependence to exist: (a) the existence of a relation of economic dependence in accordance with section 6 §2 of the CPC Law by one undertaking in relation to an undertaking that is the customer, supplier, producer, representative, distributor or commercial associate in the context of the relationship; (b) the absence of equivalent alternative solutions for the undertaking being the customer, supplier, producer, representative, distributor or commercial

283. CPC Decision 48/2012, *Complaint of Thunderworx Ltd against CYTA*, 8 Oct. 2012 (in Greek), 33.
284. Case T-65/89 *BPB Industries & British Gypsum v. Commission,* ECLI:EU:T:1993:31, para. 70.
285. France, Germany, Portugal, Latvia, Czechia, and Cyprus are among the EU Member States which provide for economic dependence in their competition legislation.
286. CPC Decision 38/2014, *Complaint filed by Great Minds Marketing & Public Relations Co. Ltd against Crabtree & Evelyn (Overseas) Ltd*, 4 Sep. 2014 (in Greek).

associate in the context of the relationship; and (c) abuse of the relationship of economic dependence. The abuse of a relationship of economic dependence can exist even as far as a specific kind of products or services is concerned, which does not have an equivalent alternative solution.

§2. Exploitative Practices

I. Excessive/Unfair Pricing

255. Excessive or unfair pricing practices by a dominant undertaking are one of the forms of abusive conduct listed as prohibited under section 6 §1 of the CPC Law. Specifically, section 6 §1(a) thereof prohibits the direct or indirect fixing of unfair purchase or selling prices or any other unfair, under the circumstances, trading conditions. Excessive or unfair pricing practices will see the dominant undertaking charging unfairly high or low prices. The landmark judgment of the CJEU in *United Brands* established the standard test for excessive pricing, in which the CJEU held that the question to be determined is: i) whether the difference between the costs actually incurred and the price charged is excessive and ii) if the answer to this question is in the affirmative, whether a price has been imposed which is either unfair in itself or when compared to competing products.[287]

256. The CPC has considered excessive pricing in a number of cases. In *Primetel/CYTA,*[288] Primetel Plc (Primetel), a telecommunications provider, lodged a complaint to the CPC against CYTA, the State-owned telecommunications incumbent, alleging that CYTA had abused its dominant position by imposing, *inter alia*, excessive pricing. Primetel's complaint derived from a contract signed between CYTA and Primetel for the purchase of the right to use of capacity in the SMW-3 submarine fibre optics cable system, for a term of twelve years. In finding that CYTA enjoyed a dominant position in the relevant market, the CPC took into account: (i) CYTA's general financial position; (ii) the fact that CYTA was operating in a protected environment since its establishment; (iii) the legal and economic barriers in submarine cable systems; (iv) the available capacity that an operator in Cyprus could purchase; and (v) the lack of alternative root systems and submarine-capable systems controlled by other telecommunications operators. The CPC held that Primetel was, at the material time, a new entrant in the broadband retail market, in which CYTA was its key rival. At the same time, CYTA was Primetel's provider of interconnection services, unbundled access to the local loop and international bandwidth via the submarine cable networks. The CPC concluded that CYTA had abused its dominant position in the international capacity supply compared with other rivals on the market imposing significantly high prices on Primetel in terms of international capacity supply. The CPC found CYTA to have infringed 6 §1(a) of the CPC Law and imposed a fine of EUR 295,277.

---

287. Case 27/76, *United Brands Company and United Brands Continentaal BV v. Commission of the European Communities*, ECLI:EU:C:1978:22, para. 252.

288. CPC Decision 6/2013, *Complaint by Primetel PLC against CYTA*, 25 Jan. 2013 (in Greek).

257. In another case involving CYTA, *CallSat/*CYTA,[289] on assessing the complaint of CallSat Telecom Ltd ('CallSat' against CYTA alleging that the latter charged unfair rates for the supply of International Private Leased Lines (IPLLs). CYTA was at the time the only functioning entity on the IPLL market in Cyprus and was thus regarded as the dominant undertaking in the relevant market. In its assessment, the CPC took into account the period during which CYTA chose to increase its IPLL prices, which was deemed crucial given that its new prices were introduced just as the market was liberalised, in which environment CallSat became active and able to purchase services from CYTA to enable CallSat to provide services to consumers. The CPC also took into account the fact that CYTA failed to offer adequate and reasonable evidence for the reasons and methods used to measure the particular prices, in connection with the fact that a few months later the CECPR placed significantly lower prices on the same services. The CPC concluded that CYTA had infringed section 6 §1(a) of the CPC Law, since it was unreasonably excessive to price IPLLs in the form of 2 Mbps, 34 Mbps, and 45 Mbps circuits.

258. In *Hertz/Hermes*,[290] Demstar Rentals (2005) Ltd, operating under the trade name Hertz, lodged a complaint with the CPC against Hermes Airports Ltd (Hermes), which was the exclusive management rights of the Larnaca and Pafos airports under a BOT concession agreement with the Republic of Cyprus. Hertz was chosen as a successful bidder and engaged as an on-airport operator under the first tendering procedure initiated by Hermes for the renting of space for car rental services; Hertz was unsuccessful under the second tender launched by Hermes in 2011. As a result, Hertz signed an Off-Airport Agreement with Hermes to ensure that car rental services are provided within the airport. The relevant product/service market was defined as the market for managing the airports Larnaca and Pafos. In addition, a secondary market for the provision of access and installation services in car rental companies at Larnaca and Pafos airports was also defined. The geographic market was defined separately as the market of the airports Larnaca and Pafos.

259. Hermes had reduced the number of licenses awarded to on-airport operators from 7 to 4 under the second tender launched in 2011, while increasing the minimum annual guarantee for each license per year and the minimum total fee paid by the successful bidders. Hermes also reserved its right to conclude off-airport agreements with those undertakings in the tender documents that may fail to secure on-airport space in the tender competition. This conduct of Hermes was found to be abuse of dominance infringing section 6 §1(a) of the CPC Law. The CPC observed that Hermes' overall behaviour was not reasonably justified. The CPC ordered Hermes to terminate the violation of section 6 § (a) of the CPC Law and recurrence in respect of on-airport and off-airport contracts. The CPC also ordered Hermes to launch a new tender for on-airport car rental contracts for Larnaca and Pafos airports to allow for the installation of at least seven car rental companies as soon as possible and in any case no later than three months before the expiry of the current

289. CPC Decision 19/2013, *Complaint of CallSat against CYTA*, 12 Apr. 2013 (in Greek).
290. CPC Decision 20/2015, *Complaint of Demstar Rentals (2005) Ltd against Hermes Airports Ltd*, 23 Jun. 2015 (in Greek).

on-airport contract. In considering the quantum of the fine, the CPC took into consideration the nature, gravity and duration of the infringement, and imposed an administrative fine of EUR 750,000 on Hermes.

260. In another case concerning Hermes, *Karydas/Hermes*,[291] the CPC found Hermes to have abused its dominant position by imposing unfair, under the circumstances, trading conditions on Y. Karydas Car Engineering & Valeting Services Ltd (Karydas), therefore infringing section 6 §1(a) of the CPC Law. Citing *Aéroports de Paris*,[292] the CPC found Hermes to hold a dominant position in the market for the management and exploitation of the Larnaca International Airport (Larnaca) and Larnaca's facilities. In the context of its presence in the said market, Hermes was offering car parking services at Larnaca and was accordingly found to enjoy a dominant position in the market for the supply of car parking spaces within Larnaca. Karydas was also active in the same market for car parking services at Larnaca.

261. Hermes was held to be under a special responsibility vis-à-vis its dominant position, due to the significant economic power towards relatively small valet services businesses, which were found by the CPC to require access to a defined space within Larnaca to be able to provide their services to their own customers. Certain practices on the part of Hermes, primarily what were found to be unjustified and non-negotiable increases to charges imposed on Karydas, as well the refusal of Hermes to renew the most recent contract between Hermes and Karydas at the material time, were found to be aimed at displacing the competitors of Hermes in the relevant market for the supply of car parking services at Larnaca, and in particular in the supply of valet parking services at Larnaca. Hermes was accordingly found to have abused its dominant position in the market for the supply of car parking spaces within Larnaca. The CPC imposed a fine of EUR 1,193,864 on Hermes for this infringement.

262. In *Theatro Ena/Cyprus Theatre Organisation,*[293] the CPC found the Cyprus Theatre Organisation (THOC), a public law body, to have abused a dominant position, therefore infringing section 6 §1(a) of the CPC Law. THOC is competent for the approval and distribution of subsidies to independent theatres, which are THOC's competitors in the market for the production and presentation of theatrical plays. The funding received by THOC from the State concerned its entire operations, whereas the subsidies that THOC itself allocated to independent theatres were allocated on a per-play basis. Without itself being under scrutiny as to its own funding, THOC was responsible for the approval and distribution of subsidies to independent theatres, which were the undertakings competing with THOC in the market for the production and presentation of theatrical plays. The CPC found THOC to be able to determine the economic power of its direct competitors in the market for the

291. CPC Decision No. 13/2018, *Complaint of Y. Karydas Car Engineering & Valeting Services Ltd against Hermes Airports Ltd* (in Greek).

292. Case C-82/01 P, *Aéroports de Paris v. Commission of the European Communities* [2002]; Judgment of 24 October 2002; ECLI:EU:C:2002:617.

293. CPC Decision No. 42/2019, *Theatro Ena/Cyprus Theatre Organisation* (in Greek).

production and presentation of theatrical plays. THOC's ability to determine these subsidies and therefore the economic power of its own competitors in the said market, was found to distort competition and constitute an abuse of THOC's dominant position. A fine of EUR 342,221.35 was imposed on THOC.

II. Discrimination

263. Section 6 §1(c) of the CPC Law prohibits the application of dissimilar conditions to equivalent transactions, thereby placing certain undertakings at a competitive disadvantage. As evident from the statutory language, discrimination can relate to 'conditions', which is not confined to pricing practices. At an EU level, both nationality-based discrimination[294] and geographical price discrimination[295] were found to be abuses of a dominant position. In *Technoplastics/Linde-Hadjikyriakos,*[296] the practice by Linde-Hadjikyriakos Gas Ltd of enforcing daily rent on gas cylinders was found to be a discriminatory practice that constituted an abuse of a dominant position, infringing section 6 §1 of the CPC Law. Discrimination is perhaps an appropriate section of the examination of exploitative practices to further consider section 6 §2 of the CPC Law. As mentioned above, the abuse of a relationship of economic dependence by one or more undertakings in relation to an undertaking that is a customer, supplier, producer, representative, distributor or commercial associate of the first undertaking, is prohibited.

264. In *Alpha Electric/Fissler,*[297] Alpha Electric House (Spyros Theodorou) Ltd (Alpha Electric) had filed a complaint with the CPC against the German-based company Fissler GmbH (Fissler). Alpha Electric alleged infringement on behalf of Fissler of section 6 §2 of the CPC Law on grounds of abuse of a relationship of economic dependence. Alpha Electric and Fissler had established a commercial relationship as of 1982, under which relationship Alpha Electric acted as a reseller and a distributor of Fissler's products in Cyprus. No written contract was ever signed between Alpha Electric and Fissler in the above respect. Following representations made by Fissler to Alpha Electric in 2008 and 2009 on the efficiency of the representation of Fissler's products in Cyprus by Alpha Electric, Fissler sent a distribution agreement, which incorporated a business plan that entailed obligatory minimum annual purchases of Fissler's products for Alpha Electric. Alpha Electric

294. Cf., *inter alia*, Case C-18/93, *Corsica Ferries Italia Srl v. Corpo dei Piloti del Porto di Genova*, ECLI:EU:C:1994:195; Case 7/82, *Gesellschaft zur Verwertung von Leistungsschutzrechten mbH (GVL) v. Commission of the European Communities*, ECLI:EU:C:1983:52.

295. Cf., *inter alia*, Case C-333/94 P, *Tetra Pak International SA v. Commission of the European Communities*, ECLI:EU:C:1996:436; Case T-228/97, *Irish Sugar plc v. Commission of the European Communities,* ECLI:EU:T:1999:246.

296. CPC Decision 29/2012, *Complaint by Technoplastics Ltd against Linde-Hadjikyriakos Gas Ltd*, 10 Aug. 2012 (in Greek).

297. CPC Decision 22/2018, *Complaint by Alpha Electric House (Spyros Theodorou) Ltd against Fissler GmbH*, 22 Jun. 2018 (in Greek).

expressed its disagreement with certain terms and provided an alternative proposal which involved the transfer of distribution of Fissler's products in Cyprus to its existing distributor in Greece.

265. Fissler then informed Alpha Electric in writing of the former's intention to terminate their commercial relationship, offering an alternative termination arrangement, whereby monetary compensation would be paid to Alpha Electric if their relationship would terminate earlier and provided that certain terms put forward by Fissler would be accepted and performed by Alpha Electric. Fissler expressed its preference for the alternative option for termination and at the same time declared it would not accept any negotiation of the material terms of such proposed arrangement, which it considered financially reasonable. Over 50% of the gross profit of Alpha Electric during the past five years originated from sales of products supplied by Fissler in the relevant geographic market. Moreover, Alpha Electric had been engaged in a long-term commercial relationship with Fissler for more than twenty years and had formulated its operations in accordance with the needs of the said relationship. As a result, Alpha Electric had carried out important investment and had created a large network of customers.

266. The CPC found Alpha Electric to be in a relationship of economic dependence as regards Fissler. In Cyprus, competitive products to Fissler's were the subject matter of existing exclusive distribution relationships with established distribution networks. As such, for Alpha Electric, there was no equivalent alternative to being the distributor of Fissler in Cyprus. The extent to which the requirement of abuse was satisfied, was determined based on the assessment as to whether the following requirements were cumulatively met: (a) the imposition of arbitrary terms by Fissler upon Alpha Electric; (b) a sudden and unjustified termination by Fissler of the long-term business relationship with Alpha Electric; and (c) a discriminative behaviour by Fissler against Alpha Electric. The CPC held that Fissler had infringed section 6 §2 of the CPC Law by abusing the relationship of economic dependence which existed between itself and Alpha Electric.

267. In *K.A.C./Henkel*,[298] the CPC dealt with an exclusive dealing arrangement. The case concerned a complaint lodged by K.A.C. Constantinides Trading Ltd (K.A.C.) against GPM-Henkel Ltd, a subsidiary of Henkel AG & Co KGaA (together, Henkel). K.A.C. was active in the parallel import of Henkel products in Cyprus. K.A.C. complained that Henkel that aimed at stopping retailers from purchasing parallel import products, which caused many K.A.C. customers to avoid buying parallel import products despite the lower prices for such goods. Henkel's conduct was alleged to have negatively impacted K.A.C.'s revenues. During the preliminary investigation procedure, the service of the CPC carried out a dawn raid at Henkel's premises and at five retail stores that sold Henkel products in Nicosia. The service of the CPC gathered evidence, such as statements of the representatives of retail stores, internal correspondence between officers of Henkel AG & Co KGaA

298. Decision No. 53/2019, *Complaint by K.A.C. Constantinides Trading Ltd v. GPM-Henkel Ltd* (in Greek).

and its subsidiaries, Henkel's notices to retail stores and to wholesalers and importers of parallel products, executive presentations, notes, sales invoices, credit notes and other documents. The CPC opened proceedings against Henkel AG & Co KGaA and its Cypriot subsidiary *GPM-Henkel Ltd*, jointly and severally, concerning a prima facie infringement of section 6 §1(b) of the CPC Law and Article 102 TFEU.

268. Henkel had sent notice letters to importers and wholesalers requesting that they cease importing Henkel goods, reserving Henkel's rights to take all appropriate legal action against them. Similar notice letters were also sent to individual retail stores that sold parallel import Henkel goods, requesting that they stop selling those items. In addition, Henkel, through individual meetings of its representatives with owners and employees of retail stores advised them to stop selling such items. The CPC defined the relevant product market as follows: (a) the market of wholesale distribution of heavy-duty laundry detergents; (b) the market of wholesale distribution of mass health and beauty products, and concluded that Henkel has holds a dominant position in the relevant wholesale market for heavy-duty detergents in Cyprus. The CPC concluded that the selling of parallel imports of Henkel goods in Cyprus was obstructed by Henkel, which had a dominant position in the relevant wholesale market for heavy-duty detergents in Cyprus.

269. The products traded in parallel were genuine Henkel products, based on the evidence gathered by the service of the CPC. It was also established that Henkel used various means of intervention, as the representatives of retail stores described, in order to achieve the objective of preventing parallel imports, namely threats to terminate its own cooperation with retail stores in case they continued to sell products from parallel imports (and in one case Henkel stopped supplying a retail store temporarily) or that the terms of their cooperation would alter, or that it would terminate discounts and other beneficial conditions. Evidence showed that Henkel offered more favourable conditions of cooperation and discounts to a retail store for such cooperation to be exclusive. Where the specific retail store continued to cooperate with K.A.C., Henkel adjusted the conditions of its own cooperation, by terminating discounts, credit and merchandising services. The CPC also found that Henkel AG & Co. KGaA became aware of the conduct of its Cypriot subsidiary. The CPC concluded that there was no reasonable reason for Henkel's actions, as there were no efficiencies that outweighed any anticompetitive impact on consumers. The CPC concluded that Henkel had infringed section 6 §1(b) of the CPC Law and Article 102 TFEU. By leveraging their dominant role in the local market, the wholesale supply of heavy-duty detergents in Cyprus had been limited to the detriment of the consumers.

§3. Exclusionary Practices

I. Predation

270. In *Hoffmann-La Roche v. Commission*,[299] the CJEU defined exclusionary practices as the concept of abuse is an objective concept relating to the behaviour of an undertaking in a dominant position which is such as to influence the structure of a market where, as a result of the very presence of the undertaking in question, the degree of competition is weakened and which, through recourse to methods different from those which condition normal competition in products or services on the basis of the transactions of commercial operators, has the effect of hindering the maintenance of the degree of competition still existing in the market or the growth of that competition.[300] The premise of predatory pricing rests with a dominant undertaking intentionally reducing prices in the face of competition from an existing competitor or a new market entrant can ultimately force those rivals out of the market. Once foreclosure is achieved, the dominant undertaking then raises its prices again, thus causing consumer harm.

II. Tying

271. Tying occurs where a dominant undertaking ties the sale of separate products by requiring customers that wish to purchase one of the products to also purchase the other product. It enables the undertaking concerned to leverage its market power to the market of the tied products in which it faces competition. Tying may be performed through contractual arrangements, discounts and bundling. Section 6 §1(d) of the CPC Law expressly prohibits making the conclusion of contracts subject to acceptance by the other parties of supplementary obligations which, by their nature or according to commercial usage, have no connection with the subject of such contracts.

III. Rebates

272. Rebates are given to customers to reward them for a particular form of purchasing behaviour. The usual nature of a conditional rebate is that the customer is given a rebate if its purchases over a defined reference period exceed a certain threshold, the rebate being granted either on all purchases (retroactive rebates) or only on those made in excess of those required to achieve the threshold (incremental rebates).[301] The rebates domain has been among the most contentious at an EU level. The European Commission's analysis traditionally revolved around an

299. Case 85/76, *Hoffmann-La Roche & Co. AG v. Commission of the European Communities*, ECLI-:EU:C:1979:36.
300. *Ibid.*, para. 91.
301. Communication from the European Commission – Guidance on the European Commission's enforcement priorities in applying Article 82 of the EC Treaty to abusive exclusionary conduct by dominant undertakings (2009/C 45/02) OJ C 45, 24.2.2009, pp. 7–20, para. 37.

'effects-based approach'.[302] In *Intel*,[303] the CJEU held that 'not every exclusionary effect is necessarily detrimental to competition'.[304] While the CJEU conceded that past cases may have condemned rebates per se when rewarding exclusivity or loyalty,[305] but stated this case law 'must be further clarified' and where a defence alleges that the scheme does not have exclusionary effects, then a full market analysis is required.[306] The *Intel* test therefore entails a two-step analysis. It must first be concluded that the rebates scheme concerned is prima facie abusive. Where the dominant undertaking concerned puts forward a defence of no capability of foreclosure, supported by evidence, then an assessment must be carried out as to whether foreclosure does arise.

273. In *Wyeth/Phadisco*,[307] the CPC found an infringement of section 6 §1(d) of the CPC Law by Wyeth Hellas SA (Wyeth) and Phadisco Ltd (Phadisco). A complaint was filed against Wyeth and Phadisco over an allegedly unfair promotion of their meningitis vaccines through the imposition of fidelity rebates. Wyeth and Phadisco provided quantitative discounts based on the volumes purchased by physicians and pharmacists of the Meningitec and Prevenar vaccines. Wyeth and Phadisco gave free Meningitec vaccines with every purchase of a certain quantity of Meningitec or with the purchase of a certain quantity of Prevenar vaccine. The CPC found Wyeth and Phadisco had abused their dominant position in the market of pneumococcal vaccines, as the quantitative discounts offered to doctors and pharmacists were not justified. Wyeth and Phadisco employed a pricing policy aimed at strengthening their dominant position in the market of meningococcal vaccines.

IV. Refusal to Deal

274. There are situations in which a dominant undertaking's refusal to supply goods or services may lead to an abuse of a dominant position. Accordingly, a refusal to deal may be found to be an infringement of section 6 §1 of the CPC Law. Such situations can arise where the dominant firm is active both upstream and downstream and it refuses to supply a competitor in the downstream market.[308] The concept of refusal to supply covers a broad range of practices, such as a refusal to

302. Communication from the European Commission – Guidance on the European Commission's enforcement priorities in applying Article 82 of the EC Treaty to abusive exclusionary conduct by dominant undertakings (2009/C 45/02) OJ C 45, 24.2.2009, pp. 7–20, IV, A. (b), generally.
303. Case C-413/14 P, *Intel Corp. v. European Commission*, ECLI:EU:C:2017:632.
304. *Ibid.*, para. 134.
305. *Ibid.*, para. 137.
306. *Ibid.*, paras 138–140.
307. CPC Decision 36/2013, *Complaint filed by Akis Panayiotou & Son Ltd Wyeth Hellas SA and Phadisco Ltd*, 12 Apr. 2013 (in Greek).
308. Cf., e.g., Joined Cases 6 and 7-73, *Istituto Chemioterapico Italiano S.p.A. and Commercial Solvents Corporation v. Commission of the European Communities*, ECLI:EU:C:1974:18.

supply products to existing or new customers,[309] refusal to license intellectual property rights,[310] including when the licence is necessary to provide interface information,[311] or refusal to grant access to an essential facility or a network.[312] Refusal to supply is a controversial topic of competition law, as it interacts with other legal domains, most notably with intellectual property rights and the freedom to trade. Advocate General Jacobs, in his opinion in *Bronner*,[313] recognised that while the laws of the Member States generally regard freedom of contract as an essential element of free trade, the competition rules of some Member States explicitly provide that an unjustified refusal to enter a binding contract may constitute an abuse of a dominant position.[314] AG Jacobs then went to say that invasion into the freedom to contract requires careful justification. As already indicated, the CPC Law can be seen as being a statutory instrument that provides for the prevention of exploitation of economic power provided, as a legitimate restriction of the right to enter into contracts, under Article 26 of the Constitution.[315]

275. The CPC has found refusals to deal as abusive conduct in a number of cases. In *Kapnisis/Misos/Limassol Licensed Porters Association/Cyprus Ports Authority*,[316] the CPC found the Limassol Licensed Porters Association (LLPA) and the Cyprus Ports Authority (CPA), the CPC found LLPA to have infringed sections 3 §1(b) and (d), 6 §1(b) and (c) of the CPC Law. The CPC found that, by refusing the Complainants access to equipment and facilities that other licensed porters by the CPA were allowed to access towards providing porter services, LLPA restricted the Complainants' free access to the relevant market, to the detriment of consumers. In employing a discriminatory approach vis-à-vis the Complainants, the decision of LLPA had an anticompetitive object in that it applied dissimilar terms in respect of equivalent transactions. As long as the anticompetitive object of the behaviour of LLPA was established, the CPC deemed it prohibited per se and no further investigation was required concerning the effect of the said conduct. The LLPA's conduct was collusive and infringed section 3 §1(b) of the CPC Law, as it restricted access

309. Joined Cases 6/73 and 7/73, *Istituto Chemioterapico Italiano and Commercial Solvents v. Commission*, ECLI:EU:C:1974:18.
310. Joined Cases C-241/91 P and C-242/91 P, *Radio Telefis Eireann (RTE) and Independent Television Publications Ltd (ITP) v. Commission*, ECLI:EU:C:1995:98; Case C-418/01, *IMS Health v. NDC Health*, ECLI:EU:C:2004:257. Those judgments show that in exceptional circumstances a refusal to license intellectual property rights is abusive.
311. Case T-201/04, *Microsoft Corp. v. Commission of the European Communities*, ECLI-:EU:T:2007:289.
312. Commission Decision No. 94/19/EC of 21 December 1993 in Case IV/34.689, *Sea Containers v. Stena Sealink – Interim Measures* (OJ L 15, 18.1.1994, p. 8) and Commission Decision No. 92/213/EEC of 26 February 1992 in Case IV/33.544 *British Midland v. Aer Lingus* – (OJ L 96, 10.4.1992, p. 34).
313. Case C-7/97, *Oscar Bronner GmbH & Co. KG v. Mediaprint Zeitungs- und Zeitschriftenverlag GmbH & Co. KG and Others*, Opinion of Advocate General Jacobs, 28 May 1998, ECLI-:EU:C:1998:264.
314. *Ibid.*, para. 53.
315. Case No. 1023/2012, *Pancyprian Organisation of Cattle Farmers (POCF) Public Ltd vs. Commission for the Protection of Competition*, 30 Nov. 2012 (in Greek).
316. CPC Decision 54/2012, *Complaint by T. Kapnisis and A. Meletiou against the Limassol Licensed Porters Association and the Cyprus Ports Authority*, 10 Oct. 2012 (in Greek).

to the relevant market, while further infringing section 3 §1(d) of the CPC Law through the application of dissimilar terms as between licensed porters of an otherwise equal standing.

276. LLPA was the only porting services provider in the Limassol Port and therefore held a monopolistic position in the relevant market. From that position LLPA, having freedom of action, restricted access to facilities essential to compete for new entrants to the relevant market porters. Moreover, this restriction extended to impose LLPA as the sole choice for any intended user of porting services. By refusing to deal with the complainants, LLPA was preventing their access to the relevant market as providers of porting services and was thus engaged in conduct that could lead to the extinction of any competition. Such access was a facility essential to compete and LLPA was thus abusing its monopolistic decision by refusing the complainants access to essential facilities, infringing section 6 §1(b) of the CPC Law. The discriminatory treatment of the complainants by LLPA, as compared to the terms other licensed porters enjoyed constituted an abuse of LLPA's dominant position and infringed section 6 §1(c) of the CPC Law.

277. This is one of the few cases in which the CPC held an association of undertakings to have infringed the provisions of both sections 3 and 6 of the CPC Law. It is also intriguing that the CPC treated LLPA as both an undertaking on its own standing and an association of undertakings. LLPA was an association representing the collective interests of its members, undertakings carrying out the economic commercial activity of porters' services. Simultaneously, on the grounds that all commercial activities of the LLPA members were carried out subject to their organisation within LLPA and LLPA was held to carry out economic activity on its own right, irrespective of whether such activity was profitable or not. *Kapnisis/ Misos/Limassol Licensed Porters Association/Cyprus Ports Authority* is also significant as it demonstrates the CPC's approach to the application of the 'essential facilities' doctrine and the criteria which the CPC takes into account in establishing its applicability. The CPC is seen to assess the following, in which case an abuse of dominance will be established: (a) the essential facility, which could be a product or service or access to a premise or a distribution system, is impossible or extremely difficult to replicate; (b) the refusal of access creates a situation where the activities of a competitor in the relevant market become impossible or substantially burdensome financially, thus creating a significant barrier to entry; (c) there is no subjective justification for such refusal, the burden of which lies with the undertaking owning the facility in question.

278. In *Golden Telemedia/MTN*,[317] the relevant service market was the market for premium-rated electronic communications services (Premium Services). Premium Services used code numbers allocated under the national numbering plan to provide, *inter alia*: (a) premium voice services and (b) premium messaging services. The complainant, Golden Telemedia Limited (GT), was active in the market

317. CPC Decision 19/2019, *Complaint by Golden Telemedia Limited against MTN Cyprus Limited* (in Greek).

for the provision of Premium Services. MTN Cyprus Limited (MTN) had refused to provide GT with blocking services relating to MTN's mobile telephony subscribers so as to enable the blocking of calls to premium voice information services, which resulted in GT not being able to provide its services to MTN subscribers. MTN's policy was to request a monetary guarantee from its subscribers towards enabling premium voice information services under their mobile telephony subscription contract. The CPC found that MTN's decision to block or impose restrictions on calls carried out by its mobile subscribers to Premium Services prevented GT from offering Premium Services to MTN's subscribers, which was to the detriment of consumers. CPC found MTN to have abused its dominant position by limiting production, distribution or technical development to the prejudice of consumers, thus infringing section 6 §1(b) of the CPC Law. The CPC Law was applied with the same outcome to similar facts concerning a complaint by Netsmart (Cyprus) Limited against CYTA.[318]

V. Margin Squeeze

279. A dominant undertaking may charge a price for the product on the upstream market which, compared to the price it charges on the downstream market does not allow even an equally efficient competitor to trade profitably in the downstream market on a lasting basis (a so-called 'margin squeeze').[319] A landmark judgment at an EU level on margin squeeze is *TeliaSonera*.[320] In that case, the Stockholm District Court referred to the CJEU a number of questions on the conditions for proving an abusive margin squeeze infringing Article 102 TFEU. The CJEU held that a margin squeeze abuse can arise even where the established conditions for an abusive refusal to supply have not been met and can be a distinct abusive conduct from a refusal to supply.[321] The absence of a regulatory obligation was deemed not relevant to the question of whether the pricing practice at issue in the main proceedings is abusive. The indispensability of the product is a factor which should be taken into account in assessing all the circumstances surrounding the pricing practice. The CJEU further held that, in assessing whether such a practice is abusive, all of the circumstances of each case should be taken into consideration and in particular: (a) as a general rule, primarily the prices and costs of the undertaking concerned on the retail services market should be taken into consideration. Only where it is not possible, in particular circumstances, to refer to those prices and costs should those of competitors on the same market be examined; and (b) it is necessary to demonstrate that, taking particular account of whether the wholesale product is indispensable,

---

318. CPC Decision 41/2012, *Complaint by Netsmart (Cyprus) Limited against CYTA*, 11 Sep. 2012 (in Greek).
319. Communication from the European Commission – Guidance on the European Commission's enforcement priorities in applying Article 82 of the EC Treaty to abusive exclusionary conduct by dominant undertakings (2009/C 45/02) OJ C 45, 24.2.2009, pp. 7–20, para. 80.
320. Case 52/09, *Konkurrensverket v. TeliaSonera Sverige AB*, ECLI:EU:C:2011:83.
321. *Ibid.*, para. 56.

that practice produces an anticompetitive effect, at least potentially, on the retail market, and that the practice is not in any way economically justified.[322]

280. In *Pittas Dairies/POCF*,[323] the CPC assess a complaint concerning margin squeeze. The case concerned a complaint lodged by Pittas Dairies Ltd and Pittas Dairy Industries Ltd (together, Pittas) against POCF for infringements of sections 6(1)(a), (b) and (c) and 6(2) of the CPC Law. Pittas also filed an application for interim measures against POCF pursuant to sections 23(2) and 28 of the CPC Law. Pittas was active in the production and distribution of dairy products based on raw cow milk. POCF was a public limited company carrying out the collective trade of raw cow milk on behalf of its members, producers of cow milk, as well as the management of the collection and distribution of cow milk. In 2012, POCF had acquired Papouis Dairies Limited (Papouis), a company that owned a milk processing factory and produced dairy products such as halloumi, kefalotyri, feta type and anari.

281. The CPC found an infringement of section 6 §1(a) of the CPC Law by POCF in relation to the imposition of unfair trading conditions, as a result of unfair and unilateral increases in the basic price of raw cow milk and the unfair and unilateral variations in the quantities of raw cow milk delivered to Pittas. Moreover, as a result of a margin squeeze between the price of raw cow milk and the price charged by POCF through its subsidiary, Papouis, in the market of production and supply of halloumi cheese, POCF was found to further infringe section 6 §1(a) of the CPC Law. The CPC imposed an administrative fine of EUR 1,038,120 on POCF for infringing section 6 §1(a) of the CPC Law as a resulting of applying unfair trading conditions to Pittas and a fine of EUR 519,060 for the infringement of section 6 §1(a) thereof by applying unfair pricing resulting in a margin squeeze. The CPC also granted the interim relief sought by Pittas, ordering POCF to supply raw cow milk to Pittas.

---

322. *Ibid.*, para. 113.

323. CPC Decision 32/2018, *Complaint by Pittas Dairies Ltd and Pittas Dairy Industries Ltd against Pancyprian Organisation of Cattle Farmers (POCF) Public Ltd*, 24 Jul. 2018 (in Greek).

Chapter 3. Concentrations

§1. Horizontal Mergers

282. 'Horizontal mergers' refer to concentrations between undertakings which are actual or potential competitors on the same relevant market. In order to assess the competition aspects and scrutiny of horizontal mergers, fundamental notions concerning the control of concentrations between undertakings must be reviewed. The Concentrations Law is the legislation regulating the control of concentrations between undertakings in Cyprus. Enforcement of the legislation rests with the CPC. It should be noted from the outset that the Concentrations Law does not apply in cases where a concentration falls within the scope of application of the Mergers Regulation. The CPC has overall responsibility for implementing the Concentrations Law and is the competent independent authority for the control of concentrations. On assessing a report prepared by its Service, the CPC declares that a concentration is compatible or incompatible with the functioning of competition in the market, pursuant to sections 20 and 21 of the Concentrations Law.

283. The European Commission has issued guidelines on the assessment of horizontal mergers (the 'Horizontal Merger Guidelines').[324] In the Horizontal Merger Guidelines, the European Commission states that there are two main ways in which horizontal mergers may significantly impede effective competition, in particular by creating or strengthening a dominant position: (a) by eliminating important competitive constraints on one or more firms, which consequently would have increased market power, without resorting to coordinated behaviour (non-coordinated effects); by changing the nature of competition in such a way that firms that previously were not coordinating their behaviour, are now significantly more likely to coordinate and raise prices or otherwise harm effective competition. A merger may also make coordination easier, more stable or more effective for firms which were coordinating prior to the merger (coordinated effects). In *Sun Chemical,*[325] the General Court held that the Horizontal Guidelines do not set out a 'checklist' of factors to be applied mechanically in every case and do not require an examination in every case of all of the factors mentioned in them.

284. In terms of non-coordinated effects of horizontal mergers, a direct effect could be the loss of competition between the undertakings concerned. Moreover, competitors of the merging undertakings would benefit from the reduction of competitive pressure where a price increase switches demand to these competitors. The reduction in these competitive constraints could lead to significant price increases in the relevant market. From a coordinated effects perspective, a merger may make coordination easier, more stable or more effective for undertakings that were already coordinating before the merger, either by making the coordination more robust or

324. Guidelines on the assessment of horizontal mergers under the Council Regulation on the control of concentrations between undertakings, *OJ C 31, 5 Feb. 2004, pp. 5–18.*

325. Case T-282/06, *Sun Chemical Group BV, Siegwerk Druckfarben AG, and Flint Group Germany GmbH v. Commission*, ECLI:EU:T:2007:203.

by permitting firms to coordinate on even higher prices.[326] The substantive test for compatibility of a concentration with competition in the market is that such concentration not significantly impede effective competition in Cyprus or in a substantial part of it, in particular as a result of the creation or strengthening of a dominant position.

285. Market shares can be seen in the CPC's practice to provide indications of the market structure and of the competitive importance of the undertakings concerned and their competitors. Market shares resulting ex post the concentration are calculated on the assumption that they comprise the sum of the market shares of the undertakings concerned ex ante the concentration. Changes in market shares over previous periods of time may provide indications on the competitive process and the likely future importance of competitors of the undertakings concerned. The relevant product markets and geographic markets determine the scope within which the market power of the participating undertakings must be assessed. In horizontal mergers, an affected market consists of all the relevant product markets and geographic markets as well as the plausible interchangeable relevant product markets and geographic markets in the territory of Cyprus where two or more of the undertakings concerned are engaged in business activities in the same product market and where the concentration will lead to a combined market share of 15% or more.

286. According to EU case law,[327] large market shares, such as 50% or more, may in themselves be evidence of the existence of a dominant market position. A horizontal merger involving a firm whose market share will remain below 50% after the concentration may also raise competition concerns in view of other factors, such as the strength and number of competitors, the presence of capacity constraints or the extent to which the products of the merging parties are close substitutes.[328] Horizontal mergers which, by reason of the limited market share of the undertakings concerned, are not liable to impede effective competition may be presumed to be compatible with the market. The overall concentration level in a market may also provide useful information about the competitive situation. To enable the CPC to measure concentration levels, the Concentrations Law requires undertakings concerned to include in their notification to the CPC the relevant Herfindahl-Hirschman Index (HHI).[329] The HHI is calculated by summing the squares of the individual market shares of all the firms in the market. While the absolute level of the HHI can give an initial indication of the competitive pressure in the market post-merger, the change in the HHI (the delta) is a useful proxy for the change in concentration directly brought about by the merger.

287. Analysis of the conditions of entry into the relevant market constitutes an important element of the overall competitive assessment. For entry to be considered

326. Horizontal Merger Guidelines, para. 39.
327. Cf., *inter alia*, Case T-221/95, *Endemol v. Commission*, ECLI:EU:T:1999:85, para. 134; Case T-102/96, *Gencor v. Commission*, ECLI:EU:T:1999:65, para. 205.
328. Horizontal Mergers Guidelines, para. 17.
329. Paragraph 7, Schedule III of the Concentrations Law.

a sufficient competitive constraint on the undertakings concerned, it must be shown to be likely, timely and sufficient to deter or defeat any potential anticompetitive effects of the merger.[330] The CPC can be expected to assess whether entry is likely or whether potential entry is likely to constrain the behaviour of incumbents ex post the concentration. For entry to be likely, it must be sufficiently profitable considering the price effects of injecting additional output into the market and the potential responses of incumbents. Potential entrants in the market may encounter barriers to entry, which are specific features of the market affording incumbent undertakings advantages over potential competitors. When entry barriers are low, the undertakings concerned are more likely to be constrained by entry when barriers to entry are low.

288. Illustrations of barriers to entry are provided by the Horizontal Mergers Guidelines as follows:[331] (a) legal advantages encompass situations where regulatory barriers limit the number of market participants by, for example, restricting the number of licences; (b) the incumbents may also enjoy technical advantages, such as preferential access to essential facilities, natural resources, innovation and R&D, or intellectual property rights, which make it difficult for any firm to compete successfully; (c) the established position of the incumbent firms on the market may make it difficult to enter a particular industry because experience or reputation is necessary to compete effectively, both of which may be difficult to obtain as an entrant. The CPC will consider efficiencies, but the undertakings concerned must show that the efficiencies generated by the merger will outweigh any anticompetitive effects and that they will benefit consumers.

§2. Vertical Mergers

289. Vertical concentrations involve undertakings operating at different levels of the supply chain, such as an undertaking at an upstream level with an undertaking in a downstream level. In vertical mergers, an affected market consists of all the relevant product markets and geographic markets as well as the plausible interchangeable relevant product markets and geographic markets in the territory of Cyprus, where any of the undertakings concerned are engaged in business activities in a product market which is upstream or downstream of a product market in which any other party to the concentration is engaged (vertical relationship) and provided any of the individual or combined market shares of these undertakings is 25% or more (regardless of whether there is or is not any existing supplier-customer relationship between the undertakings).[332] Contrary to horizontal mergers, vertical mergers cannot result in loss of competition between direct competitors. As the European Commission recognises in its Guidelines on the assessment of non-horizontal mergers

330. Horizontal Mergers Guidelines, para. 68.
331. Horizontal Mergers Guidelines, para. 71.
332. Paragraph 3, Schedule I of the Concentrations Law.

under the Council Regulation on the control of concentrations between undertakings (the 'Vertical Mergers Guidelines'),[333] a characteristic of vertical mergers is that the activities and/or the products of the companies involved are complementary to each other and their integration can produce significant efficiencies and be pro-competitive.[334]

290. In assessing the competitive effects of a vertical merger, the CPC can be expected to compare the competitive conditions that would result from the notified merger with the conditions that would have prevailed without the merger. As confirmed by its own practice, the CPC will take into account the Vertical Mergers Guidelines.[335] According to the Vertical Mergers Guidelines, there are two main ways in which vertical mergers may significantly impede effective competition: non-coordinated effects and coordinated effects.[336] Non-coordinated effects may principally arise when non-horizontal mergers give rise to foreclosure, namely where actual or potential rivals' access to supplies or markets is hampered or eliminated as a result of the merger, thereby reducing these companies' ability or incentive to compete. As a result of such foreclosure, the undertakings concerned may be able to profitably increase their prices. Such instances give rise to a significant impediment to effective competition and are therefore referred to hereafter as 'anti-competitive foreclosure'.[337] In May 2020, the General Court held[338] that non-coordinated effects, that is unilateral effects, can only lead to a significant impediment to effective competition test if they produce effects equivalent to the creation or strengthening of a dominant position. Therefore, the effect of reducing competitive pressure on remaining competitors may not be sufficient, in itself, to demonstrate a significant impediment to effective competition in the context of non-coordinated effects.

291. The Vertical Mergers Guidelines distinguish between two forms of foreclosure:[339] (1) input foreclosure – where the merger is likely to raise the costs of downstream rivals by restricting their access to an important input and (2) customer foreclosure – where the merger is likely to foreclose upstream rivals by restricting their access to a sufficient customer base. Input foreclosure arises where, post-merger, the new entity would be likely to restrict access to the products or services that it would have otherwise supplied absent the merger, thereby raising its downstream rivals' costs by making it harder for them to obtain supplies of the input under similar prices and conditions as absent the merger. This may lead the merged

333. *Guidelines on the assessment of non-horizontal mergers under the Council Regulation on the control of concentrations between undertakings*, OJ C 265, 18.10.2008, pp. 6–25.
334. *Ibid.*, para. 13.
335. Cf., *inter alia*, CPC Decision 26/2019, *Acquisition of Blue Circle Engineering Ltd by Hellenic Petroleum Cyprus Holding (HPCH) Ltd*, 22 April 2019; CPC Decision 31/2016, *Acquisition of LUKOIL CYPRUS LTD by CORAL A.E.*, 22 December 2016.
336. Vertical Mergers Guidelines, para. 17.
337. Vertical Mergers Guidelines, para. 18.
338. Case T-399/16, *CK Telecoms UK Investments Ltd v. European Commission*, ECLI:EU:T:2020:217.
339. Vertical Mergers Guidelines, para. 30.

entity to profitably increase the price charged to consumers, resulting in a significant impediment to effective competition.[340]

292. Customer foreclosure may occur when a supplier integrates with an important customer in the downstream market. Because of this downstream presence, the merged entity may foreclose access to a sufficient customer base to its actual or potential rivals in the upstream market (the input market) and reduce their ability or incentive to compete. In turn, this may raise downstream rivals' costs by making it harder for them to obtain supplies of the input under similar prices and conditions as absent the merger. This may allow the merged entity profitably to establish higher prices on the downstream market.[341] Coordinated effects arise where the vertical merger changes the nature of competition in such a way that firms that previously were not coordinating their behaviour, are now significantly more likely to coordinate to raise prices or otherwise harm effective competition. A merger may also make coordination easier, more stable or more effective for firms which were coordinating prior to the merger.[342]

§3. Pure Conglomerate Mergers

293. Conglomerate mergers are mergers between undertakings which are in a relationship which is neither purely horizontal nor vertical. As the Vertical Mergers Guidelines note, in practice the focus is on mergers between companies that are active in closely related markets.[343] Concentrations which can be seen as conglomerate mergers would involve suppliers of complementary products or products which belong to a range of products purchased by the same set of customers for the same end use. In assessing the competitive effects of a conglomerate merger, the CPC can be expected to take into account both the possible anticompetitive effects arising from conglomerate mergers and the possible pro-competitive effects stemming from efficiencies substantiated by the parties. As confirmed by its practice, the CPC will take into account the Vertical Mergers Guidelines.[344]

294. The primary concern in conglomerate mergers is foreclosure. The combination of products in related markets may confer on the merged entity the ability and incentive to leverage a strong market position from one market to another by means of tying or bundling or other exclusionary practices.[345] The assessment of conglomerate mergers can therefore be expected to entail whether the undertakings concerned would have the ability to foreclose their rivals, whether they would have the economic incentive to do so and whether a foreclosure strategy would have a

340. Vertical Mergers Guidelines, para. 31.
341. Vertical Mergers Guidelines, para. 58.
342. Vertical Mergers Guidelines, para. 19.
343. Vertical Mergers Guidelines, para. 91.
344. Cf., *inter alia*, CPC Decision 26/2019, *Acquisition of Blue Circle Engineering Ltd by Hellenic Petroleum Cyprus Holding (HPCH) Ltd*, 22 April 2019; CPC Decision 31/2016, *Acquisition of LUKOIL CYPRUS LTD by CORAL A.E.*, 22 December 2016.
345. Vertical Mergers Guidelines, para. 93.

significant detrimental effect on competition, thus causing harm to consumers.[346] Tying and bundling are often the means through which foreclosure can be achieved ex post conglomerate mergers. The effects of bundling or tying can only be expected to be substantial when at least one of the merging parties'' products is viewed by many customers as particularly important and there are few relevant alternatives for that product, such as because of product differentiation.[347] The incentive to foreclose rivals through bundling or tying depends on the degree to which this strategy is profitable.[348] Conglomerate mergers may in certain circumstances facilitate anti-competitive coordination in markets, even in the absence of an agreement or a concerted practice.[349]

§4. Joint Ventures

295. Establishing full functionality of a joint venture may prove particularly challenging where it only takes over one specific function within the parent company business activities, without the joint venture having its own access to or presence in the market. The strong presence of parent companies in upstream/downstream plays a crucial role in assessing the full functionality of a joint venture, where this presence results in substantial sales or purchases between the parents and the joint venture. Given that the basic function of an outsourcing joint venture is normally to supply the outsourcing parent, the essential question is whether, regardless of these sales, the joint venture is able to play an active role in the market. The joint venture's full functionality will not normally be affected by an initial period of sales exclusively to its parents. Indeed, such a start-up period may be necessary in order to establish the joint venture in a market. The joint venture should inevitably have sufficient resources to build up such market presence within a reasonable time frame. Where sales from a joint venture to the parent companies are intended to be made on a lasting basis, the essential question is whether, regardless of these sales, the joint venture is geared to play an active role in the market and can be considered economically autonomous from an operational viewpoint.

296. Joint control is characterised by a deadlock situation resulting from the power of two or more parent companies to reject proposed strategic decisions of the joint venture. In *EDS/Lufthansa*[350] EDS acquired a 25% minority stake in Lufthansa Systems, an IT service subsidiary of Lufthansa. Their agreement required unanimity for important strategic matters, such as the annual budget and the business plan. The European Commission held that these elements did not deprive the joint venture of its full functionality or its economic autonomy from an operational viewpoint and held that even where Lufthansa, being the joint controlling parent of the

346. Cf., *inter alia*, Case T-210/01, *General Electric v. Commission*, ECLI:EU:T:2005:456, paras 327, 362–363, 405.
347. For example, Commission Decision in Case No COMP/M.3732 – *Procter & Gamble / Gillette*, of 15 Jul. 2005, point 110.
348. Vertical Mergers Guidelines, para. 105.
349. Vertical Mergers Guidelines, para. 119.
350. Case IV/M.560 – EDS/Lufthansa, Decision of 11 May 1995.

joint venture in that case, remained the main customer of the joint venture in the medium term, the joint venture's dependence on its parent would only be temporary. In addition, the services provided by the joint venture to its parent were priced on an arm's length basis.

297. As clearly illustrated by *EDS/Lufthansa* and as is expressly stated in the European Commission's Consolidated Jurisdictional Notice,[351] for a joint venture to be a full-function undertaking and therefore economically autonomous from an operational viewpoint, the joint venture does not have to be autonomous as regards the adoption of its strategic decisions.[352] The criterion of full-functionality would be satisfied so long as the joint venture is autonomous from an operational aspect. In *Hitachi/NECDRAM/JV*,[353] the European Commission considered that a joint venture, the functioning of which would be implemented in three stages over a period of at least two years, was full function. This was because at the end of this period the joint venture would have established an independent sale channel, would have exclusive use of its own brand and access to the necessary intellectual property rights. In *PRSfM/STIM/GEMA/JV*,[354] the joint venture was held to be fully functional given the equity contributions of the parent companies and the provision of existing back-office structures and all intellectual property.

298. A joint venture may be considered full-function even if it does not own the resources that it needs in order to operate on the market, provided it has sufficiently firm access to such resources. In *Celanese/Degussa*,[355] ownership of certain production facilities that were to be used by the joint venture was retained by one of the parents, for technical reasons. Despite this, the Commission confirmed that the joint venture was full function, as it would have exclusive access to the production capacity of the plant in question. In *Eastman Kodak/Sun Chemical*[356] the joint venture was initially established for a period of ten years, but this was found to be on a lasting basis as there were automatic options to renew the agreement for further periods of five years. In the VLPG case,[357] in which the CPC carried out a full investigation, clearance was granted subject to commitments by the undertakings concerned. The case concerned the creation of a joint venture by Hellenic Petroleum Cyprus Ltd, Petrolina (Holdings) Public Ltd, Intergaz Ltd and Synergkaz Ltd, to which venture the said undertakings shifted part of their activities relating to the storage and handling of liquefied petroleum gas (LPG) to the joint venture. The joint

---

351. European Commission Consolidated Jurisdictional Notice under Council Regulation (EC) No. 139/2004 on the control of concentrations between undertakings, OJ C 95, 16 Apr. 2008, pp. 1–48.
352. *Ibid.*, para. 93.
353. Case No. COMP/JV.44 – Hitachi/NEC – DRAM/JV, Decision of 3 May 2000.
354. Case M.6800-*PRSfM/STIM/GEMA/JV, Decision of 16 Jun. 2015.*
355. Case COMP/M.3506 – Celanese/Degussa/JV (European Oxo-Chemicals), *Decision of* 11 Jun. 2003.
356. Case No. IV/M.1042 – Eastman Kodak/Sun Chemical, Decision of 15 Jan. 1998.
357. CPC Decision 35/2017, *Hellenic Petroleum Cyprus Ltd, Petrolina (Holdings) Public Ltd, Intergaz Ltd and Synergkaz Ltd*, 27 Jul. 2017 (in Greek).

venture was held to potentially have the ability and motivation to exploit its dominant position and to hinder the expansion of other companies and potential competitors.

299. The CPC has also highlighted the potential for significant obstruction of competition as a result of the creation of the joint venture's dominant position. The concentration was eventually cleared subject to a number of remedies, including the exclusion of members of the boards of the parent undertakings from sitting on the board of the joint venture, confidentiality undertakings by the joint venture in relation to the parent undertakings, the appointment of a trustee and the introduction of criteria for the assessment of storage capacity requests from third parties, together with providing any new entrant that constructs LPG storage facilities in the area, access to the anchor and unloading pipes, to the extent that it will be under the control of the joint venture.

300. In the *Limassol Port (LOT 3) case*,[358] which saw the creation of the joint venture DP World Limassol Ltd by DP World FZE and G.A.P. Vassilopoulos Multipurpose Port Services Ltd, the CPC found that due to the existence of vertical relationships between the services offered by the target undertaking and one of the undertakings controlling the joint venture, the concentration raised serious doubts as to its compatibility with the functioning of competition in the markets where G.A.P. Vassilopoulos Public Ltd was active. The presence of a certain director on the board of directors of the joint venture, appointed by G.A.P. Vassilopoulos Multipurpose Port Services Cyprus Ltd and was at the same time a member in boards other companies belonging to G.A.P. Vassilopoulos Public Ltd was held by the CPC, at first instance, as a presence that could lead to the elimination or reduction of competition in downstream or upstream markets, in relation to the markets where the joint venture would be active. This was the case as the said director would be able to acquire confidential or sensitive information on the competitors of G.A.P. Vassilopoulos Public Ltd. The provision of advisory services by G.A.P. Vassilopoulos Public Ltd to the joint venture were considered as potentially impeding competition to a significant extent in the markets where G.A.P. Vassilopoulos Public Ltd was active, as the latter would be able to acquire confidential or sensitive information on its competitors.

301. The CPC eventually cleared the concentration on the basis of commitments by the undertakings concerned, among which were the following: (a) a commitment to amend the relevant joint venture agreement and its by-laws so that the director appointed by G.A.P. Vassilopoulos Multipurpose Port Services Cyprus Ltd to the board of the joint venture will not participate or be present in discussions at the board of the joint venture nor have any voting rights in relation to any matter, agreement or proposed agreement GAP Vassilopoulos Public Ltd or any member of its group of companies may have a substantial commercial interest or a conflict of interests; (b) a commitment that the director appointed by G.A.P. Vassilopoulos

358. CPC Decision 29/2016, *Acquisition of the management of the Multi-Purpose Terminal of Limassol Port (LOT3) by DP World Limassol*, 16 Dec. 2016 (in Greek).

Multipurpose Port Services Cyprus Ltd to the board of the joint venture will not acquire any confidential and/or sensitive business information or business secrets held by the joint venture concerning competitors of GAP Vassilopoulos Public Ltd; (c) an independent third party will verify compliance of the joint venture with these commitments and inform the CPC annually; (d) the joint venture will conduct its activities through the provision of services, facilities and goods in the multipurpose terminal of Limassol port on a basis that will ensure non-discrimination in relation to the access to services, infrastructure, facilities and goods, their quality, and the regulated and non-regulated tariffs; (e) any transaction carried out by GAP Vassilopoulos Public Limited or any of its subsidiaries, will be conducted under certain conditions that ensure that no discrimination takes place (arm's length basis); (f) the joint venture will publish standard terms and conditions and its price list (for regulated and non-regulated charges) on its website; and (g) the joint venture will inform the market regarding its rebate mechanism.

Part III. Administrative Procedure

Chapter 1. Administrative Investigations Before the Antitrust Authority

§1. Initiative

I. General Sectors Inquiries

302. The power of the CPC to hold general sector inquiries is provided for by section 32A of the CPC Law.[359] Section 32A of the CPC Law is analogous to the respective powers of the European Commission pursuant to Article 17 of the Modernisation Regulation. The CPC may conduct inquiry in a particular sector of the economy, or in particular types of agreements in several sectors, when the trend of trade, the rigidity of prices, or other circumstances, create suspicion that competition may be restricted or distorted in the Republic. The CPC may request the necessary information for the application of sections 3 and/or 6 of the CPC Law, and/or the corresponding Articles 101 and/or 102 TFEU, as well as conduct any inspection to this effect. The Commission may, in particular, request the undertakings or associations of undertakings to communicate to it any agreement, decision or concerted practice. The CPC may further publish a report on the results of its inquiry into particular sectors of the economy or particular types of agreement in several sectors, and use the evidence, resulting from the inquiry, in cases of investigation of possible infringements of sections 3 and/or 6 of the CPC Law and/or the corresponding Articles 101 and/or 102 TFEU.

303. Sector inquiries are a powerful tool at the disposal of the CPC, that may be set in motion whenever the CPC has reasons to believe that a specific market is not performing as well as it should, and this is, at least partly, due to infringement of the competition law rules. The sector inquiry may better inform the understanding of the CPC for a particular sector from the point of view of competition policy, and may lead to subsequent specific investigations in order to ensure the respect of EU rules on restrictive agreements and abuse of dominant position. However, specific investigations are not a necessary outcome of a sector inquiry. The most important decision so far to carry out a sector inquiry referred to the petrol oil sector. On 17 December 2014 the CPC announced its decision to conduct a sector inquiry, after

359. Section 32A was added by Law 41(I)/14.

reviewing several press releases, and after its Service carried out a preliminary study, which showed that the prices of petrol oil in Cyprus remained steady, despite the fact that during 2014 the respective prices globally had been significantly reduced. The CPC noted that there were several complaints by consumers, who argued that prices of petrol oil increased immediately whenever there was an increase of import costs. However, the reverse did not occur whenever there was a decrease of import costs. This is known as 'Rockets and Feathers', where prices tend to rocket, but then fall slowly like a feather. The inquiry covered all aspects of the market, i.e., import, transport, storage, wholesale and retail, and all relevant actors participating in the market.

II. Ex-Officio Investigations

304. The CPC may, at its own discretion, hold ex-officio investigations, i.e., investigations decided *ex proprio motu*, without the existence of a complaint. The CPC may exercise its power to hold an ex-officio investigation in any case where it considers there might be prohibited collusion, or abuse of dominant position in violation of either the domestic law, or of the respective provisions of Modernisation Regulation. The powers that the CPC may exercise in case of ex-officio investigations are substantially the same as those exercised in an investigation initiated pursuant to a complaint.

III. Complaints

305. Pursuant to section 35 of the CPC Law, any natural or legal person who has a legitimate interest to this effect, shall be entitled to lodge a complaint of infringement of the provisions of section 3 and/or 6 of the CPC Law and/or Articles 101 and/or 102 TFEU. A person has a legitimate interest if he can prove that he has suffered, or there is a serious or possible risk that he will suffer, a substantial financial injury, or that he will, or there is a serious or possible risk that he will, be placed at a disadvantage regarding competition, as a direct result of the infringement. The complaint shall be lodged in writing to the CPC and shall be signed by the complainant, or the legal adviser, or an authorised representative of the complainant. The said complaint should include all the information referred to in the Annex to the CPC Law, so that the CPC is in a position to investigate the complaint lodged. Where the complaint does not include all the information of the Annex, the CPC may nevertheless accept it, if it deems that the information submitted is satisfactory for the investigation of the complaint lodged.

306. The Annex requires that the complaint should include a solemn statement that all the information stated in the complaint is true, as well as the following information:

(1) Particulars of the person lodging he complaint: full name and surname, postal and electronic address, number of telephone and fax of the person lodging the

complaint. In the case of a legal person, full business name must be stated. There should also be full particulars of the person who shall be responsible for the provision of additional information and/or clarifications on behalf of the person lodging the complaint. Where the person lodging the complaint is a legal person, the group of companies where it belongs, the holding and/or subsidiary companies thereof must be stated. There should be a brief description of the nature, scope and professional activities of the person lodging the complaint. The relationship between the person lodging the complaint and the undertaking or association of undertakings against which the complaint is lodged must also be stated (i.e., competitor, client).

(2) Particulars of the person against whom the complaint is lodged: full business name and address of the undertaking or association of undertakings, including information in relation to the group of companies where it belongs, the holding and/or subsidiary companies thereof. There should also be a brief description of the nature, scope and professional activities of the undertaking or association of undertakings against which the complaint is lodged.

(3) Nature of the relevant market: this includes determination of the nature of the products affected by the alleged infringements, number of suppliers of the said products, the total (in value) of sales of the said products, the dimensions of the competition existing in the relevant market, the possibilities for new competitors to enter the said market, whether there are other substitutes for the relevant products, determination, in the best possible way, of the relevant market and the shares in the market of the undertaking and/or undertakings against which the complaint is lodged, and determination, in the best possible way, of the geographic extension of the alleged infringement and explanation of the degree to which trade among Member States is being affected due to the alleged infringements.

(4) Details of the alleged infringement and proof: there should be a detailed indication of all the facts which show and/or prove infringement of sections 3 and/or 6 of the CPC Law of the CPC Law and/or Articles 101 and/or 102 TFEU, provision of every information available on the agreements, decisions or practices or concerted practices of the undertakings or associations of undertakings against whom the complaint is being lodged (i.e., text of the agreement, minutes of the meetings or negotiations, terms of transactions, business documents, circulars, correspondence, etc.), submission of statistical or other data which are in the possession of the person lodging the complaint and which are relevant to the facts under dispute (i.e., changes in prices, quantities, reductions, technical development, entrance bars, etc.), and submission of names and addresses of the persons who intend to be summoned as witnesses in order to testify in relation to the facts under dispute, as well as of the persons who have been affected by the alleged infringements.

(5) Legitimate interest: the person lodging the complaint must state in detail the way he has been affected and/or may be affected by the alleged infringements and whether he is justified to lodge the complaint.

307. Where a complaint concerns an act, omission, or behaviour, which does not fall within the competence of the CPC pursuant to the provisions of the CPC Law, the CPC shall inform the person who submitted the complaint accordingly. Furthermore, where a complaint concerns an act, omission or behaviour which does not fall within the CPC priorities, the CPC shall also inform the person who submitted the complaint accordingly. Upon receiving the complaint, the CPC shall instruct the Service to carry out preliminary investigation of the suspected infringement referred to in the complaint. It should be noted that the CPC has an obligation to examine all complaints submitted before it; this is not discretionary.[360] If, following the preliminary investigation of the Service, the CPC ascertains that the complaint lodged does not fall within the scope of application of the CPC Law and/or that there is not a reasonable ground for suspected infringement of sections 3 and/or 6 of the CPC Law, and/or Articles 101 and/or 102 TFEU, based on the information before it, then the CPC shall issue a relevant decision. Where the CPC, after a proper preliminary investigation carried out by the Service, ascertains that a prima facie case for the infringement mentioned in the complaint is made out, then further proceedings shall take place.

§2. Powers

I. Requests for Information

308. Pursuant to section 30 of the CPC Law, the CPC may collect information that is necessary for the exercise of its competences, powers and duties, both on its behalf as well as on behalf of other competition authorities, by addressing to that effect a written request to undertakings, associations of undertakings or other natural person or public or private entity. The powers of the CPC are analogous to the respective powers of the European Commission pursuant to Article 18 of the Modernisation Regulation. The CPC may further exercise analogous powers with regard to the assessment of concentrations, pursuant to section 42 of the Concentrations Law. When sending a request, the CPC shall specify the required information, the provisions of the CPC Law, or of the Modernisation Regulation on which the request is based, the reasoning of the request, a reasonable time limit fixed for the provision of information which may not be less than twenty days and the possible sanctions in the event of non-compliance with the obligation for the provision of information. The person, the undertaking or the association of undertakings, or the public or private entity to whom the request by the CPC is addressed to, shall be bound to provide in full and accurately, the required information within the time limit fixed. However, public entities may deny to provide the information requested, where this would be contrary to a provision of EU law or secondary legislation which aims at the harmonisation with EU Law.

309. Where the reply and/or the information provided by the person, the undertaking, the association of undertakings, the public or private entity, to whom the request is addressed, are incomplete, ambiguous or need further clarifications and/

360. Case 256/13, *Cyprus Telecommunications Authority v. Commission for the Protection of Competition*, 22 Dec. 2016 (in Greek).

or investigation, the CPC may submit a new request addressed to the said person, undertaking, association or undertakings, public or private entity in order to obtain all the information required and/or clarifications and/or explanations necessary. In the said request, there shall be specified a time limit for the provision of this information and/or clarifications which may not be less than seven days, as well as the possible sanctions in the event of non-compliance with the above obligation. In case of submission of a request pursuant to the above: (a) all the members of the managerial or administrative board or committee arranging the affairs of the legal person, (b) the general manager or director or managing director of the legal person, and (c) the persons who, according to the law or articles of association, are authorised to represent companies or associations having no legal personality, shall be bound to provide, in full and accurately, all the information required on behalf of the person, the undertaking or association of undertakings concerned, within the fixed time limit.

310. Lawyers duly authorised, may also supply on behalf of their clients all the information required, provided that the natural and legal persons who are obliged to provide information shall remain fully responsible for the full and in a timely manner provision of the said information. In case of omission to provide the required information within the time limit fixed, and/or of intentional or negligent provision of false, incomplete, inaccurate or misleading information, the CPC may impose on an undertaking, association of undertakings, natural or legal persons or private entities, an administrative fine of up to 1% of their turnover in the preceding financial year. In case of omission to provide the required information within the time limit fixed, the CPC may additionally impose on an undertaking, association of undertakings, natural or legal persons or private entities an administrative fine up to 5% of the average daily turnover during the preceding financial year for each day during which the infringement continue.

311. The information provided to the CPC in the exercise of its functions under this section may be used only for the purpose for which the information was required, with the exemption of those cases where this proves necessary for the application of the EU competition law. Furthermore, the person, the undertaking or the association of undertakings, the public or private entity to whom the request is addressed, with the provision of the information requested, may indicate documents, statements and any material it considers to contain confidential information and/or business secrets justifying its opinion, and providing a separate, non-confidential version within the time limit set by the CPC for notification of his opinion. If the person, the undertaking or the association of undertakings, or the private entity does not exercise its right to characterise any material as confidential, then the CPC may consider that the relevant documents, statements and the rest of the material do not contain confidential data and/or confidential information.

II. Investigating and Search Powers

312. The powers of the CPC to investigate and search are extremely wide, and far-reaching. Pursuant to section 30A of the CPC Law,[361] the CPC may, in the exercise of its competences, powers and duties, conduct interviews with every natural or legal person that consents to, in order to take statements regarding the subject of the investigation that it is conducting. The relevant interview may be conducted with all available means, and the CPC may register, in any form, the statements it takes from the interviewees, provided it informs them accordingly. Before the interview starts, the CPC notifies the intended interviewee, of the legal basis and the purpose of the interview, reminds him of its consensual nature and informs that that the interview is recorded. A copy of the recorded interview is available to the interviewee, who signs it after approving it. The powers of the CPC are analogous to the respective powers of the European Commission pursuant to Article 19 of the Modernisation Regulation. The CPC may further exercise analogous powers with regard to the assessment of concentrations, pursuant to section 43 of the Concentrations Law.

313. The CPC may also, in accordance with section 31 of the CPC Law, carry out, in the exercise of its competences, powers and duties, all necessary inspections of undertakings or associations of undertakings and for this purpose: (a) enter any office, premises, land and means of transport of undertakings and associations of undertakings, as well as in any other business premise with the exemption of residences; (b) examine the records, books, accounts, and other records related to the business, irrespective of the medium on which they are stored; (c) take or acquire, in any form, a copy or an extract form the records, books, accounts and any other document of business activity, irrespective of the medium in which they are stored, and wherever these are kept; (d) seal any business premises and records, books, accounts and other business records, for the period and to the extent necessary for the inspection; and (e) request any representative or member of staff of the undertaking or association of undertakings, for explanations on facts or documents relating to the subject matter and purpose of the inspection and record the answers. The powers of the CPC are analogous to the respective powers of the European Commission pursuant to Article 20 of the Modernisation Regulation.

314. Competent officers of the Service shall carry out inspections and exercise the relevant powers, at the request of the CPC. If deemed necessary by the CPC, the said officers shall be accompanied by other officers, namely public officers and/or officers of the wider public sector, and/or persons with special knowledge who may be employed by the CPC. The CPC's request shall be in writing and shall accurately specify the subject matter and purpose of the inspection, fix the date on which it is to begin, the provision on which this power of the CPC is based and the possible sanctions where the undertaking or association of undertakings refuses to comply with the CPC request. The inspections shall be carried out without prior notification of the undertaking or association of undertakings concerned, unless the

361. The section was added by the amending Law 41(I)/14.

CPC deems that the notification will assist the inquiry. The CPC may further, where appropriate, request the assistance of the police so as to become capable to exercise its powers. The undertaking or association of undertakings in which the inspection is conducted may consult its lawyer during the inspection, but his presence is not legally required for the validity of the inspection and/or defence for defective or non-compliance with the CPC request.

315. The CPC may impose on an undertaking or association of undertakings an administrative fine up to 1% of the turnover of the preceding financial year, where, either intentionally or negligently it produces the required records, books, accounts or other business records in incomplete or falsified manner, or where the undertaking or association of undertakings refuses to comply with the CPC's request for inspection. The CPC may additionally impose on the undertaking or association of undertakings concerned, an administrative fine up to 5% of the average daily turnover during the preceding financial year for each day it omits to comply with an order of the CPC to conduct an inspection. The information received by the CPC in the exercise of its competences may be used only for the purpose for which the inspection is allowed, with the exemption of those cases where this proves necessary for the application of the EU competition law. Every undertaking or association of undertakings which is subject to an inspection and every person to whom questions are submitted, or from whom explanations are requested, shall have the obligation to provide the investigating officer, as long as the latter reasonably demands, with any facilitation, any information, and any declaration on whether the information he provides to the investigating officer is true, whereas the investigating officer may demand and receive such facilitation, information and declaration.

316. The CPC may further carry out on-the-spot inspection of other premises, land and means of transport, upon the issue of a duly reasoned judicial warrant, pursuant to section 32 of the CPC Law. The powers of the CPC are analogous to the respective powers of the European Commission pursuant to Article 21 of the Modernisation Regulation. The CPC may further exercise analogous powers with regard to the assessment of concentrations, pursuant to section 44 of the Concentrations Law. The CPC may apply to the District Court to issue a warrant, ordering the conduct of an inspection, as long as there are reasonable suspicions that in that place there are records, accounts, books, other records related to the business or other particulars relating to the investigation of the case. If the Court is satisfied that the application submitted is justified by the facts stated on it, it shall issue a warrant, allowing the CPC to exercise, *mutatis mutandis*, the powers it may exercise when carrying out inspections in residences or any other premises, land and means of transport. The procedure of submission and hearing of the application shall be governed by a rule of court made by the Supreme Court, but until the making of such rule, the application should be supported by an affidavit of an authorised officer. No specialised rule of court has yet been made. Every search warrant shall be under the hand of a judge issuing the same, shall bear the date and time of issue, as well as a declaration of the judge that he has been justifiably satisfied on the need for the issue of the said warrant.

317. Article 22 of the Modernisation Regulation further provides that the competition authority of a Member State may, in its own territory, carry out any inspection or other fact-finding measure under its national law on behalf and for the account of the competition authority of another Member State in order to establish whether there has been an infringement of Article 101 or Article 102 TFEU. Any exchange and use of the information collected shall be carried out in accordance with Article 12 of the Modernisation Regulation. Article 12 provides that the information, including confidential information, may be used in evidence for the purpose of applying Article 101 or Article 102 TFEU, and in respect of the subject matter for which it was collected by the transmitting authority. However, where national competition law is applied in the same case and in parallel to EU competition law and does not lead to a different outcome, the information exchanged may also be used for the application of national competition law. The information exchanged can only be used in evidence to impose sanctions on natural persons where: (a) the law of the transmitting authority foresees sanctions of a similar kind in relation to an infringement of Articles 101 or 102 TFEU or, in the absence thereof; (b) the information has been collected in a way which respects the same level of protection of the rights of defence of natural persons as provided for under the national rules of the receiving authority. However, in this case, the information exchanged cannot be used by the receiving authority to impose custodial sanctions.

318. Moreover, pursuant to Article 22 §2 of the Modernisation Regulation, at the request of the European Commission, the competition authorities of the Member States shall undertake the inspections which the European Commission considers to be necessary, or which it has ordered by decision pursuant to Article 20 of the Modernisation Regulation. The officials of the competition authorities of the Member States who are responsible for conducting these inspections, as well as those authorised or appointed by them, shall exercise their powers in accordance with their national law. If so requested by the European Commission or by the competition authority of the Member State in whose territory the inspection is to be conducted, officials and other accompanying persons authorised by the European Commission may assist the officials of the authority concerned.

III. Cooperation with Other State Institutions

319. Section 23B of the CPC Law,[362] provides that the CPC may cooperate with regulatory or other authorities that exercise control in specific sectors of the economy of the Republic and offer its assistance, upon their request. The CPC may further request the assistance of the above regulatory or other authorities, when exercising its powers, and may conclude memoranda of cooperation with other national competition authorities. The Modernisation Regulation further introduces detailed provisions on cooperation between the European Commission and the competition authorities of the Member States. Article 11 of the Modernisation Regulation provides that the European Commission and the competition authorities of the

362. The section was added by the amending Law 41(I)/14.

Member States shall apply the EU competition rules in close cooperation. The European Commission shall, for this purpose, transmit to the competition authorities of the Member States copies of the most important documents it has collected with a view to applying its powers under the Modernisation Regulation. At the request of the competition authority of a Member State, the European Commission shall further provide it with a copy of other existing documents necessary for the assessment of the case.

320. When the competition authorities of the Member States are acting under Article 101 or Article 102 TFEU, they should inform the European Commission in writing before, or without delay after, commencing the first formal investigative measure. This information may also be made available to the competition authorities of the other Member States. They should further inform the European Commission no later than thirty days before the adoption of a decision requiring that an infringement be brought to an end, accepting commitments or withdrawing the benefit of a block exemption Regulation. To that effect, they shall provide the European Commission with a summary of the case, the envisaged decision or, in the absence thereof, any other document indicating the proposed course of action. This information may also be made available to the competition authorities of the other Member States. At the request of the European Commission, the acting competition authority shall make available to the European Commission other documents it holds which are necessary for the assessment of the case. The information supplied to the European Commission may be also made available to the competition authorities of the other Member States. National competition authorities may also exchange between themselves information necessary for the assessment of a case that they are dealing with under Article 101 or Article 102 TFEU. The competition authorities of the Member States may further consult the European Commission on any case involving the application of EU law.

321. The initiation by the European Commission of proceedings for the adoption of a decision shall relieve the competition authorities of the Member States of their competence to apply Articles 101 and 102 TFEU. If a competition authority of a Member State is already acting on a case, the European Commission shall only initiate proceedings after consulting with that national competition authority. Moreover, Article 13 of the Modernisation Regulation provides that where the competition authorities of two or more Member States have received a complaint, or are acting on their own initiative under Article 101 or Article 102 TFEU, against the same agreement, decision of an association or practice, the fact that one authority is dealing with the case shall be sufficient grounds for the others to suspend the proceedings before them or to reject the complaint. The European Commission may likewise reject a complaint on the ground that a competition authority of a Member State is dealing with the case. Where a competition authority of a Member State or the European Commission has received a complaint against an agreement, decision of an association or practice which has already been dealt with by another competition authority, it may reject it.

322. A representative from the CPC, as well as other competition authorities of the Member States further participates in the Advisory Committee on Restrictive Practices and Dominant Positions, that the European Commission should consult prior to the taking of decisions pursuant to Article 14 of the Modernisation Regulation.[363] Section 29 of the CPC Law provides that the CPC shall participate in the meetings of the Advisory Committee with a member of the CPC, or of the staff of the Service, designated by the CPC. The consultations of the Advisory Committee may take place, pursuant to Article 14 of the Modernisation Regulation, at a meeting convened and chaired by the European Commission, together with a summary of the case, an indication of the most important documents and a preliminary draft decision. The Advisory Committee shall deliver a written opinion on the European Commission's preliminary draft decision. It may deliver an opinion even if some members are absent and are not represented. At the request of one or several members, the positions stated in the opinion shall be reasoned. Consultation may also take place by written procedure. However, if any Member State so requests, the European Commission shall convene a meeting. The European Commission should take the utmost account of the opinion delivered by the Advisory Committee, and should inform the Committee of the manner in which its opinion has been taken into account. Where the Advisory Committee delivers a written opinion, this opinion shall be appended to the draft decision. If the Advisory Committee recommends publication of the opinion, the European Commission shall carry out such publication taking into account the legitimate interest of undertakings in the protection of their business secrets.

323. At the request of a competition authority of a Member State, the European Commission should further include on the agenda of the Advisory Committee, cases that are being dealt with by a competition authority of a Member State under Article 101 or Article 102 TFEU. The European Commission may also do so on its own initiative. In either case, the European Commission shall inform the competition authority concerned. A request may in particular be made by a competition authority of a Member State in respect of a case where the European Commission intends to initiate proceedings with the effect of relieving the national competition authority of its competences to further pursue the matter. It should be noted, however, that the Advisory Committee shall not issue opinions on cases dealt with by competition authorities of the Member States.

324. The competition authorities of the Member States, acting on their own initiative, may also cooperate with the national courts of their Member States, pursuant to Article 15 §3 of the Modernisation Regulation. They may accordingly submit written observations to the national courts of their Member State on issues relating to the application of Article 101 or Article 102 TFEU, and with the permission of the court in question, they may also submit oral observations. Where the coherent application of Article 101 or Article 102 TFEU so requires, the European Commission, acting on its own initiative, may also submit written observations to courts of

363. *See also* Working Arrangements for the Functioning of the Advisory Committee on Restrictive Practices and Dominant Position Annex C (2019) 23 10 final.

the Member States, and with the permission of the court in question, it may also make oral observations. The competition authorities of the Member States and the European Commission may request the relevant court of the Member State to transmit or ensure the transmission to them of any documents necessary for the assessment of the case, but only for the purpose of the preparation of their observations only, the competition.

325. In view of the need to safeguard the uniform application of EU competition law, Article 16 of the Modernisation Regulation provides that when the competition authorities of the Member States rule on agreements, decisions or practices under Article 101 or Article 102 TFEU, which are already the subject of a European Commission decision, they cannot take decisions which would run counter to the decision adopted by the European Commission. Similarly, when national courts rule on agreements, decisions or practices under Article 101 or Article 102 TFEU, which are already the subject of a European Commission decision, they cannot take decisions running counter to the decision adopted by the European Commission. They must also avoid giving decisions which would conflict with a decision contemplated by the European Commission in proceedings it has initiated. To that effect, the national court may assess whether it is necessary to stay its proceedings.

§3. Right of Defence

I. Content and Notification of Opening Decisions

326. The CPC shall, pursuant to section 17 of the CPC Law, decide to initiate proceedings for the investigation of an infringement, as long as it finds, following a proper preliminary investigation, that there is possible infringement of the provisions of sections 3 and/or 6 of the CPC Law and/or Articles 101 and/or 102 TFEU. If this is the case, then the CPC shall prepare a written statement in order to inform the undertakings or associations of undertakings on the objections raised to their detriment. The said statement of objections shall be served on them, or on a person duly authorised by the said undertakings or associations of undertakings, in any manner of summon which is permissible under section 45 of the CPC Law. Section 45 allows for the summons of undertakings or associations of undertakings or any other person before the CPC: (a) by the dispatch of a double-registered letter to the principal place of business of the undertaking, the association of undertakings or the person summoned; (b) through fax or any other electronic way to the principal place of business of the undertaking, the association of undertakings or the person summoned; or (c) by hand delivery to a director, or official or authorised person of the undertaking, the association of undertakings or the person summoned, irrespective of the place he was found. Where the existing information before the CPC is changed, or new information arises, the CPC may proceed to the modification of any objections raised against the undertakings or associations of undertakings concerned and the preparation and communication of a modified statement of objections to the undertakings or associations of undertakings concerned.

II. Proceedings: Hearings, Access to File, and Briefs

327. During the proceedings before the CPC for the ex-officio investigation of infringements, or for the investigation of complaints lodged pursuant to the CPC Law, the following shall be allowed to be present upon invitation from the CPC: (a) the persons who lodged the complaint, personally, through an authorised lawyer or personally with an authorised lawyer; (b) the persons involved in the proceedings and/or the complaint before the CPC; (c) any person, who may, at the CPC's discretion, help in the investigation of the infringement and/or the complaint. In addition, any member of the staff who serves at the Service may be present. All guests should withdraw before the beginning of the consultation of the CPC to reach its decision; however, it would seem that members of the Service may remain even after the beginning of the consultation of the CPC to reach its decision, as a statutory exception from the general principles of administrative law. Section 21 §2 of the General Principles of Administrative Law, Law 158(I)/99 (Principles of Administrative Law), provides that employees should leave prior to the beginning of the consultation for reaching a decision by the administrative organ; however, statute may introduce further exceptions and this seems to be such a case.

328. The CPC should set a reasonable, under the circumstances, time limit to the persons summoned. The time limit may be justifiably extended. The CPC should grant every possible opportunity to the persons present before it, to submit written observations on the objections raised to their detriment and, to this effect, a reasonable time limit shall be set, which may be justifiably extended. Persons submitting written observations should clearly indicate any confidential information and/or business secrets. The CPC shall not, however, be bound to take into account written observations, submitted after the expiration of the set time limit. Where the undertaking or association of undertakings, on which the statement of objections was served, omits and/or refuses to submit any written observations in respect of the objections raised against it within the time limit set, the CPC may proceed to the issue of a decision for the alleged infringements included in the statement of objections. The interested persons shall also be entitled to request that they further expand on the arguments they submitted with their written observations, in the context of oral proceedings before the CPC. In such a case the CPC may, by its decision, set a time limit for the development of oral arguments.

329. The CPC shall not be bound to communicate to the undertaking or association of undertakings against which the complaint or the ex-officio investigation is turned to, the whole file formed by it on the case; however, it shall be bound to communicate to it all of those documents of the file on which it intends to base its decision, with the exception of those documents constituting business secrets. If the documents are already available to the undertaking or association of undertakings, the CPC must indicate them to the undertaking in writing, so that this undertaking or association of undertakings be informed in due course of all the documents that shall be used by the CPC as evidence. The CPC shall not be allowed to base its decision on a document that has not been communicated or indicated to the undertaking or association of undertakings against which the complaint or the ex-officio investigation is turned to. During the proceedings before the CPC, if the CPC intends to base its decision on a document that it has not communicated or indicated to the undertaking or association of undertakings against which the complaint or the ex-officio investigation is turned to, then it shall be to communicate the said document to the said undertaking or association of undertakings and shall grant to it reasonable time to examine the said document. The internal workings of the CPC shall be determined by the CPC itself, subject to the Principles of Administrative Law.

III. Decision

330. Section 18 of the CPC Law provides that the decision of the CPC should be duly reasoned, and should be communicated to every undertaking or association of undertakings concerned and published in the Official Gazette of the Republic. The decision should not, however, disclose any information that has been characterised as being of a confidential nature. The decisions of the CPC shall take effect from the date of their communication, provided that a defective communication or publication shall not affect the validity of the decision.

Chapter 2. Voluntary Notifications and Clearance Decisions Merger Control

§1. Preliminary Filing Obligations

I. Criteria and Thresholds

331. The Concentrations Law applies to all concentrations of major importance. Section 3 of the Concentrations Law defines an act of concentration of undertakings as one of major importance, where: (a) the aggregate turnover achieved by each of at least two of the participating undertakings is more than EUR 3,500,000, and at least two of the participating undertakings achieve turnover within the Republic of Cyprus, and at least EUR 3,500,000 out of the aggregate turnover of all the participating undertakings is achieved within the Republic of Cyprus, or (b) this is declared as such by an order of the Minister of Energy, Commerce, and Industry. The Minister may declare a concentration as one of major importance, pursuant to sections 5 and 35 of the Concentrations Law, even if it does not fulfil the criteria of (a) above, if he considers that the concentration is one of major public interest regarding the effect it may have on public security, the pluralism of the media and the principles of sound administration. The Council of Ministers may, following a reasoned opinion of the CPC, amend from time to time the minimum turnovers by order published in the Official Gazette of the Republic.

332. The Concentrations Law does not apply in cases where a concentration falls within the scope of application of the Mergers Regulation. The Mergers Regulation applies to concentrations which have a Community dimension, namely where: (a) (i) the combined aggregate worldwide turnover of all the undertakings concerned is more than EUR 5,000 million, (ii) the aggregate Community-wide turnover of each of at least two of the undertakings concerned is more than EUR 250 million, (iii) unless each of the undertakings concerned achieves more than two-thirds of its aggregate Community-wide turnover within one and the same Member State; or (b) (i) the combined aggregate worldwide turnover of all the undertakings concerned is more than EUR 2,500 million, (ii) in each of at least three Member States, the combined aggregate turnover of all the undertakings concerned is more than EUR 100 million, (iii) in each of at least three Member States included for the purpose of (ii) above, the aggregate turnover of each of at least two of the undertakings concerned is more than EUR 25 million, and (iv) the aggregate Community-wide turnover of each of at least two of the undertakings concerned is more than EUR 100 million, (v) unless each of the undertakings concerned achieves more than two-thirds of its aggregate Community-wide turnover within one and the same Member State.

II. Turnover Calculation

333. For the purposes of applying the thresholds, the turnover shall be calculated in accordance with the provisions of Schedule II of the Concentrations. These correspond to the provisions for calculating turnover found in Article 5 of the Mergers Regulation. The aggregate turnover shall comprise the amounts derived from the sale of products and the provision of services by the undertakings concerned during the preceding financial year and corresponding to the ordinary activities of the undertakings, after deduction of sales rebates, of value added tax and other taxes directly related to turnover. Where the concentration consists of the acquisition of parts of one or more undertakings, whether or not constituted as legal entities, only the turnover relating to the parts which are the subject of the transaction shall be taken into account with regard to the seller or sellers. For a bank or other credit institution, the 1/10 of the balance sheet of the last financial year shall be used instead of turnover. For an insurance company, the value of the gross premiums during the last financial year shall be used instead of turnover. This shall comprise all amounts received or receivable in respect of insurance contracts concluded by it or on its behalf, including outgoing reinsurance premiums and after deduction of taxes and parafiscal contributions or levies charged by reference to the amounts of individual premiums or the total volume of premiums.

334. The aggregate turnover of a participating undertaking shall not include internal transactions carried out between any of the undertakings referred to in paragraph 4 of Schedule II of the Concentrations Law, namely: (a) the undertakings concerned; (b) those undertakings in which the undertaking concerned directly or indirectly: (i) owns more than half the capital or business assets, or (ii) has more than half of the voting rights, or (iii) has the power to appoint more than half the members of the supervisory or administrative board or the bodies legally representing the undertakings concerned, or (iv) has the right to manage the affairs of the undertakings; (c) those undertakings which have in the undertaking concerned the rights or powers referred to in (b) above; (d) those undertakings in which an undertaking as referred to in (c) above has the rights or powers referred to in (b) above; (e) those undertakings in which two or more undertakings as referred to in subparagraphs (a)–(d) above jointly have the rights or powers referred to in subparagraph (b) above.

335. Where undertakings participating in the concentration jointly have the rights or powers listed in (b) above, in calculating the turnover of the participating undertakings no account shall be taken of the turnover resulting from the sale of products or the provision of services between the joint undertaking and each one of the participating undertakings or any other undertaking connected with any one of them, within the meaning of (b)–(e) above. Account shall be taken of the turnover resulting from the sale of products or the provision of services between the joint undertaking and any third undertaking. The said turnover shall be apportioned equally among the undertakings concerned. The financial data requested in the notification form is expressed in Euro and on the basis of the average exchange rate for the years or other periods of reference.

III. Market Share Calculation

336. The affected markets for calculating the market share are defined in Schedule I of the Concentrations Law. A relevant product market comprises all products and/or services, which are regarded as interchangeable or substitutable by the consumer by reason of their characteristics, prices and intended use. A relevant product market may, in certain cases, be composed of specific individual products and/or services which present to a large extent identical physical or technical characteristics and are interchangeable. Factors relevant to the assessment of the relevant product market include, among others, the analysis of the reasons for which certain products or services are included in these markets and why others are excluded on the basis of the abovementioned definition and taking into consideration, for example, the possibility of substitutability of products and services, the prices, the cross-price elasticity of demand or other relevant factors (e.g., the possibility of substitutability from the demand side in appropriate cases).

337. The relevant geographic market comprises the area in which the participating undertakings are involved in the supply and demand of relevant products or services, in which the conditions of competition are sufficiently homogeneous and which can be distinguished from neighbouring geographic areas because, in particular, conditions of competition are appreciably different in those areas. Factors relevant to the assessment of the relevant geographic market are, indicatively, the nature and characteristics of the relevant products or services, the existence of entry barriers into the market, the consumer preferences, the substantial differences in the undertakings' market shares between neighbouring geographic areas and substantial price differences.

338. Affected markets consist of all the relevant product markets and geographic markets as well as the plausible interchangeable relevant product markets and geographic markets in the territory of the Republic, where: (a) two or more of the parties to the concentration are engaged in business activities in the same product market (horizontal relationship), and where the concentration will lead to a combined market share of 15% or more; or (b) any of the parties to the concentration are engaged in business activities in a product market which is upstream or downstream of a product market in which any other party to the concentration is engaged (vertical relationship) and provided any of the individual or combined market shares of these undertakings is 25% or more, regardless of whether there is or is not any existing supplier-customer relationship between the parties to the concentration.

339. Further to the affected markets, the notified concentration may have significant implications in other markets as well, for example when: (a) Any of the participating parties has a market share of more than 25% and any other participating party is a potential competitor in the said market. An undertaking may be considered as a potential competitor, particularly, if it plans to enter into the market or if it has developed or pursued such plans during the last three years; (b) any of the participating parties has a market share of more than 25% and any other participating party holds important intellectual property rights in the said market; (c) any of the participating parties is active in a neighbouring product market which is closely related to a product market, which is a neighbouring market closely related to a product market in which any other participating party is active, and the individual or combined market shares of the parties in any of the said markets is at least 25%. The product markets are closely related neighbouring markets, if the products are complementary to each other or if they belong in a spectrum of products which are generally purchased by the same group of clients for the same end use.

§2. Structure of Proceedings

I. Preliminary Assessment and Full Investigation

A. *Notification*

340. Acts of concentration of major importance to which the Concentrations Law applies, should, by virtue to section 10 of the Concentrations Law, be notified to the Service of the CPC in writing, prior to their implementation and following the conclusion of the agreement, the announcement of the public bid or the acquisition of a controlling interest. Notification may also be made where the participating undertakings demonstrate to the CPC a good faith intention to conclude an agreement or, in the case of a public bid, where they have announced an intention or final decision to make such a bid, provided that the intended agreement or bid would result in a concentration of a major importance. The acts of concentration which must be notified in accordance with the above, and constituting a merger or acquisition of joint control, shall be notified jointly or separately by those who participate in these acts; in all other cases the obligation of notification shall be borne by the person or undertaking acquiring control. The Service shall publish the fact of the notification in the Official Gazette of the Republic indicating the names of the participating undertakings, the nature of the concentration and the economic sectors involved. In so doing, the Service should take into account, as far as possible, the legitimate interest of the affected undertakings in the protection of their business secrets. The Service should further inform the Minister in relation to the concentration as soon as it is received, pursuant to section 16 of the Concentrations Law.

341. The notifications of concentrations should contain the information referred to in Schedule III of the Concentrations Law. The person who has the obligation for notification should state in relation to every participating undertaking, their name and address, the nature of the commercial activity in which they are engaged, the name, address, telephone number and fax number of the person through whom one may communicate with the undertaking and the position the said person holds in it. When one or more representatives have been authorised to sign the notification on behalf of one or more of the participating undertakings, the notification must be accompanied by the relevant receipt and each one of the representatives should be identified by his name, address, telephone number and fax number and the passport or ID number. The completed notification should further be accompanied by the following supporting documents: (a) copies of the final or most recent documents bringing about the concentration, whether by agreement or following a public announcement of the intention or final decision of acquisition proposal; (b) in the case of final decision of acquisition proposal, a copy of the public announcement and of the offer document, if this is available, and in the case of a public bid, a copy of the public announcement of the intention of a bid. If those documents are not available at the time of notification, then, copies of those documents should be submitted as soon as possible and, in any case, not later than when they are posted to those to whom they must be sent; (c) copies of the most recent annual reports and audited financial statements of all the parties to the concentration; (d) copies of reports or analyses prepared for the purposes of the concentration from which information has been acquired for the fulfilment of the conditions, (e) a list and a short description of the contents of all the other analyses, reports, studies and surveys prepared by or for any of those who have the obligation for notification for the purpose of assessing or analysing the proposed concentration with respect to the conditions of competition, the competitors (actual and potential) and the market conditions. Each document in the list must include the name and position held by its author.

342. The notification should be submitted in one of the official languages of the Republic, i.e., Greek or Turkish. However, the supporting documents may be submitted in English, instead of Greek. If these documents have been written in original language other than these languages, the document should be submitted both in the original language as well as in translation into one of the official languages of the Republic. The supporting documents may be originals or copies of the originals. In the latter case, the notifying party shall confirm that the said copies are true and complete. The person who has the obligation for notification must submit to the offices of the CPC in print two copies and in electronic form all the documents of the notification. The copy of the agreement required for the purposes of the Concentrations Law should be stamped, unless the agreement was concluded in a country where the national legislation does not require the stamping of agreements.

343. The notification should further contain details of the concentration, namely: (a) summary description of the nature and scope of the concentration, including details of: (i) the instances referred to in sections 3 and 6 of the Concentrations Law which created the circumstances from which the concentration arose, (ii) whether the whole or parts of the undertakings are subject to the concentration, (iii) in the case of a public tender, whether the tender for the shares of one party by another party has the support of the administrative board or of the legal representative of the former party; (b) explanation of the purpose of the concentration; (c) whether the concentration has been notified to other competition authorities of the Member States, and if yes, to which, when, and whether it has received approval; (d) a description of the financial and structural details of the concentration, including: (i) any financial or other support received from any source (including public authorities) by any of the participants in the concentration, (ii) the proposed structure of ownership and control after the completion of the concentration, (iii) the proposed or expected date of appearance of any major events designed to bring about the completion of the concentration; (e) details for each of the undertakings regarding the turnover in the Republic of Cyprus and worldwide turnover, and for every participant in the concentration regarding profits before the deduction of taxes and the number of persons employed within and outside the Republic of Cyprus.

344. For each of the parties to the concentration, details must be given about all undertakings belonging to the same group, mentioning in each case the nature of the controlling interest and the ways in which it has been acquired. For each group of undertakings details must be given about any other undertakings which are active in the affected markets: (a) in which the group holds, either alone or together with other groups, at least 10% of the shares or voting rights, or (b) which have as members of their boards of directors the members of the boards of directors of this group, mentioning in each case the names of the members concerned. There should also be a description and analysis of all the relevant product markets and relevant geographic markets, as well as of all the reasonable alternative definitions of relevant product and geographic markets concerning the concentration, and a description and analysis of the affected markets and other markets where the notified concentration might have significant implications.

345. On the basis of the definitions given for every affected market and for every other market where the notified concentration might have significant implications the person who has the obligation for notification should mention or estimate, where necessary: (a) the value of the turnover in the market and, when it is deemed expedient, the volume in production units (excluding exports, but including imports), the basis and the sources of calculations and, where available, documents for the confirmation of these calculations shall be mentioned; (b) the expected development of demand; (c) the turnover of each group of undertakings; (d) the market share of each one of the competitors of each of the parties to the concentration and the name, address, telephone and fax numbers of each one of these competitors (where known); (e) by estimation, the HHI index, before and after the concentration, and the percentage of the market shares used as a basis for the calculation of the HHI; (f) the value of the imports into this market and their origin, including the proportion of these imports which is effected by the groups of undertakings; (g) the tariff and non-tariff barriers to imports; (h) the importance of economies of scale for the production or distribution of the products in the affected markets; (i) the way that the planned concentration might affect the interests of intermediate and ultimate consumers.

346. The person who has the obligation for notification should further state whether there has been any significant entry of any undertaking in the market in the last five years and whether any such entry is likely in the following five years, and describe the factors which affect the entry into the market, taking into account the cost of entry on a viable production scale, the need for government authorisation or compliance with specific legal or institutional standards or controls, the access to raw materials, and the existence and importance of patents or agreements on technical know-how in the market. They should further describe the importance of R&D to the extent that they affect the ability of the undertaking operating in the market to compete in the long term and explain the nature of the R&D in the market carried out by groups of undertakings, and: (a) estimate the cost of R&D as a percentage of the turnover; (b) describe the major innovations that have been resulted from the R&D in the last five years and mention the undertakings which brought about these innovations in the market; and (c) describe the extent to which the groups of undertakings or the undertakings included therein are franchisers or holders of patents or participate in know-how agreements which affect the market. It is also their obligation to explain the distribution systems and the services networks that exist on the market, mentioning in particular any undertakings constituting part of the groups of undertakings and providing distribution or maintenance services to a significant extent. Furthermore, they should describe the structure of supply and demand mentioning in particular, any easily definable categories of suppliers or customers, and the extent to which public authorities, government services or state undertakings are suppliers or customers, provide details of the five largest suppliers of the parties to the concentration and of their individual shares as regards the supplies purchased by these parties, provide details of the five largest customers of the parties to the concentration and of their individual shares as regards the sales of the parties to the concentration to these customers. Finally, they should record the names, addresses and telephone and fax numbers of the main commercial contacts in the market.

347. In case of acquisition of undertakings, it must be answered whether two or more parent undertakings retain to a significant extent activities in the same market with the joint venture, or in a market which is downstream or upstream from that of the joint venture, or in a neighbouring market closely related to this market. In case of an affirmative answer, it should be indicated for each one of the said markets: (a) the turnover of each parent undertaking in the preceding year; (b) the economic significance of the activities of the joint venture in relation to this turnover; (c) the market share of each parent undertaking. It should further be justified why the creation of the joint venture does not lead to coordination between independent undertakings that restricts competition within the meaning of section 3 of the Concentrations Law, in order for the CPC to be in position to fully appraise the case. Similarly, if the answer is negative, the answer should be justified.

348. Where any of the information included in the notification is considered as confidential, or as a business secret, by the parties concerned by the concentration because its disclosure will damage the undertakings concerned by the concentration, this must be clearly marked as confidential or as a business secret and the reasons justifying why this information should not be published or disclosed must be mentioned. Such information may, in exceptional cases, be submitted in a separate envelope and due reference must be made in the text of the notification. All the parties to the concentration must attach to the notification a signed statement by them certifying that all the information included in this notification is to the best of their knowledge and belief true, that all estimates are the best that may be given and ascertained, that all the opinions expressed are sincere and that they are aware of the potential administrative sanctions. Finally, for the notification to be accepted, a fee of EUR 1,000 should be paid. The full investigation proceedings will commence upon the payment to the CPC of a fee of EUR 6,000. The Minister of Energy, Commerce, and Industry may, by virtue of section 12 §3 of the Concentrations Law, with an order published in the Official Gazette of the Republic, amend the notification fees, pursuant to a reasoned opinion of the CPC.

349. The participating undertakings may revoke the notification of concentration provided that they submit to the CPC a request for revocation, pursuant to section 18 of the Concentrations Law. The CPC shall publish its decision of approval of the request for revocation of concentration in the Official Gazette of the Republic and shall, at the same time, inform the Minister. Where a concentration which must be notified is not notified, but comes to the knowledge of the Service in another way, the Service should, pursuant to section 13 of the Concentrations Law, immediately inform those who have the obligation to notify about their obligation to notify pursuant to the Concentrations Law, and upon receipt of the notification, proceed as if the conditions had been met from the start, provided that for the purposes of calculating further time limits the actual date of receipt of the notification is taken into account.

B. Preliminary Assessment

350. Where an act of concentration is notified to the Service, the Service shall examine it in order to ascertain whether it complies fully with the conditions of Schedule III and, if it is ascertained that a notification does not comply fully with such conditions, the Service shall immediately request, by virtue of section 15 of the Concentrations Law, the additional information required for securing compliance. The Service should examine the notification as soon as it is received and after ascertaining that the notification fully complies with the conditions of Schedule III, it shall carry out a preliminary evaluation and shall prepare a written report to the CPC, pursuant to section 17 of the Concentrations Law, in which it shall include its reasoned opinion, as follows: (a) The concentration notified does not fall within the scope of application of the Concentrations Law, and/or within the meaning of concentration; or (b) the concentration notified, despite falling within the scope of application of the Concentrations Law and within the meaning of concentration, does not raise serious doubts as to its compatibility with the functioning of competition in the market and it can be declared as being compatible with the functioning of competition in the market; or (c) the concentration notified falls within the scope of application of the Concentrations Law and the meaning of concentration, raises serious doubts as to its compatibility with the functioning of competition in the market and it is recommended to initiate the full investigation proceedings.

C. Full Investigation

351. Where the CPC decides to initiate the full investigation proceedings, it shall instruct the Service to carry out a full investigation in relation to the concentration, pursuant to section 25 of the Concentrations Law. In such a case, the Service shall as soon as possible: (a) obtain from the notifying party or from other participants in the concentration or from other third persons, any additional information which it deems necessary for the completion of the investigation; (b) notify the participating undertakings that they may modify the concentration or offer commitments, in order for the doubts as to the compatibility of the notification with the requirements of market to be removed; the modifications and commitments suggested by the undertakings concerned by the concentration shall be submitted to the Service within the time limit defined by the Service, according to Schedule IV; (c) in light of the additional information it may have obtained, and any suggested modifications and/or commitments, examine whether and to what extent the doubts have been removed, and if these doubts have not been removed, the Service may, if it finds any differentiations or modifications in the circumstances under which the concentration has been established which may result in the removal of the doubts, commence negotiations with the participating undertakings.

352. In the case of a concentration for which a full investigation is carried out, the Service may, by virtue of section 26 of the Concentrations Law, and following an application by persons who may be affected directly by the decision of the CPC, but who do not participate in the concentration, afford to them a suitable opportunity of expressing their views regarding the concentration in such a manner and at such time as not to violate the time limit. On completion of the above actions, the Service shall prepare a report of findings to be submitted to the CPC, pursuant to section 27 of the Concentrations Law, making reference to its findings regarding: (a) whether the doubts have been removed or may be removed as a result of additional information that may have been obtained, and/or any amendments to the concentration and/or the suggested commitments, and/or any negotiations undertaken, or (b) whether the doubts continue to remain.

353. Commitments by the undertakings concerned should be notified to the CPC pursuant to Schedule IV of the Concentrations Law. The undertakings should provide detailed information on the object of the commitments offered, and the conditions for their implementation. In cases where the commitments offered consist in the divestiture of a business, the specific information should be included. The undertaking should provide evidence proving the suitability of the commitments offered, to remove the significant impediment of effective competition identified by the CPC. The undertaking should thus provide a non-confidential summary of the nature and scope of the commitments offered and why, in their view, they are suitable to remove any significant impediment to effective competition. The CPC may use this summary for the market test of the commitments offered with third parties.

354. There should be further information on a business to be divested In case the commitments offered consist in the divestiture of a business, and in particular general information on the business to be divested, including: (a) a description of the business to be divested, in general, including the entities belonging to it, their seat and place of management, other locations for production or provision of services, the general functional structure and any other relevant information relating to the administrative structure of the business to be divested; (b) a report and description of any legal obstacles for the transfer of the business to be divested or the assets to be sold, including third-party rights and administrative authorisations required; (c) a list and description of the products manufactured or services provided, in particular their technical and other characteristics, the brand names involved, the turnover generated with each of these products or services, and any innovations or new products or services planned; (d) a description of the level on which the essential functions of the business to be divested are operated if they are not operated on the level of the business to be divested itself, including such functions as R&D, production, marketing and sales, logistics, customers, suppliers, and IT systems. The description should contain the role performed by those other levels, the relations with the business to be divested and the resources (personnel, assets, financial resources, etc.) involved in the function; (e) a description in detail of the links between the business to be divested and other undertakings controlled by the notifying parties(irrespective of the direction of the link), such as: (i) supply, production, distribution, service or other contracts, (ii) shared tangible or intangible assets, (iii) shared or seconded personnel, (iv) shared IT systems or other systems, and (v) shared customers; (f) a description, in general terms, of all relevant tangible and intangible assets used and/or owned by the business to be divested, including, in any case, IP rights and brand names; (g) an organisational chart mentioning the number of personnel currently working in each of the functions of the business to be divested and a list of those employees who are indispensable for the operation of the business to be divested, describing their functions; (h) A description of the customers of the business to be divested, including a list of customers, a description of the corresponding records available, provision of the total turnover generated by the business to be divested with each of these customers (in Euro and as percentage of the total turnover of business to be divested); (i) the financial data for the business to be divested, including the turnover and the Earnings Before Interest, Tax, Depreciation and Amortisation (EBITDA) achieved in the last two years, and the forecast for the next two years; (j) Identification and description of any changes that have occurred in the last two years, in the organisation of the business to be divested or in the links with other undertakings controlled by the notifying parties; (k) identification and description of any changes, planned for the next two years, in the organisation of the business to be divested or in the links with other undertakings controlled by the notifying parties. There should also be included general information on the business to be divested as described in the commitments, a description of the areas where the business to be divested as set out in the commitments offered differs from the nature and scope of the business as currently operated, and an analysis of the reasons why, the business will be acquired by a suitable purchaser in the time-frame proposed in the commitments offered.

II. Time Framework

355. The implementation of a concentration, which falls within the scope of application of the Concentrations Law, is prohibited, until: the notifying party receives a notice of approval from the Service, or the time limit expires without the notice having been forwarded by the Service. The Service should, by virtue of section 23 of the Concentrations Law, inform the interest parties of the preliminary decision of the CPC within one month from the date of receipt of the notification from the Service or, as the case may be, from the date on which the Service receives the additional information which is necessary for securing compliance of the notification with the conditions of Schedule III. In case where the notification fee has not been paid, the time limit will commence to count from the date on which the notification fee is paid. Where due to the exceptional volume or complexity of the information forwarded in the relevant notification, the Service ascertains that the time limit cannot be kept, it has the obligation, without delay and, in any case, within seven days at the latest before the expiry of the said time limit, after consultation with the Chair of the CPC, to inform the notifying party that the said time limit is extended by fourteen days. When the time limit expires, without the notice having been forwarded by the Service to the notifying party, the concentration in question is considered to have been declared compatible with the market, by virtue of section 24 of the Concentrations Law.

356. The Service has an obligation to submit to the CPC the report of its findings within three months at the latest from the date of receipt of the notification from the Service or, as the case may be, from the date on which the Service received the additional information which is necessary for securing compliance with the conditions of Schedule III. Where the notification fee has not been paid, the time limit with regard to the report of the Service will commence to count from the date on which the notification fee is paid. Where due to the exceptional volume or complexity of the information forwarded in the relevant notification, the Service ascertains that the time limit cannot be met, it has the obligation, pursuant to section 30 of the Concentrations Law, to inform the notifying party that the said time limit is extended by fourteen days. The information must be given without delay, and, in any case, within seven days at the latest before the expiry of the time limit, after consultation with the Chairperson of the CPC. If any delay in the fulfilment by the Service or the CPC of any of their obligations is due to an omission on behalf of any of the participants in the specific concentration or any representative thereof, the time limits shall be subject to such extension as in the opinion of the CPC is reasonably necessary for the fulfilment of the said obligations.

III. Right of Defence

357. Before taking any decision, and subject always to the time limits referred to in previous paragraphs, the CPC may, if it considers expedient, carry out negotiations, hearings or discussions with any person who, at the discretion of the CPC, may help at the appraisal of the concentration. Furthermore, a right to a hearing before the CPC is granted pursuant to section 33 of the Concentrations Law. Before taking any decision, the representatives of the participating undertakings, in person or by proxy or in person and with proxy and/or any interested or other persons who may be affected directly by the decision of the CPC, shall appear before the CPC, upon a written request, to present their arguments in the context of an oral hearing.

358. In case of any infringements of the provisions of the Concentrations Law, the CPC shall, by virtue of section 34 of the Concentrations Law, prepare a statement of objections, and shall issue a summons to the persons against whom the statement of objections has been addressed and to any person who, at the discretion of the CPC, may help at the examination of the infringement requiring them to appear before it for a hearing. A statement of objections shall be communicated to the persons against whom it has been addressed. The CPC may further communicate the statement of objections to any other person summoned to appear before it for a hearing. The persons to whom the statement of objections has been communicated shall be given every possible opportunity of submitting written observations on the statement of objections of the CPC, and to this effect, a reasonable time limit shall be set, which may be justifiably extended. The CPC shall not, however, be bound to take into account written observations submitted after the expiry of the set time limit. When submitting their written observations, the persons shall clearly define any confidential information and/or any business secrets, analysing the reasons why they should not be published or disclosed as well as the reasons why their disclosure will damage the undertakings, submitting at the same time the non-confidential version of their written observations. In case where the persons to whom the statement of objections has been communicated, omit and/or refuse to submit any written observations in relation to the statement of objections of the CPC within the time limit set, the CPC may proceed to take a decision on the matter.

359. The persons summoned shall have, within the context of the written observations submitted by them, the right to request the development of their arguments in the context of an oral hearing before the CPC. The CPC may, by its decision, set a time limit for the development of the arguments. In the context of the proceedings, the CPC shall not be bound to communicate to the person to whom the statement of objections has been addressed the whole file formed by it on the concentration; however, it shall be bound to communicate to this person all of those documents of the file, that will be used by it as evidence for the compilation of the statement of objections and then for the taking of its decision, with the exception of those documents constituting business secrets; or if those documents are already accessible to the said person, it shall indicate them to him in writing, so that this person or other third person concerned be informed in due course of all the documents that will be used by the CPC. Moreover, the CPC shall not be allowed to base its decision on a document that has not been communicated or indicated to a person to whom the statement of objections has been addressed. If the CPC intends, during the proceedings before it, to base its decision on a document that it has not communicated or indicated to a person to whom the statement of objections has been addressed, it shall be bound to communicate the said document to the said person and shall grant to it reasonable time to examine it.

§3. Clearance and Conditional Clearance

I. Conditions and Undertakings

A. Content

360. In making its appraisal, the CPC shall take into account, by virtue of section 19 of the Concentrations Law: (a) the need to maintain and develop conditions of effective competition within the relevant markets in view of, among other things, the structure of the affected markets, the structure of other markets where the notified concentration might have significant implications and the actual or potential competition from undertakings located either within or out of the Republic of Cyprus; (b) the market position of the participating undertakings and of the undertakings connected with them in one of the ways referred to in Schedule II, the economic and financial power of the said undertakings, the alternative supply sources of the products and services which are the commercial object in the affected markets and/or in other markets where the notified concentration might have significant implications and their substitutes, the supply and demand trends for all the products and services, any barriers to entry in the affected markets and/or in other markets where the notified concentration might have significant implications, the interests of the intermediate and ultimate consumers of the relevant products and services, and the contribution on the development of technical and economic progress provided that it is to consumers' advantage and does not form an obstacle to competition.

361. To the extent that the creation of a joint venture constituting a concentration, has as its object or effect the coordination of the competitive behaviour of undertakings that remain independent, such coordination shall be appraised in accordance with the criteria of sections 3 and 4 of the Concentrations Law, which refer to prohibited restrictive agreements, with a view to ascertaining whether or not the operation is compatible with the functioning of the competition in the market. In making the appraisal, the Service shall take into account in particular: (a) whether two or more parent companies retain, to a significant extent, activities in the same market as the joint venture or in a market which is downstream or upstream from that of the joint venture or in a neighbouring market closely related to this market; (b) whether the coordination which is the direct consequence of the creation of the joint venture affords the participating undertakings the possibility of eliminating competition in respect of a substantial part of the products or services in question.

362. A concentration which would significantly impede effective competition in the Republic of Cyprus or in a substantial part of it, in particular as a result of the creation or strengthening of a dominant position, shall be declared incompatible with the functioning of competition in the market, by virtue of section 20 of the Concentrations Law. Alternatively, a concentration which would not significantly impede effective competition in the Republic or in a substantial part of it, in particular as a result of the creation or strengthening of a dominant position, shall be declared compatible with the functioning of competition in the market, pursuant to section 21 of the Concentrations Law. The CPC shall take into account the written report of the Service and shall examine the notification and reach a decision as follows: (a) where it concludes that the concentration notified does not fall within the scope of application of the Concentrations Law, and/or within the meaning of concentration, it shall make a decision to that effect, pursuant to section 22 of the Concentrations Law; (b) where it decides that the concentration notified, although falling within the scope of application of the Concentrations Law, and within the meaning of concentration, does not raise serious doubts as to its compatibility with the functioning of competition in the market, it shall not oppose it and shall declare that it is compatible with the functioning of competition in the market; (c) where it finds that the concentration notified falls within the scope of application of the Concentrations Law and the meaning of concentration and raises serious doubts as to its compatibility with the functioning of competition in the market, it shall decide to initiate the full investigation proceedings and shall invite the undertakings which have the obligation for notification, to pay the notification fee. The decision of the CPC is communicated to the participating undertakings and the Minister without delay.

363. If the case proceeds to a full investigation, the CPC shall examine the report of findings of the Service and, then shall, by virtue of section 28 of the Concentrations Law: (a) either declare the concentration in question as compatible with the functioning of competition in the market subject to any specific terms and relevant commitments made by the participants in the concentration for the observance of these terms; or (b) declare the concentration in question as incompatible with the functioning of competition in the market. Before taking any decision, the CPC shall compile a report with the objections ascertained in relation to the incompatibility of the concentration with the functioning of competition in the market, for informing the participating undertakings. The report shall be communicated to the participating undertakings or to a duly authorised person. The Service shall further inform the Minister about the decision of the CPC, without delay.

364. The CPC reserves the power, pursuant to section 31 of the Concentrations Law, to grant a derogation from the obligation to not implement the concentration. This may granted upon request by one or more of the undertakings concerned by the concentration, which is notified simultaneously to all the undertakings concerned by the concentration. The request for a temporary approval of the concentration must be reasoned and it must prove that the undertakings which submit the request are likely to suffer serious damages due to further delay in the materialisation of the concentration. In deciding on the request, the CPC shall take into account, *inter alia*, the effects of the suspension on one or more undertakings concerned by the concentration or on a third party and the threat to competition posed by the concentration. The CPC shall communicate its decision to the undertakings concerned by the concentration and in case it grants the derogation, such derogation may be made subject to conditions and obligations imposed by the CPC in order to ensure conditions of effective competition. The Service shall inform the Minister of Energy, Commerce, and Industry about the decision of the CPC without delay. At any event, the temporary approval of a concentration shall not affect the content of the subsequent decision of the CPC.

365. Where the Minister of Energy, Commerce, and Industry has issued a reasoned order declaring that a notified concentration shall be deemed to be of major public interest, the CPC shall submit its decision to the Minister in relation to the compatibility of the concentration with the functioning of competition in the market, by virtue of section 36 of the Concentrations Law. The decision of the CPC shall be published in the Official Gazette of the Republic and shall be communicated to the notifying party. In case where the CPC considers that the notified concentration is compatible with the functioning of competition in the market, the Service shall so inform the notifying party. In case the CPC considers that the notified concentration is compatible with the functioning of competition in the market, the Minister, after weighing the public interest grounds and the need for the protection of competition in the market, shall, pursuant to section 37 of the Concentrations: (a) either state in writing that he agrees with the decision of the CPC, in which case the CPC shall communicate this written statement to the notifying party, or (b) in case where he disagrees with the decision of the CPC, refer this decision to the Council of Ministers, as soon as possible, for examination.

366. The Council of Ministers shall, by virtue of section 38 of the Concentrations Law, decide without delay, weighing the public interest grounds and the need for the protection of competition in the market, whether it will approve or not the concentration and, then, shall issue a relevant reasoned order, which shall be published in the Official Gazette of the Republic and be forwarded by the CPC to the notifying party. In cases where the CPC considers that the notified concentration is compatible with the functioning of competition in the market, this concentration shall not apply, unless: (a) either the written statement of the Minister that he does not object to the decision of the CPC is communicated to the notifying party, or (b) the reasoned order of the Council of Ministers by which it approves the concentration is communicated to the notifying party.

367. The CPC reserves the power, pursuant to section 45 of the Concentrations Law, to revoke any decision taken in relation to the compatibility of any concentration with the functioning of competition in the market or to amend the terms of the decision if it ascertains: (a) that false or misleading information has been supplied or that necessary information relating to this concentration has been withheld by the notifying party or by any other participant in the concentration or by any interested person; or (b) that any term imposed on the participants in the concentration by the said decision has not been satisfied or has ceased to be satisfied. In the above cases, the CPC may further, by virtue of section 46 of the Concentrations Law, and after carrying out a due investigation and the submission of the relevant report of the Service, order the dissolution or partial dissolution of a concentration, in order to secure the restoration of the functioning of competition in the market. The CPC may further order the dissolution or partial dissolution of a concentration, when it ascertains that a concentration has been implemented in violation of its obligation for notification, or in violation of the obligation to not implement it prior to approval.

368. The dissolution or partial dissolution of a concentration shall be accomplished: (a) by the deprivation of any participations, shares, assets or rights acquired by anyone who participated in the concentration; or (b) by the cancellation of any contracts which created the conditions of the concentration or which arose from it; or (c) by a combination of the ways described above, or with other ways as the CPC deems necessary. Any measures imposed by the CPC should not, however, exceed those which are reasonably necessary for the restoration of the functioning of competition in the market. A test of proportionality should therefore be applied. Where any measures are imposed, the CPC should fix a reasonable period of time within which these measures must be implemented by the participating undertakings, taking into account the nature and extent of the relevant measures. The Service should further immediately notify in writing the participants in the concentration and any other interested party about the decision to take the measures, and should take all the necessary measures to ensure compliance therewith

B. Timing

369. The decision of the CPC after the completion of the full investigation proceedings shall be forwarded to the notifying party within four months at the latest from the date of receipt of the notification by the Service or, as the case may be, from the date of receipt by the Service of the additional information which is necessary in order to secure compliance of the notification with the conditions of Schedule III of the Concentrations Law. Where the notification fee has not been paid, the time limit with regard to the decision of the CPC, will commence to count from the date on which the notification fee is paid. If the time limits are not met in relation to a specific concentration, this concentration shall be considered to be compatible with the functioning of competition in the market, by virtue of section 29 of the Concentrations Law. The Minister of Energy, Commerce, and Industry should reach his own decision within fifteen days from the communication of the CPC decision to him. If the Minister states in writing that he agrees with the decision of the CPC, the CPC should communicate this written statement to the notifying party as soon as possible and in any case within seven days at the latest after the date of communication of the written statement of the Minister to the CPC. The order of the Council of Ministers should be forwarded by the CPC to the notifying party as soon as possible and, in any case, within seven days at the latest after the date of communication of the order to the CPC by the Council of Ministers.

370. Section 53 of the Concentrations Law further provides that if in the context of judicial review, a decision of the CPC, or a written statement of the Minister of Energy, Commerce, and Industry, or an order of the Minister or of the Council of Ministers, has been annulled, the time limits shall apply anew as from the date upon which the decision was pronounced, but they shall be suspended if an appeal is made before their expiry and in case of dismissal of the appeal or of the decision on the appeal which does not result in the complete lifting of the annulment, they shall apply anew as from the date upon which the decision on the appeal, was pronounced.

§4. Relations with Other Merger Control Authorities

I. Other Authorities Within the Local Jurisdiction

371. The CPC shall cooperate with both CECPR and CERA, where appropriate. However, it has consistently been held that competition law rules may apply where the sector-specific legislation does not preclude the undertakings it governs from engaging in autonomous conduct that prevents, restricts or distorts competition.[364] This is particularly so in the case of complaints submitted to the CPC regarding possible violations of the EU competition rules. In such cases the European CPC has a duty to investigate, and if necessary to order appropriate remedies. Moreover, the obligations under the Concentrations Law apply irrespective of the sectoral legislation. Cases might thus be subject to both competition rules, and to national or European sector-specific measures. Compliance with the sector-specific measures does not absolve the undertakings from their obligations imposed in accordance with the CPC Law. Furthermore, the mere fact that the CECPR has acted in a specific manner does not preclude the examination of the case by the CPC pursuant to the CPC Law.

II. International Coordination

372. The CPC has an obligation to cooperate with the European Commission and the competition authorities of other Member States for issues relating to the control of concentrations between undertakings, pursuant to section 54 of the Concentrations Law. In cases where a particular concentration is being examined simultaneously by another competition authority of a Member State, the participating undertakings may submit with the notification a statement of voluntary waiver of the right of confidentiality for the purpose of supplying confidential information and/or business secrets, by virtue of section 50 and Schedule V of the Concentrations Law. The waiver forms an agreement to waive the confidentiality right preventing the CPC from disclosing confidential information to the European Commission or to any other competition authority of a Member State concerning the suggested concentration and to consent to the CPC forwarding to the European Commission or to a competition authority of a Member State of any relevant documents, statements, data and information, the written report prepared by the CPC and/or the Service. The European Commission and the competition authority of the Member State concerned will, however, also be bound by a duty of confidentiality to not disclose any information to third parties.

373. Prior to the notification of a concentration with Community dimension, for which the European Commission is the competent organ, by virtue of Article 4 of the Mergers Regulation, the persons or undertakings concerned may inform the European Commission, by means of a reasoned submission, that the concentration

364. Joined Cases C-359/95 and C-379/95, *P Commission and France v. Ladbroke Racing*, ECLI-:EU:C:1997:531, para. 34, with further references.

may significantly affect competition in a market within a Member State which presents all the characteristics of a distinct market and should therefore be examined, in whole or in part, by that Member State. The European Commission shall transmit this submission to all Member States without delay. The Member State referred to in the reasoned submission shall, within 15 working days of receiving the submission, express its agreement or disagreement as regards the request to refer the case. Where that Member State takes no such decision within this period, it shall be deemed to have agreed. Unless that Member State disagrees, the European Commission, where it considers that such a distinct market exists, and that competition in that market may be significantly affected by the concentration, may decide to refer the whole or part of the case to the competent authorities of that Member State with a view to the application of that State's national competition law.

374. The decision whether or not to refer the case shall be taken within 25 working days starting from the receipt of the reasoned submission by the European Commission. The European Commission shall inform the other Member States and the persons or undertakings concerned of its decision. If the European Commission does not take a decision within this period, it shall be deemed to have adopted a decision to refer the case in accordance with the submission made by the persons or undertakings concerned. If the European Commission decides, or is deemed to have decided, to refer the whole of the case, national competition law shall apply.

375. For a concentration which does not have a Community dimension, and which is capable of being reviewed under the national competition laws of at least three Member States, the persons or undertakings concerned shall, before any notification to the competent authorities, inform the European Commission by means of a reasoned submission that the concentration should be examined by the European Commission. The European Commission shall then transmit this submission to all Member States without delay. Any Member State competent to examine the concentration under its national competition law may, within 15 working days of receiving the reasoned submission, express its disagreement as regards the request to refer the case. Where at least one such Member State has expressed its disagreement within the period of 15 working days, the case shall not be referred. The European Commission shall, without delay, inform all Member States and the persons or undertakings concerned of any such expression of disagreement. Where no Member State has expressed its disagreement within the period of 15 working days, the concentration shall be deemed to have a Community dimension and shall be notified to the European Commission. In such situations, no Member State shall apply its national competition law to the concentration.

376. Pursuant to Article 9 of the Mergers Regulation, the European Commission may, by means of a decision notified without delay to the undertakings concerned and the competent authorities of the other Member States, refer a notified concentration to the competent authorities of the Member State concerned. Within 15 working days of the date of receipt of the copy of the notification, a Member State, on its own initiative or upon the invitation of the European Commission, may inform the European Commission, which shall inform the undertakings concerned, that: (a) a concentration threatens to affect significantly competition in a market within that Member State, which presents all the characteristics of a distinct market, or (b) a concentration affects competition in a market within that Member State, which presents all the characteristics of a distinct market and which does not constitute a substantial part of the common market.

377. If the European Commission considers that, having regard to the market for the products or services in question and the geographical reference market, there is such a distinct market and that such a threat exists, either (a) it shall itself deal with the case in accordance with the Mergers Regulation or (b) it shall refer the whole or part of the case to the competent authorities of the Member State concerned with a view to the application of that State's national competition law. If, however, the European Commission considers that such a distinct market or threat does not exist, it shall adopt a decision to that effect which it shall address to the Member State concerned, and shall itself deal with the case in accordance with the Mergers Regulation. To this end, the European Commission should obtain information from the competent authority of the Member State and give it the opportunity to make known its views at every stage of the procedure up to the adoption of a decision; to that end it shall give it access to the file.

378. In cases where a Member State informs the European Commission that a concentration affects competition in a distinct market within its territory that does not form a substantial part of the common market, the European Commission shall refer the whole or part of the case relating to the distinct market concerned, if it considers that such a distinct market is affected. A decision to refer or not to refer shall be taken as a general rule within 35 working days, where the European Commission has not initiated proceedings, or within 65 working days at most of the notification of the concentration concerned where the European Commission has initiated proceedings, without taking the preparatory steps in order to adopt the necessary measures to maintain or restore effective competition on the market concerned. If within the 65 working days the European Commission, despite a reminder from the Member State concerned, has not taken a decision on referral, nor has taken the preparatory steps, it shall be deemed to have taken a decision to refer the case to the Member State concerned.

379. The competent authority of the Member State concerned shall decide upon the case without undue delay. Within 45 working days after the European Commission's referral, the competent authority of the Member State concerned shall inform the undertakings concerned of the result of the preliminary competition assessment and what further action, if any, it proposes to take. The Member State concerned may exceptionally suspend this time limit where necessary information has not been provided to it by the undertakings concerned as provided for by its national competition law. Where a notification is requested under national law, the period of 45 working days shall begin on the working day following that of the receipt of a complete notification by the competent authority of that Member State. The geographical reference market shall consist of the area in which the undertakings concerned are involved in the supply and demand of products or services, in which the conditions of competition are sufficiently homogeneous and which can be distinguished from neighbouring areas because, in particular, conditions of competition are appreciably different in those areas. This assessment should take account in particular of the nature and characteristics of the products or services concerned, of the existence of entry barriers or of consumer preferences, of appreciable differences of the undertakings' market shares between the area concerned and neighbouring areas or of substantial price differences. The Member State concerned may take only the measures strictly necessary to safeguard or restore effective competition on the market concerned.

380. At the request of the European Commission, the competent authorities of the Member States shall undertake, pursuant to Article 12 of the Mergers Regulation, the inspections which the European Commission considers to be necessary for the exercise of its powers. The officials of the competent authorities of the Member States who are responsible for conducting these inspections, as well as those authorised or appointed by them, shall exercise their powers in accordance with their national law. If so requested by the European Commission or by the competent authority of the Member State within whose territory the inspection is to be conducted, officials and other accompanying persons authorised by the European Commission may assist the officials of the authority concerned.

381. The European Commission shall, by virtue of Article 19 of the Mergers Regulation, transmit to the competent authorities of the Member States copies of notifications within three working days and, as soon as possible, copies of the most important documents lodged with or issued by the European Commission pursuant to the Mergers Regulation. Such documents shall include commitments offered by the undertakings concerned vis-à-vis the European Commission with a view to rendering the concentration compatible with the common market. The European Commission shall further carry out the procedures set out in this Regulation in close and constant liaison with the competent authorities of the Member States, which may express their views upon those procedures. An Advisory Committee on concentrations shall be consulted before any decision is taken, with the exception of provisional decisions. This Advisory Committee shall consist of representatives of the competent authorities of the Member States. Each Member State shall appoint one or two representatives; if unable to attend, they may be replaced by other representatives. At least one of the representatives of a Member State shall be competent in matters of restrictive practices and dominant positions.

382. Consultation at the level of the Advisory Committee shall take place at a joint meeting convened at the invitation of and chaired by the European Commission. A summary of the case, together with an indication of the most important documents and a preliminary draft of the decision to be taken for each case considered, shall be sent with the invitation. The meeting shall take place not less than 10 working days after the invitation has been sent. The European Commission may in exceptional cases shorten that period as appropriate in order to avoid serious harm to one or more of the undertakings concerned by a concentration. The Advisory Committee shall deliver an opinion on the European Commission's draft decision, if necessary by taking a vote. The Advisory Committee may deliver an opinion even if some members are absent and unrepresented. The opinion shall be delivered in writing and appended to the draft decision. The European Commission shall take the utmost account of the opinion delivered by the Advisory Committee, and shall communicate the opinion of the Advisory Committee, together with the decision, to the addressees of the decision. It shall make the opinion public together with the decision, having regard to the legitimate interest of undertakings in the protection of their business secrets.

383. One or more Member States may request the European Commission, pursuant to Article 22 of the Mergers Regulation, to examine any concentration that does not have a Community dimension, but affects trade between Member States and threatens to significantly affect competition within the territory of the Member State or States making the request. Such a request shall be made at most within 15 working days of the date on which the concentration was notified, or if no notification is required, otherwise made known to the Member State concerned. The European Commission shall inform the competent authorities of the Member States and the undertakings concerned of any such request. Any other Member State shall have the right to join the initial request within a period of 15 working days of being informed by the European Commission of the initial request. All national time limits relating to the concentration shall be suspended until it has been decided where the concentration shall be examined. As soon as a Member State has informed the European Commission and the undertakings concerned that it does not wish to join the request, the suspension of its national time limits shall end.

384. The European Commission may, at the latest 10 working days after the expiry of the above period, decide to examine, the concentration where it considers that it affects trade between Member States and threatens to significantly affect competition within the territory of the Member State or States making the request. If the European Commission does not take a decision within this period, it shall be deemed to have adopted a decision to examine the concentration in accordance with the request. The European Commission shall inform all Member States and the undertakings concerned of its decision. It may further request the submission of a notification. The Member State or States having made the request shall no longer apply their national legislation on competition to the concentration. Moreover, the European Commission may opt to inform one or several Member States that it considers a concentration, although not having a Community dimension, affects trade between Member States and threatens to significantly affect competition within the territory of the Member State or States informed. In such cases, the European Commission may invite that Member State or those Member States to make a request for the European Commission to examine the concentration.

Chapter 3. Challenging of the Administrative Decision

§1. Competent Courts

385. Article 146 §1 of the Constitution used to provide that the Supreme Constitutional Court shall have exclusive jurisdiction to adjudicate finally on a resource made to it on a complaint that a decision, an act or omission of any organ, authority or person, exercising any executive or administrative authority is contrary to any of the provisions of the Constitution or of any law or is made in excess or in abuse of powers vested in such organ or authority or person. Jurisdiction to review administrative action was therefore vested exclusively to the Supreme Constitutional Court and since 1964 to the Supreme Court on the basis of the doctrine of necessity. However, the Eighth Amendment of the Constitution, Law 130(I)/2015, amended Article 146 of the Constitution, so that a newly established Administrative Court would exercise the administrative jurisdiction at first instance. The Establishment and Function of the Administrative Court Law 131(I)/2015 established the Administrative Court which functions as of 2016. The Supreme Court continues to exercise the appellate administrative jurisdiction in benches of three judges and maintains the power to refer any case to the Full Bench of the Supreme Court if it considers it necessary.

386. No other Court can review the legality of administrative action either directly or indirectly. A Court exercising civil or criminal jurisdiction has no jurisdiction to question the validity of an administrative act or decision; accordingly, a District Court exercising civil or criminal jurisdiction or even the Supreme Court while exercising such jurisdiction, shall accept any administrative act as valid and shall not, under any circumstances, question the validity of such administrative act. If such administrative act has been taken contrary to the Constitution or any law or the principles of administrative law, this should be examined by the Administrative Court and provided that the applicant has filed a resource in accordance with the provisions of Article 146 of the Constitution.

387. Recourse may be filed before the Administrative Court against a decision, an act or omission of the administration which falls within the public domain. The Supreme Court has defined organs or authority of the Republic as those: 'specific juridical creations bearing the features of individual and concrete organic institutions of government and functioning for and on behalf of a primary legal entity, such as the Republic of Cyprus, of which they are organs or authorities in the ordinary meaning of such terms'.[365] In view of the above, the term 'organ' or 'authority' of the Republic includes not only organs or authorities of the central administration of the State which exercise executive or administrative power, such as the various ministries or departments, but also semi-governmental organisations and legal persons of public nature.

365. *Celaleddin and Others v. The Council of Ministers* 5 RSCC 102.

388. There are various criteria that the Supreme Court considers in order to decide whether a legal person is an organ or authority of the Republic in accordance with Article 146 of the Constitution; these include considerations whether the legal person has been founded for the public interest, the power to exercise public authority, for example, by imposing taxes or levies, or collecting public revenues, or ordering compulsory acquisition of land; whether the status of the employees should be considered as analogous to that of public servants; whether the supervision of the State over the legal person is extraordinary; or whether the State participates in the management of the legal person. It is not sufficient that the act, decision or omission has been taken by an organ, authority or person of the administration; the act should also emanate from the exercise of powers in the public domain, namely the exercise of executive or administrative authority. Cypriot administrative law thus applies a twofold criterion in order to determine whether an act is administrative for the purposes of Article 146 of the Constitution, by considering both the nature of the authority from which the act or decision emanates, and the nature of the act or decision in question.[366]

389. The Supreme Court has held that the unilateral expression of the will of the administration is the crucial factor in determining whether the act or decision is an administrative one; the State should exercise its *imperium*, by conferring rights or imposing obligations upon persons. The test to determine whether the act or decision falls within the ambit of Article 146 of the Constitution is whether the act or decision intends to promote a public purpose, so as to interest the public at large or a substantial part of such public. A public purpose is one in which the public at large or a noticeable section of it has an interest in the sense that its proper promotion has repercussions extending beyond those immediately affecting the parties directly affected thereby. The CPC is an administrative organ.

390. Paragraph 2 of Article 146 of the Constitution provides that a recourse may be made by a person whose existing legitimate interest, which is adversely and directly affected by such decision or act or omission.[367] The applicant should prove *legitimatio ad causum*, namely that the decision or act under review has damaged or negatively influenced his own interests. The applicant's relationship to the act, from which relationship his interest flows, has to exist already when the act has been challenged, and his injury must have already taken place or appear reasonably unavoidable. Thus, the legitimate interest must be existing at all stages of the trial.[368] The existence of a legitimate interest shall be examined by the Administrative Court *ex proprio motu*. It has been held that for legitimate interest to exist, such interest should be in accordance with the law; otherwise, it could not be legitimate.[369] Interested parties may also intervene in the procedure. It has been held that when an undertaking files a recourse against the decision of the CPC to impose an

366. *The Greek Registrar of the Co-Operative Societies v. Nicolaides* [1965] 3 CLR 164.

367. A. Emilianides, *Legitimate Interest in the Administrative Trial: A Review of the Case-Law*, Cyprus & European L. Rev 10, 631–699 (2009) (in Greek).

368. *Maratheftis v. Municipality of Limassol* [2003] 3 CLR 228 (in Greek), *Chrysostomides v. The Greek Communal Chamber* [1964] CLR 397; *Republic v. Pericleous* [1972] 3 CLR 63.

369. *Constantinou v. Municipality of Paphos* [1998] 3 CLR 707 (in Greek).

administrative fine for infringing competition, the complainant has a legitimate interest to intervene as an interested party.[370]

§2. Time Limits

391. Article 146 §3 stipulates that a recourse has to be made within seventy-five days of the date when the decision or act was published or, if not published, and in the case of an omission, when it came to the knowledge of the person making the recourse. The seventy-five day period stipulated in the Constitution is of a mandatory nature, and accordingly no recourse may be made after such period has elapsed; this requirement may be examined by the Court *ex proprio motu*. The period may not be extended by the fact that the applicant is a minor or ill; however, it might be extended in cases of force majeure. The onus of proof that an applicant came to the knowledge of the act or omission impeached, if such an act has not been published, rests on the party who alleges that the recourse is out of time. In case of doubt, the Court has to lean in favour of the applicant.

392. It has been held that the knowledge is complete if it allows the person interested to ascertain with certainty and precision the material and moral damage that he suffers from the published or communicated act. The communication must be complete, because if the interested person does not become aware of the whole of the contents of the act, he cannot judge and decide about the exercise or not of his right to file the recourse. Therefore, the communication of only the operative part without the reasoning for the act is not complete and the time does not run. Complete knowledge may be inferred from a statement or action of the interested person, especially from the submission of an application for remedy, containing the defects of the impeached act or omission.

§3. Scope of Judicial Review

393. Article 146 §4 of the Constitution provides that upon a recourse the Administrative Court may, by its decision: (a) confirm, either in whole or in part, the impugned decision or act or omission, and (b) declare, either in whole or in part, such decision or act to be null and void and of no effect whatsoever, or declare that such omission, either in whole or in part ought to have been made and that whatever has been omitted should have been performed. The Administrative Court, when exercising its jurisdiction by virtue of Article 146 of the Constitution, is essentially a court of review and not a court of substance. Whereas, it has power to confirm or annul the decision, act or omission under review, it has no power to amend it, or to substitute it with another decision or act, or to decide what the administration ought to have done. Accordingly, the Administrative Court shall not substitute the discretion of the administrative organ with its own discretion, and shall not interfere with

370. Case 2019/12, *Cyprus Telecommunications Authority v. Commission for the Protection of Competition and another*, 12 Apr. 2013 (in Greek).

the decision of the administration so long as such could have been reasonably taken in accordance with the law and the general principles of administrative law. Moreover, the Administrative Court shall not review the substance of matters of a technical nature (such as expert opinion, the findings of a medical board, or the report of a technical committee) so long as the administrative organ has properly exercised its discretion in accordance with the general principles of administrative law.

394. Courts have adopted the above-mentioned restrictive approach to judicial review with regard to competition law cases.[371] It has accordingly been held that the CPC should enjoy a wide margin of discretion and that the Court would not normally interfere with its decisions of a technical nature. The Court should not therefore interfere with the exercise of technical judgment by the CPC, but may determine whether the facts of the case satisfy the proper application of the statutory provisions. What constitutes a decision of a technical nature has been interpreted in an extremely wide manner, with issues, such as the determination of the relevant market being declared a technical issue, where the power of the Court to review the decision is limited.[372] In other cases, the Courts held that they should not review whether an administrative fine imposed was a severe one, which would entail a review of substance, but rather should restrict themselves to examine whether the CPC had acted beyond the proper limits of the exercise of its discretion.[373] The Court may assess whether the CPC has properly evaluated all material facts in order to calculate the fine to be imposed.[374] It will not, however, reassess facts where the investigation was a proper one. The CPC therefore functions as an administrative organ, and not as a court or tribunal. It has been held that the requirements of a fair trial are fulfilled if there is revisional control by an independent and impartial court or tribunal, such as the administrative court.[375]

395. The case law of the Supreme Court has developed several general principles for the proper application of administrative law. It has been repeatedly held that no decision or act of the administration may be inconsistent with the general principles of administrative law. Such general principles have been codified in a

371. For example, Case 1782/12, *Stylianou v. Commission for the Protection of Competition*, 30 Jun. 2014 (in Greek), Case 1023/12, *Pancyprian Organization of Cattle Public Company Ltd v. Commission for the Protection of Competition*, 30 Nov. 2012 (in Greek), Case 5550/13, *Belanco Ltd v. Commission for the Protection of Competition*, 17 Dec. 2018 (in Greek), Case 5665/13, *Cyprus Telecommunications Authority v. Commission for the Protection of Competition*, 10 Jan. 2019 (in Greek).

372. Case 612/09, *Ioannou v. Commission for the Protection of Competition*, 23 Sep. 2010 (in Greek), Case 2004/12, *Cyprus Telecommunications Authority v. Commission for the Protection of Competition and another*, 29 Sep. 2015 (in Greek), Case 1/09, *Cyprus Telecommunications Authority v. Commission for the Protection of Competition and another*, 18 Feb. 2011 (in Greek), Cases 5669–5670/13, *Pfizer Hellas-Cyprus Branch and another v. Commission for the Protection of Competition*, 12 Sep. 2016 (in Greek).

373. Case 2019/12, *Cyprus Telecommunications Authority v. Commission for the Protection of Competition and another*, 25 Jul. 2016 (in Greek).

374. Case 2056/12, *Fissler GmbH v. Commission for the Protection of Competition*, 12 Sep. 2016 (in Greek).

375. Cases 5669–5670/13, *Pfizer Hellas-Cyprus Branch and another v. Commission for the Protection of Competition*, 12 Sep. 2016 (in Greek).

single statutory act, the Principles of Administrative Law.[376] The main principles will be assessed in the following paragraphs. The principle of legality of administrative action derives from the principle of the rule of law. Section 8 of the Principles of Administrative Law stipulates that the acts of the administration must be consistent to the law in force. An administrative act or decision which has been taken without a law empowering the organ or authority of the administration to take such decision, or by an organ which is not competent to take such act shall be void. Section 17 §3 of the Principles of Administrative Law expressly states that the illegality of an act issued by an incompetent administrative organ may not be remedied even if the competent organ subsequently approves of such an act. Administrative action outside or beyond the powers conferred upon the administration by law would amount to an act or decision taken in excess or abuse of power. Excess or abuse of power also constitute separate grounds for the annulment of administrative acts. When the administrative organ issues an administrative act, on the basis of an application by the subject, it must be based on the status of the law at the time the administrative act is issued, irrespective of whether it was different at the time of application; if, however, the administration had failed to examine the application within reasonable time, then the status of the law at the time of application may be taken into account instead.

396. Section 10 of the Principles of Administrative Law expressly states that administrative organs should exercise their competences and issue their decisions within a reasonable time and without undue delay. However, the time limits fixed for the issue of an administrative act are in principle only indicative for the administration. An act may be declared as invalid only if excessive time has passed from the expiry of the time limit, so as to have substantially affected the factual and legal circumstances of the case.[377] On the contrary, the time limits fixed for the submission of applications by the persons subject to the administration are mandatory, by virtue of section 11 of the Principles of Administrative Law. It should be noted that administrative acts may not have retrospective effect, by virtue of section 6 of the Principles of Administrative Law, unless the requirements of section 7 of Principles of Administrative Law apply, namely: (a) the law conferring the competences to the administrative organ expressly authorises such retrospective effect; (b) the administrative act is issued in order to comply with a court judgment of the and retrospective effect is required in order to fully restore legality; (c) the administrative organ reissues an act which had been annulled for formal grounds, so long as the new decision has the same content as the first one and is issued within a reasonable time from the first and on the basis of the same legal and factual considerations; (d) the administrative act revokes an illegal act of the administration; (e) the sole content of the act is to ascertain a factual situation without prejudicing existing situations; (f) retroactivity is required in order to rectify an injustice occurred towards a person due to the omission of the administration.

---

376. *See* A. Angelides, *The General Principles of Administrative Law Act and the Subsequent Case-Law of the Supreme Court of Cyprus* (House of Representatives 2008, in Greek).
377. *Tingiridou v. Republic* [1987] 3 CLR 1811.

397. Administrative authorities should exercise their discretionary powers properly, within the limits provided by law and without abusing their rights. The Administrative Court shall examine whether the administrative organs have exercised their discretion within the proper limits of such discretion and, if not, the administrative decision is subject to invalidation. Whereas, the administrative organ should not decide a priori and in a general way the manner in which it shall exercise its discretionary powers in future cases, it may nevertheless exercise its powers on the basis of a general policy or criteria it has predetermined for similar cases, so long as such policy or criteria are consistent with the legislation and so far as it also examines whether the particular facts of a given case might justify a different approach. The administrative organ may further be guided by circulars or administrative guidelines of a general character which were issued by a hierarchically superior administrative organ, in so far as those circulars or guidelines are not inconsistent with the legislation.

398. The principles of proper administration impose to the administrative organs, by virtue of section 50 of the Principles of Administrative Law, to exercise their discretion in accordance with a concept of fairness and equity, so as to avoid unfair and unjust solutions. The administrative organs may not pursue aims which are inconsistent with the aims of the legislation,[378] or act in bad faith. The obligation of the administration to act in good faith is of cardinal importance for the trust of the citizens; accordingly the administrative organs should not alter the manner in which they exercise their discretion, thus prejudicing the interested person, unless there is a good reason. The methods used by the administration should be proportionate to the aims pursued, and any interference with the rights of the citizen shall be excused only where such is necessary or justified for the public interest. The administration is not permitted to act in a manner which is inconsistent or contradictory, or to invoke its own shortcomings in order to ignore a situation which is favourable for the citizen.

399. The administration has an obligation to carry out an investigation into all relevant circumstances and to reach its decision only after having conducted the inquiry reasonably necessary for the purpose of ascertaining fully all the relevant fact. Reasonable and due inquiry is an essential step in the administrative process whose lack would lead to the annulment of an administrative decision (section 45 of the Principles of Administrative Law).[379] There is, however, a presumption that the administrative organ has considered all the material facts which were before it, including recommendations of lower organs and the material submitted by the applicant or other persons.[380] This is in accordance with the general presumption of regularity of administrative organs.[381] Thus, the mere fact that a collective organ adopted the opinion or recommendation of another organ does not imply that there was no

378. *Michaelides v. The Attorney-General* [1984] 3 CLR 1596.
379. *Nicolaides v. The Greek Registrar of the Co-Operative Societies* [1965] 3 CLR 585.
380. *Ierides v. The Republic* [1980] 3 CLR 165.
381. *Georghios Zachariades Ltd v. Ports Authority of Cyprus* [1996] 3 CLR 269 (in Greek); *Gavriel v. Attorney-General* [1989] 3 CLR 3067 (in Greek).

due inquiry.[382] The applicant thus has the burden of disproving the presumption of legality of the administrative act[383] and of convincing the Court that such was taken because the administrative organ failed to conduct a reasonable inquiry or take into account material facts.[384]

400. Misconception of the administration as to the legal principles (or their proper interpretation) governing the administrative decision,[385] or misconception of facts materially affecting the decision,[386] shall result to the invalidation of the decision in question, by virtue of section 46 of the Principles of Administrative Law. Whereas, the assessment of the facts lies with the administrative organs and the Court shall not interfere with such evaluation so long as it was reasonably open to the administration,[387] the Court shall declare the decision to be void when there is even a possibility of material misconception.[388] Such material misconception may arise if the administrative organ has taken into account non-existing material or has failed to take into account existing material and would also imply that there is lack of a reasonably inquiry. It is further provided that the administrative organs should abide to the formalities which the law requires for the issue of an administrative act; however, section 13 of the Principles of Administrative Law distinguishes between those formalities which are material for the decision taken and those which are immaterial and did not have any effect to the outcome of the decision. The former render the administrative act invalid, whereas the latter do not.

401. It is a paramount principle of administrative law that administrative decisions must be duly reasoned. The object of the rule requiring reasons to be given for administrative decisions is to enable the persons concerned and the Court on review to ascertain in each case, whether the decision is well founded in fact and in law. Accordingly, the reasons must be stated clearly and unambiguously, they must be read in the sense in which reasonable persons affected thereby would understand them, and they should be supported by reasons which fulfil the object of the relevant legislation. Mere repetition of the text of the enactment concerned, either in a negative form or otherwise, is not sufficient (section 28 of the Principles of Administrative Law).[389] The extent of reasoning which is required in each particular case depends upon the nature of the decision in question. Reasoning is not based on length; a lengthy decision might lack justification, whereas a brief decision might be duly reasoned.[390] Full reasoning shall be given if the administrative authorities

382. *Phylaktou v. The Republic* [1973] 3 CLR 444; *Morphis v. The Republic* [1975] 3 CLR 255.

383. *Vasiotis Constructions Ltd v. Municipality of Limassol* [1989] 3 CLR 3193 (in Greek).

384. *Hadjiyiorki v. The Republic* [1977] 3 CLR 144; *Demetriou v. The Municipal Committee of Larnaca* [1986] 3 CLR 2171; *Violari v. Republic* [1988] 3 CLR 2170.

385. *Demades & Sons Ltd v. The Republic* [1964] CLR 167.

386. *Pavlides v. The Republic* [1967] 3 CLR 223.

387. *Hji Michael v. The Republic* [1972] 3 CLR 246.

388. *Kontos v. The Republic* [1974] 3 CLR 112; *Daphnides v. The Republic* [1964] CLR 180; *Municipality of Strovolos v. Pitta* [2001] 3 CLR 55 (in Greek).

389. *Christou v. The Republic* [1972] 3 CLR 32; *Bagdades v. The Central Bank of Cyprus* [1973] 3 CLR 417; *Rallis v. The Greek Communal Chamber* [1963] RSCC 11; *Zavros v. The Council for Registration of Architects and Civil Engineers* [1969] 3 CLR 310.

390. *Marangos v. The Republic* [1983] 3 CLR 682.

sufficiently explains how it applied the law or its discretion on the basis of the facts of the case in order to reach its decision;[391] the reasons for reaching a specific conclusion have to be sufficiently explained.

402. The Administration may not rely generally on the public interest in order to justify its decision; the grounds why the Administration considered that a specific decision was for the public interest have to be explained.[392] It is not lawful for the Administration to rely on 'education grounds' or 'public policy grounds' without explaining sufficiently what these grounds are.[393] Nor is it lawful for the Administration to simply announce that a petition is rejected, without offering any justification.[394] The decision should contain all the material facts on which the decision is based, as well as all the relevant legal provisions that the administrative organ considered in order to reach its decision.[395] However, the Administration may opt not to refer to every single detail of the case, if this has not been crucial for its decision.[396] If, however, the reasoning may be found in documents which were before the administrative organ when it reached its decision, such as opinions of hierarchically lower organs which the superior organ adopted, it is not necessary to repeat such reasoning in the decision itself.[397] The reasoning of an administration decision may not, under any circumstances, be supplemented by material which was not before the administrative organ at the time when the decision was taken,[398] or by the arguments submitted by advocates on behalf of the Administration.[399]

403. Collective organs are under a duty to keep proper minutes in accordance with section 24 of the Principles of Administrative Law. The inadequacy of recording a decision deprives the Court of the ability to examine how and why it was reasonably open to the administrative organ to decide in such a manner. If no minutes have been recorded the administrative act shall unavoidably be annulled.[400] Similarly, if the administrative file does not contain material documents on which the administrative organ supposedly based its decision, the decision shall be

391. *Georghiou v. Republic* [1989] 3 CLR 589 (in Greek); *Nicolas v. Republic* [1989] 3 CLR 228 (in Greek).
392. *Kazamias v. The Republic* [1982] 3 CLR 239; *Adamides v. The Republic* [1982] 3 CLR 343.
393. *Carayiannis v. The Republic* [1969] 3 CLR 341; *Dekathlon Shipping Co Ltd v. The Republic* [1980] 3 CLR 630.
394. *Andreou v. The Republic* [1978] 3 CLR 85.
395. *Papazachariou v. The Republic* [1972] 3 CLR 486; *Hadjiconstantinou v. The Republic* [1973] 3 CLR 65.
396. *Savva v. The Republic* [1985] 3 CLR 694; *Orictaco Co Ltd v. The Republic* [1985] 3 CLR 1327.
397. *Georghiou v. Republic* [1989] 3 CLR 589; *Louca v. Republic* [1986] 3 CLR 1640; *Republic v. Myrtiotis* [1975] 3 CLR 484; *Peratica Trading Ltd v. Republic* [2002] 3 AAΔ 445 (in Greek).
398. *Tsikkinis v. Republic* [1984] 3 CLR 1577.
399. *Metalock (Near East) Limited v. The Republic* [1969] 3 CLR 351; *Frangou v. Republic* [1998] 3 CLR 270 (in Greek).
400. *Medcon Construction v. Republic* [1968] 3 CLR 535; *Stylson Engineering Co Ltd v. Republic* [1995] 3 CLR 491 (in Greek).

annulled.[401] If the decision of a collective organ was reached by majority, rather than unanimously, the requirement to provide sufficient reasoning is even more obvious.[402]

404. The reasoning provided by the administrative organ should in any event be in accordance with the law. The Administration may not rely on extra-legal criteria, which are inconsistent with the relevant legal provisions governing the case.[403] It should be noted, however, that if part of the reasoning is lawful and it is sufficient in order to justify the decision, the mere fact that part of the reasoning is incorrect shall not automatically lead to the annulment of the administrative decision (section 31 of the Principles of Administrative Law).[404] The above principles may only apply if the fact that part of the reasoning is faulty does not also lead to lack of proper inquiry or material factual misapprehension. In any event, the reasoning should be consistent with the material facts of the case.[405]

405. The principles of natural justice should always govern the action of the administration. An administrative organ which participates in the making of an administrative act should warrant both integrity and impartiality. By virtue of section 42 of the Principles of Administrative Law, any person who has a special relationship or is related, either by blood or affinity within the fourth degree or has intense hostility towards the person who is affected by the administrative act, or any person who has an interest (monetary or of another kind) in the outcome of the administrative act, should not participate in its making. The question whether objectivity exists should be considered in an objective manner and thus, the decisive criterion in not whether bias actually existed, but whether an outsider might reasonably conclude that there was partiality.[406] It is therefore immaterial whether the person acted in good faith.[407] The principle of impartiality is consistent with the Latin maxim *nemo judex in causa sua*; the only case where a person should participate in the making of an administrative act despite the fact that he has an interest or special relationship in the making of the act, is when the said act may not be lawfully issued by any other organ, or where the competent collective organ could not otherwise convene because of lack of a quorum.

406. The second principle of natural justice consists of the right to be heard by the administrative organ. By virtue of section 43 of the Principles of Administrative Law, any person who is affected by the issue of an administrative act or by the taking of an administrative measure which is of a disciplinary or an adverse nature, has

---

401. *Michael v. The Republic* [1981] 3 CLR 147; *Georghiades v. The Republic* [1980] 3 CLR 487, *Eracleous v. The Republic* [1985] 3 CLR 740.
402. *Georghiades v. The Republic* [1967] 3 CLR 653; *Papageorghiou v. The Republic* [1984] 3 CLR 1348.
403. *Emilios Ellinas & Co Ltd v. Ministry of Finance* [1990] 3 CLR 181 (in Greek).
404. *Pikis v. The Republic* [1967] 3 CLR 562; *Ioannou v. The Ministry of Interior* [1987] 3 CLR 1549.
405. *Jacovides v. The Republic* [1966] 3 CLR 212.
406. *Republic v. Solomou* [1998] 3 CLR 769 (in Greek).
407. *Kallouris v. The Republic* [1964] CLR 313.

the right to be heard prior to the act being issued.[408] If an administrative organ intends to support its decision on allegations which have been submitted against a person, it should give that person the right to present his views regarding such allegations. However, the right to be heard is not necessarily an oral one; the person may in principle submit his views in writing. The extent of the right to be heard should always be considered on the basis of the actual circumstances of the case, the nature of the investigation that the administration needs to carry out and the object of the inquiry.[409] In cases of decisions of a purely administrative nature, however, which are not of a disciplinary or an adverse nature and which do not have the character of a sanction, such as compulsory acquisition, or public procurement or registration of vehicles, the right to be heard is normally not required, unless provided by law, or unless the circumstances of the case would so require.[410]

407. The constitutional prohibition of discrimination extends also to the action of the administration. Article 28 of the Constitution and section 38 of the Principles of Administrative Law which safeguard the principle of equality of citizens entail that the administration must treat in an equal and uniform manner all citizens who are under the same or similar circumstances.[411] It has repeatedly been held that the principle of equality safeguarded by Article 28 of the Constitution does not convey the notion of exact arithmetical equality, but it safeguards only against arbitrary differentiations and does not exclude reasonable distinctions which have to be made in view of the intrinsic nature of things.[412] The Court has to assess the material facts and particular circumstances of each case in order to conclude whether there has been unequal treatment and bearing in mind that if it was reasonably open to the Administration to treat the cases differently, the Court should not interfere by substituting its own views.[413]

408. However, Article 28 of the Constitution is violated only when the differentiation is not based on an objective and reasonable justification. The existence of such justification must be assessed in relation to the aim and effects of the measure under consideration, regard being had to the principles which normally prevail in democratic societies. Article 28 is likewise violated when it is clearly established that there is no reasonable relationship on proportionality between the means employed and the aim sought to be realised. Bare equality of treatment regardless of the inequality of realities is neither justice nor homage to the constitutional principle. Where objects, persons or transactions essentially dissimilar are treated uniformly, discrimination may result.[414] Whenever the Administration decides to handle a case in a different manner than it had dealt with other similar cases in the past, such decision should be part of a wider justified new policy decision on the

---

408. *Louca v. The Republic* [1986] 3 CLR 1640.
409. *Kyprianou v. The Public Service Commission* [1973] 3 CLR 206.
410. *Savvides v. Republic* [1989] 3 CLR 2595; *Hjiloucas v. The Republic* [1971] 3 CLR 96.
411. *Jacovides v. The Republic* [1966] 3 CLR 212.
412. *Kantara Shipping Ltd v. The Republic* [1969] 3 CLR 95; *Georghiades v. The Republic* [1979] 3 CLR 146.
413. *Kyriacou v. The Greek Communal Chamber* [1968] 3 CLR 280.
414. *The Republic v. Maria Christoudia* [1988] 3 CLR 2622.

manner in which the Administration exercises its discretion; otherwise, the difference in treatment might be considered as arbitrary. [415] It should be noted, however, that there is no right of equal treatment with respect to illegal action of the Administration. The mere fact that the Administration had acted contrary to the law in previous cases does not entail a right of the applicant to request that the Administration also acts illegally in his case.[416] Accordingly, the refusal by the Administration to act illegally does not entail discrimination under any circumstances.[417]

409. Following the annulment of an administrative act, the Administration is called upon to reach a new administrative decision on the basis of the findings of the Supreme Court. Paragraph 5 of Article 146 provides that the decision of the Court is binding on all courts and all organs or authorities in the Republic and shall be given effect to and acted upon by the organ or authority or person concerned. However, it is only the operative findings of the decision which are binding on the administrative. Accordingly, the fact that the applicant has been successful in annulling the administrative fine imposed to them does not preclude that the CPC may re-examine the case and potentially reach the decision to impose a new administrative fine, to the extent that this is permissible on the basis of the operative findings of the Administrative Court. it might be that the administrative organ decides again that the same person as before ought to be promoted, after a thorough investigation of the factual circumstances, or taking into account material facts which it had failed to take into account, or giving due reasoning for its decision, depending on the operative findings of the Supreme Court in the case at hand. New Article 146 §5A of the Constitution provides that a law may provide that the Administrative Court may determine whether there has been compliance with its judgment and impose penalties in case of non-compliance. However, no such law has yet been enacted.

§4. Confidential Information

410. The issue of disclosure of information characterised as confidential by the CPC has been considered in some detail by the Supreme Court.[418] The petitioner was the complainant in proceedings before the CPC. CYTA, against who the compliant had been lodged, had provided to the CPC data and information, which it specifically requested that they should treat as confidential information and business secrets. It should be noted that the information had not been used by the CPC for the evaluation of the complaint, or the determination of the infringement. The CPC

415. *Drousiotis v. The Cyprus Broadcasting Corporation* [1984] 3 CLR 546.

416. *Voyiazanos v. The Republic* [1967] 3 CLR 239; *Ioannides v. The Republic* [1973] 3 CLR 117, *Shamassian v. The Republic* [1973] 3 CLR 341.

417. *Lanitis v. The Republic* [1988] 3 CLR 87; *Proestou v. The Republic* [1981] 3 CLR 314, *Ioannou v. The Republic* [1982] 3 CLR 1002; *Christodoulides v. The Republic* [1985] 3 CLR 357, *Koniotis v. The Republic* [1967] 3 CLR 376; *Karayianni v. The Educational Service Committee* [1979] 3 CLR 371.

418. *Cyprus Telecommunications Authority and another v. Commission for the Protection of Competition*, Rev. App. 141/15, 9 Oct. 2017 (in Greek).

examined the complaint accordingly and found that CYTA had infringed the statutory provisions. CYTA filed a recourse against the decision of the CPC and the petitioner was an interested party in the recourse. In their written address before the Court, CYTA referred to confidential documents and information, but unilaterally omitted to disclose them. The petitioner argued that this amounted to a violation of the principle of fair trial and equal treatment of the parties and requested the Court to order the disclosure of all the relevant data and argumentation. The First Instance Court held that the information and documents should be disclosed. CYTA appealed.

411. It was common ground that the Republic of Cyprus has not introduced any specific provisions regarding the confidentiality of information in proceedings before the courts, in so far as competition law is concerned. The Court referred to the ECJ (as it then was) judgment in *Varec*[419] which held that the right to recourse does not provide for unqualified access to information which could be used to distort competition or to prejudice the legitimate interests of economic operators who participated in the contract award procedure concerned. Such an opportunity could even encourage economic operators to bring an appeal solely for the purpose of gaining access to their competitors' business secrets. Hence, whereas the adversarial principle means, as a rule, that the parties have a right to a process of inspecting and commenting on the evidence and observations submitted to the court, in some cases it may be necessary for certain information to be withheld from the parties in order to preserve the fundamental rights of a third party or to safeguard an important public interest.

412. The protection of business secrets and of confidential information must therefore be observed in such a way as to reconcile it with the requirements of effective legal protection and the rights of defence of the parties to the dispute, and, in the case of judicial review or a review by another body which is a court or tribunal within the meaning of Article 234 EC, in such a way as to ensure that the proceedings as a whole accord with the right to a fair trial. Accordingly, it must be ensured that the confidentiality and business secrecy are safeguarded in respect of information contained in files communicated to that body by the parties to an action, particularly by the contracting authority, although it may apprise itself of such information and take it into consideration. It is for the review body to decide to what extent and by what process it is appropriate to safeguard the confidentiality and secrecy of that information, having regard to the requirements of effective legal protection and the rights of defence of the parties to the dispute and, in the case of judicial review, so as to ensure that the proceedings as a whole accord with the right to a fair trial.

413. There were two plurality judgments, each supported by two of the justices. The first plurality judgment referred to the CJEU case law and held that documents and information may be characterised as confidential, if there is a specific request by the interested party and after the respective interests of all parties are taken into

419. C-450/06, *Varec SA v. Belgian State*, 14 February 2008, EU:C:2008:91.

account. Whereas, the petitioner had a right to be given all the documents of the procedure, this right was not absolute, but had to be balanced against the interests of CYTA to safeguard its confidential information and trade secrets. The procedure both before the CPC and before the courts should therefore respect the right to a fair trial, and this balance may be achieved only if the Court had before it all relevant information, including the trade secrets and confidential information in question. Taking all factors into account, it was held that the First Instance Court had failed in its obligation to ensure that all respective interests are weighed.

414. The second plurality opinion, also supported by two of the justices, held that whereas it is not for the party to unilaterally determine what is confidential information, in this case the omission to disclose did not refer to evidence presented before the Court, but to argumentation. A party enjoys some discretion as to the manner which to present their written address and argumentation, and in this case the information not disclosed corresponded to information which had been held to be confidential by the CPC itself. In view of the above, the First Instance Court had acted prematurely in ordering the disclosure of the information, since it had not weighed the respective interests of the parties. Disclosure under these circumstances might negatively impact the application of competition rules, since the petitioner had not convincingly argued that such information was necessary for their defence. The issue should accordingly be assessed, after carefully balancing the respective interests of the parties.

Selected Bibliography

In Greek

Agisilaou, P., D. Kalli, & K. Kleanthous. *Competition Policy in Cyprus 1989-2009.* Athens: Nomiki Vivliothiki, 2011.

Emilianides, A. 'The Problem of Prohibition of Concerted Practice in Community Competition Law'. *Greek Review of European Law* 24 (2009): 739–753.

Koui, K. 'The Role of State Authorities and Services in the Protection of Competition and Consumer in Cyprus'. *Lysias* 2 (2009): 20–25.

Polyviou, P. *Administration and Justice. The Commission for the Protection of Competition and the Cyprus Securities and Exchange Commission.* Chrysafinis and Polyviou: Nicosia 2016.

Stamelos, P. *European Competition Law with Application to Greece and Cyprus.* Athens: Nomiki Vivliothiki, 2020.

Timotheou, F. 'Law of Free Competition in Cyprus'. *Cyprus Law Tribune* 3 (2001): 81–123.

Tryfonidou, A. 'Observations in the Case Netmed v. Commission for Protection of Competition'. *Lysias* 1 (2008): 51–54.

In English

Antoniou, A. 'The Essential Facilities Doctrine Before the European Community Courts: Ostracised or Expanded?' *Cyprus and European Law Review* 11 (2010): 77–101.

Christoforou, C. 'Competition'. In *Introduction to Cyprus Law.* 3rd edn. Andreas Neocleous & Co LLC, Limassol, 2010.

Christoforou, V. 'Harmonising Competition and State Aid Rules'. In *Cyprus and the EU: The Road to Accession*, edited by C. Stefanou. Ashgate: Aldershot, 2005.

Selected Bibliography

Index

The numbers here refer to paragraph numbers.

Abuse, 34, 48, 79, 82, 90, 93, 98, 111, 112, 197, 242, 252, 253, 254, 259, 262, 263, 264, 266, 270, 274, 276, 277, 279, 303, 304, 385, 395
Administrative court, 38, 385, 386, 387, 390, 393, 394, 397, 409
Administrative fines, 53, 131, 139, 142, 143, 147, 150, 151, 152, 233
Anticompetitive agreement, 84, 94
Antitrust, 32, 33, 42, 44, 52, 84, 163, 164, 166, 168, 169, 170, 171, 172, 174, 175, 176, 177, 253
Arrangement, 13, 64, 105, 164, 184, 188, 197, 199, 200, 201, 213, 215, 219, 221, 231, 232, 234, 239, 265, 267, 271
Assessment, 102, 143, 144, 145, 149, 158, 167, 189, 219, 220, 232, 247, 250, 257, 266, 272, 283, 287, 289, 294, 299, 308, 312, 316, 319, 320, 324, 336, 337, 379, 400

Bid-rigging, 195, 198
Block exemption, 54, 89, 207, 209, 210, 222, 223, 238, 244, 246, 247, 248, 320

Cartel, 36, 53, 145, 150, 176, 184, 185, 199, 200, 218, 240
Collective boycott, 202
Collusion, 53, 89, 97, 105, 107, 131, 134, 150, 151, 154, 184, 185, 187, 188, 193, 198, 204, 221, 225, 229, 304
Complaint, 39, 75, 130, 131, 132, 134, 135, 138, 148, 159, 188, 231, 256, 257, 258, 264, 267, 273, 278, 280, 303, 304, 305, 306, 307, 321, 327, 329, 371, 385, 410
Composition, 36, 39, 113, 119, 121, 122, 124, 189
Concentration, 40, 43, 58, 91, 95, 96, 99, 105, 113, 114, 115, 116, 129, 134, 141, 142, 180, 181, 190, 282, 284, 285, 286, 287, 289, 293, 299, 300, 301, 308, 312, 316, 331, 332, 333, 334, 335, 336, 338, 339, 340, 341, 342, 343, 344, 345, 346, 347, 348, 349, 350, 351, 352, 353, 355, 356, 357, 358, 359, 360, 361, 362, 363, 364, 365, 366, 367, 368, 369, 370, 371, 372, 373, 375, 376, 378, 381, 382, 383, 384
Concerted practice, 32, 34, 46, 47, 54, 79, 84, 88, 89, 92, 94, 97, 105, 106, 107, 108, 184, 185, 186, 189, 190, 191, 192, 203, 205, 221, 294, 302, 306
Confidential, 68, 134, 164, 165, 169, 181, 188, 190, 191, 205, 300, 301, 311, 317, 328, 330, 348, 353, 358, 372, 410, 413, 414
Conglomerate mergers, 293, 294
Council of Ministers, 8, 9, 22, 23, 32, 34, 35, 36, 37, 54, 76, 89, 96, 117, 118, 119, 121, 124, 125, 126, 127, 207, 222, 331, 365, 366, 369, 370
Cumulative effect, 85

Damages, 44, 59, 160, 163, 164, 166, 168, 169, 170, 171, 172, 174, 175, 176, 177, 364
De minimis, 84, 87
Discrimination, 72, 102, 252, 263, 301, 407, 408
Dissimilar conditions, 46, 48, 88, 90, 110, 263
Distort competition, 32, 34, 137, 262, 411
Distribution, 12, 32, 47, 74, 78, 85, 89, 90, 94, 109, 110, 112, 188, 218, 220, 221, 224, 225, 226, 227, 229, 230, 231, 232,

233, 234, 262, 264, 266, 268, 277, 278, 280, 345, 346, 354
Dominant position, 34, 48, 76, 77, 79, 82, 83, 90, 93, 96, 98, 103, 104, 111, 112, 197, 250, 251, 252, 253, 256, 260, 261, 262, 263, 268, 270, 273, 274, 276, 278, 283, 284, 290, 298, 299, 303, 304, 322, 362, 381

Economic dependence, 90, 93, 111, 192, 253, 254, 263, 264, 266
Equivalent, 34, 46, 48, 70, 83, 88, 90, 110, 111, 129, 140, 154, 181, 254, 263, 266, 275, 290
Energy, 74, 117, 133, 136, 331, 348, 364, 365, 369, 370
Excessive pricing, 252, 255, 256
Exclusionary practices, 252, 270, 294
Exclusive dealing, 220, 228, 267
Exclusive distribution, 225, 226, 227, 229, 266
Exclusive rights, 50 80 237
Ex-officio investigation, 39, 130, 188, 226, 304, 327
Exploitative practices, 252, 263

Franchising, 234, 236

Group boycott, 202

Horizontal mergers, 282, 283, 284, 284, 285, 286, 288, 289, 290

Immunity, 53, 150, 151, 152, 153, 154, 156, 172, 173, 237
Independent, 2, 8, 34, 61, 63, 66, 113, 117, 120, 121, 133, 182, 233, 262, 282, 297, 301, 347, 361, 394
Information exchange, 186, 189, 203, 204, 205, 242
Infringement, 39, 44, 49, 52, 93, 98, 111, 131, 136, 139, 141, 142, 143, 144, 145, 146, 147, 148, 149, 150, 151, 153, 154, 155, 156, 157, 158, 159, 160, 162, 163, 164, 170, 171, 172, 173, 174, 175, 176, 177, 181, 184, 186, 202, 232, 239, 252, 254, 259, 261, 264, 267, 273, 274, 280, 281, 302, 303, 305, 306, 307, 310, 317, 320, 326, 327, 328, 358, 410.
Inspection, 55, 102, 139, 141, 147, 150, 151, 302, 313, 314, 315, 316, 317, 318, 380
Interim measures, 55, 69, 73, 131, 139, 159, 160, 180, 280
Investigating powers, 130
Investigation, 39, 53, 55, 75, 84, 91, 122, 130, 134, 135, 142, 145, 147, 148, 171, 182, 188, 189, 190, 226, 267, 275, 298, 302, 303, 304, 305, 307, 309, 312, 316, 326, 327, 329, 348, 350, 351, 352, 362, 363, 367, 369, 394, 399, 406, 409

Joint venture, 99, 116, 200, 213, 214, 295, 296, 297, 298, 299, 300, 301, 347, 361
Joint production agreements, 209, 210, 214
Joint purchasing agreements, 215, 216, 217
Joint selling agreements, 218, 219

Legitimate interest, 164, 305, 306, 322, 340, 382, 390, 411
Leniency, 53, 145, 150, 153, 154, 166, 168, 173
Limitation period, 147, 171, 177

Margin squeeze, 279, 280, 281
Market allocation, 85, 194, 195
Market share, 84, 85, 101, 103, 104, 144, 172, 190, 201, 207, 208, 209, 219, 223, 224, 225, 228, 232, 238, 251, 285, 286, 289, 336, 337, 338, 339, 345, 347, 379
Market sharing, 194, 195, 196
Misconception, 1
Monopoly, 12, 50, 80, 104, 232

Natural justice, 122, 405, 406

Oligopoly, 96

Price-fixing, 186, 188, 189, 192, 193, 195, 199, 212, 218
Price increase, 102, 175, 185, 187, 284
Product market, 100, 101, 191, 210, 268, 285, 289, 336, 338, 339, 344
Production limitation, 199, 200
Prohibited conduct, 40, 98
Proportionality, 65, 94, 96, 164, 166, 167, 368, 408
Public interest, 35, 94, 119, 127, 182, 198, 331, 365, 366, 388, 398, 402, 411

Quorum, 128, 405

Rebates, 187, 273, 333, 187
Recourse, 29, 30, 35, 98, 270, 387, 390,

391, 392, 393, 410, 411
Refusal to deal, 274
Research and development agreements, 206
Restrictive agreements, 212, 303, 361

Sector inquiries, 130, 302, 303
Selective distribution, 109, 224, 225, 229, 230, 231, 232, 233
Specialisation agreements, 209, 210
Standardisation agreements, 211, 212
Substitutability, 101, 102, 336
Supplementary obligations, 46, 48, 88, 90, 271

Technology licensing, 238, 249
Term of office, 124, 125, 127
Threshold, 84, 85, 87, 115, 224, 232, 272, 333
Turnover, 115, 139, 140, 141, 146, 157, 158, 160, 222, 310, 315, 331, 332, 333, 334, 335, 343, 345, 346, 347, 354
Tying, 271, 294

Unfair pricing, 255, 281

Vertical agreements, 54, 220, 221, 222, 223, 224, 231, 235
Vertical mergers, 289, 290, 291, 292, 293

Index

www.ingramcontent.com/pod-product-compliance
Lightning Source LLC
Chambersburg PA
CBHW071445230926
51846CB00001B/348
* 9 7 8 9 4 0 3 5 3 8 2 4 2 *